Alaska

OFF THE BEATEN PATH™

I0668246

Alaska

MIKE MILLER

A Voyager Book

Old Saybrook, Connecticut

Illustrations by Carole Drong

Off the Beaten Path is a trademark of The Globe Pequot Press, Inc.
Cover map copyright © DeLorme Mapping

Library of Congress Cataloging-in-Publication Data
Miller, Mike,
    Alaska: off the beaten path / by Mike Miller. — 1st ed.
        p.   cm.   —   (Off the beaten path series)
    "A voyager book."
    Includes index.
    ISBN 1-56440-749-7
    1. Alaska—Guidebooks.   I. Title.   II. Series.
F902.3.M55   1995
917.9804'5—dc20   95-23871
                                                                              CIP

Manufactured in the United States of America
First Edition/Third Printing

To Travis, Marnita, Merijke, Ori, and David—
each of you young and full of life and promise,
like the Great Land in which you live.

FAR NORTH

INTERIOR

United States

Canada

YUKON

SOUTHWEST

SOUTHCENTRAL

Canada

SOUTHEAST

ALASKA

Contents

Introduction viii

Southeast Alaska 1

Canada's Yukon 53

Southcentral Alaska 75

Interior Alaska 119

Alaska's Far North 147

Southwestern Alaska 167

Additional Sources of Information 185

Statewide Outfitters and Tour Organizations 185

Indexes

    General 187

    National and State Parks 196

    Museums 196

INTRODUCTION

A funny thing happened on our way around the world.

Our goal early in marriage—wife Marilyn's and mine—was simple. We'd move here a while, there a while, but never really settle down. We'd spend maybe a year (or a couple of years, max) in any one place. Eventually we'd sample the pleasures of living in a dozen or so states and nations. Then we would make our lifetime decision.

Trouble is, we moved to Alaska first.

That was 40 years ago, and though story-gathering assignments over the decades have taken us pleasurably to five continents at last count, we've never wanted to live any other place. Even for our own vacation travels we choose, more often than not, to explore an Alaska or Canadian Yukon locale.

Part of the reason we've chosen to stay in Alaska is—as they say in the real estate business—"location...location...location." We like off the beaten path places to see and off the beaten path things to do and absolutely the whole state of Alaska fits nicely in that category. There's still the feel of the frontier even in our larger cities. And outside of these communities (sometimes only a few minutes or a few miles outside) the wilderness character of Alaska is more than a feeling. It's reality.

Even the passengers aboard mammoth cruise ships, luxuriously ensconced in spacious stateroom suites and lacking not a single creature comfort, find themselves being transported through sea-lanes past islands and forests and glaciers that haven't changed appreciatively since the days when navigators such as Bering, Cook, and Vancouver came calling in centuries past. Of course, travelers who spend a day (or a week) in small cruisers or kayaks will experience the wildness closer still—perhaps viewing bears, deer, and other wild creatures on forested shores separated from their craft by only a few yards of water. Maybe they'll actually share their water environment with seals or sea lions or whales of several species.

Motorists can travel Alaska's modern paved highways alongside thousands of square miles of near-virgin forest/mountain/glacier country; by turning off onto lesser-used roads and byways they can immerse themselves in huge tracts of terrain still largely unpeopled, untrammeled, and unoccupied except by moose, caribou, grizzly bears, and other such animals.

And talk about far horizons—you can drive north of the Arctic Circle virtually to the Arctic Ocean. Many do, each year. If flying's your thing, Alaska's legendary bush pilots can drop you off—as they have Marilyn and me—alongside alpine lakes teeming with fish, or in remote Arctic villages where subsistence hunting and fishing is still a treasured way of life, or in river headwaters that offer some of the most glorious wilderness rafting on earth.

For all its wildness and wilderness, Alaska is an easy place to get around and visit, even in the bush and backcountry. We've traveled Alaska's roads by RV, auto, motorcoach, and bicycle (including one memorable pedal trip during which we awoke one morning to find fresh grizzly bear tracks beside our tent). We've experienced the speed and convenience of jet travel between Alaska's major communities and the thrill of flying over—and actually landing on—icy glaciers. We've paddled kayaks on outings in coastal waters and we've enjoyed the sight of huge paddles propelling a stern-wheeler on the Chena and Tanana rivers in the Interior. Alaska's noteworthy system of coastal ferry vessels has been a particular delight; these large and little ships sail regularly between major cities and villages in Southeast Alaska and in Prince William Sound. In the Southwest region they connect mainland ports with fabled Kodiak Island and the Aleutian Islands chain beyond.

For the hiker or walker, whether an avid backcountry backpacker or simply an afternoon trekker of trails, Alaska is pure heaven. Only inches beyond the municipal limits of larger cities or little towns you can be walking along wild ocean beaches or hiking beside big lakes, rivers, or sparkling creeks. You can be gently (or vigorously) ascending valley inclines to mountain tops where awesome views in any direction take in the likes of glaciers, water bodies, endless forests, and countless other peaks and valleys. Or you can walk along century-old gold rush trails and roads that still resonate with the excitement of the quest for rich ore.

Even within modern communities you can take a casual stroll and come upon marvelous sights and sites, as in Wrangell where within easy walking distance of downtown you can come upon ancient petroglyph rock drawings so old that no one knows who etched them.

Walking, driving, cruising, flying...however and wherever you get around in Alaska you'll find it marvelously offbeat, upbeat, and richly rewarding.

You'll not wonder why we settled here.

A Very Small Sketch of a Very Big State

"All Gaul," declared Julius Caesar in *De Bello Gallico*, "is divided into four parts."

With Alaska it takes five.

All of Alaska, of course, is located north and west of what geographers call "the contiguous states" of the U.S. The Canadian Province of British Columbia lies between. The southernmost of Alaska's five regions, and closest to the "Lower 48," as Alaskans call these sister states, is **Southeast Alaska.** It's a place of thousands of forested Islands plus a long sliver of mainland abutting northern British Columbia. **Southcentral Alaska** forms an arch around the top of the Gulf of Alaska and extends inland roughly to the Alaska Range of mountains, a towering wall of peaks and masses that separates Southcentral from **Interior Alaska.** Interior, in turn, forms the huge middle of the state, bordering Canada's Yukon Territory on the east. Its westerly border stops just short of the Bering Sea. Farther north, in fact as far north as you can get and still be in North America, lies **Far North Alaska.** Finally, **Southwestern Alaska** takes in the westernmost approaches of the Alaska mainland, the Alaska Peninsula, Kodiak Island, the long, long string of Aleutian Islands which extends almost to Japan, plus the Pribilof Islands and others of the Bering Sea.

In this book I've added a sixth region, **Canada's Yukon Territory,** because—since it is adjacent both to Southeast and Interior Alaska—you cannot drive from the Alaska panhandle to the main body of Alaska without going through this friendly, fascinating portion of Canada.

Some Notes and Cautions

First, a bit about the Alaska lifestyle and dress. Because we are off the beaten path, things are pretty informal all over the state. Friendly is a way of life up here and you never have to worry about asking an Alaskan for help, or directions, or for the answer to what you think may be a dumb question. "Comfortably casual" is the dress code of the day, every day, even in big city hotels and restaurants. M'lady, if she'd feel more comfortable, can certainly wear a cocktail dress or dressy pantsuit in the evening, and her escort can likewise wear a coat and tie if he'd like, but it really isn't necessary.

For outdoor wear, comfortable walking shoes (or broken-in boots if you're a hiker) are a must. The weather can vary wildly all over the state, so plan to do what Alaskans do: dress in layers that start with light cotton shirts and/or undershirts then graduate to heavier shirts, sweaters, and even ski-type parkas. The latter are especially useful if you plan glacier cruises, campouts, or travel in the Arctic. Layering allows you to add protection or to peel off excess clothing as the weather dictates. *Very important:* A lightweight combination windbreaker/raincoat should always be at the top of your pack or suitcase.

Now about money: Truth to tell, the cost of living is higher in Alaska than in most other states, but the differences are narrowing all the time. Depending on where you are (in a large easily accessible city or a remote bush community), costs for lodging and food could be the same as you're accustomed to paying, or only a few percentage points higher—or they could be a great deal more. I have tried to show prices for most admissions, meals, overnights, and other costs. At the time of this writing all the prices (plus telephone numbers, addresses, and other such data) were current. But things can change; hotel and meal prices, in particular, may well be higher when you make your trip. When a hotel or B&B price is quoted here it's usually for a double. Singles may (or may not) be less; extra guests in a room usually cost more. There is no statewide sales tax in Alaska but most municipalities impose one on goods, services, and overnight accommodations. Sales taxes are not included in the prices quoted in this book.

Remember that when you travel in the Yukon, distances are measured in metric kilometers, not miles; when speed limits are posted at 90 kilometers per hour, that's the same as 55 mph in the U.S. Likewise, our Canadian friends pump gasoline in liters, not gallons. Happily there's one metric conversion you don't have to worry about: You can still order a "Quarter-Pounder" at the Yukon's single McDonald's outlet in Whitehorse. Can you imagine asking for a "113-Grammer With Cheese"?

Friends from Outside often ask "When is the best time to visit Alaska?" The answer is, anytime you want to come. Summer obviously ranks as Alaska's most popular season but the "shoulder" months of May, September, and early October offer the advantages of fewer crowds, often discounted prices, and an unhurried, more relaxed pace of living.

Winter, perhaps surprisingly, is coming into its own with an active statewide agenda of downhill and cross-country skiing, sled dog mushing and racing, winter carnivals, and viewing the eerie and spectacular *aurora borealis,* the northern lights. Obviously you have to dress for the season (snug long johns, heavy sweaters, and extra-warm outerwear for tours and activities out of doors) but if you use common sense and take the advice of the locals you, too, can happily and safely experience Alaska during the time of year many Alaskans enjoy their state the most.

Finally...it seems incredible but, more than three and a half decades after becoming the forty-ninth state of the United States, Alaskans still get asked if we use U.S. currency and stamps. The answer, of course, is emphatically yes—though if you arrive here with Canadian dimes, quarters, and other small change in your pocket or purse, merchants will accept them at face value. Canadian dollars, on the other hand, will be discounted according to current value on the international money exchanges.

Now, enough of technical stuff. Read on. Come. Visit. Enjoy!

The prices and rates listed in this guidebook were confirmed at press time. We recommend, however, that you call establishments before traveling to obtain current information.

SOUTHEAST ALASKA

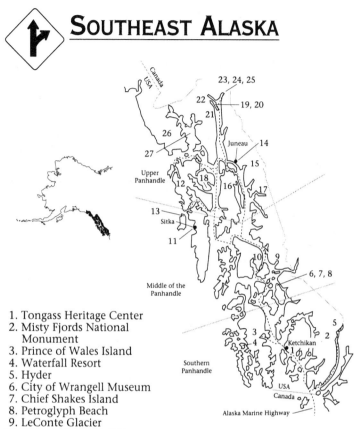

23, 24, 25

22
21
19, 20

26
27

Upper
Panhandle
12 18 16 14
Juneau
15
17
13
Sitka

11

Middle of the
Panhandle

6, 7, 8

5
3
4
Ketchikan
2
1

Southern
Panhandle

USA
Canada

Alaska Marine Highway

10 9

1. Tongass Heritage Center
2. Misty Fjords National
   Monument
3. Prince of Wales Island
4. Waterfall Resort
5. Hyder
6. City of Wrangell Museum
7. Chief Shakes Island
8. Petroglyph Beach
9. LeConte Glacier
10. Clausen Memorial Museum
11. Sheldon Jackson Museum
12. White Sulphur Springs cabin
13. Sea Otter and Wildlife Quest
14. Wickersham House
15. East Turner Lake and West
    Turner Lake Forest Service
    Cabins
16. Pack Creek
17. Tracy Arm Fjord
18. Tenakee Springs
19. Sheldon Museum and
    Cultural Center

20. Fort William Henry Seward
21. Chilkat State Park
22. Alaska Chilkat Bald Eagle
    Preserve
23. Klondike Gold Rush National
    Historical Park
24. White Pass & Yukon Route
25. Trail of '98 Museum
26. Glacier Bay National Park
    and Preserve
27. *Spirit of Adventure*

SOUTHEAST ALASKA

Incredible place, Southeast Alaska. (Or Southeastern, as Alaskans often call it.) It's a place of islands—more than 1,000—and a land of lush forests, snow-capped mountains, cascading waterfalls, steep-walled fjords, and magnificent glaciers. From these latter fall tens of thousands of huge and minuscule icebergs that dot the seascape and glitter within great bays and inlets. It is a region of proud and skillful Tlingit, Haida, and Tsimshian native peoples, whose totems and other works of art are only now beginning to receive the recognition they deserve. It is a land, too, with a colorful, gutsy gold rush past and a place where today huge salmon, monster halibut, and bountiful trout await the angler's lure in saltwater, lakes, and streams.

It's an easy place to get to. Literally scores of elegant cruise ships embark each week in summer from West Coast ports en route to the Southeast Alaska panhandle. Stateroom-equipped ferryliners of the Alaska Marine Highway System likewise ply these waters from Bellingham, Washington, and from Prince Rupert, British Columbia. And of course the jets of Alaska Airlines, plus Delta in the summer, depart daily from Seattle and other cities in the "Lower Forty-eight" states en route to the land that nineteenth-century naturalist John Muir called "one of the most wonderful countries in the world." Here's what Southeast Alaska holds in store for visitors these days.

SOUTHERN SOUTHEAST

Alaskans call Ketchikan their First City because it's the first Alaskan port of call for cruise ships, ferries, yachts, and many airlines en route to the forty-ninth state. Spread out along the shores of Revillagigedo Island (the name is Spanish and almost unpronounceable; locals just say Revilla), the town is just a few blocks wide, but it's miles long. The hustling, bustling city's economy lies in commercial fishing, timber, and tourism. Sportfishing for salmon, halibut, and freshwater species can be superb. So is the sight-seeing at local totem parks and from the decks of small cruisers that explore nearby islands and waters.

For travelers who seek a cruiselike experience, the small ships of half a dozen companies offer comfortable vessels with staterooms,

2

dining rooms, ample decks, observation lounges, and bars—but not the Vegas-like theaters, ballrooms, casinos, boutiques, and crowds of the big liners. It's great the way a number of these boats can nose into small bays and inlets for close-up looks at bears, deer, and other wildlife. Also pleasureable are the whales. When they are in the vicinity, the skipper can cut the engine and drift for a half hour or more to watch the water acrobatics of the great beasts. **Alaska Sightseeing/Cruise West** (800–426–7702) operates three such ships on weekly cruises from Seattle as well as the *Spirit of Glacier Bay* from Juneau to Glacier Bay and the *Sheltered Seas* between Ketchikan and Juneau, with nights ashore in Petersburg. **Glacier Bay Tours and Cruises'** speedy forty-nine-passenger catamaran *Executive Explorer* sails between Ketchikan, Juneau, and Glacier Bay. Call (800) 451-5952 for more information.

You'll discover more authentic Native-carved totem poles around Ketchikan than any place else in the world. One of the outstanding collections stands at **Saxman Native Village**, 2½ miles south of Ketchikan on South Tongass Highway. Deeply carved figures represent eagles and ravens, bears and killer whales, and even the figure of a hapless, drowning Indian youth caught in the bite of a giant rock oyster as the tide comes in. Elsewhere in the park you'll find a traditional Beaver Clan community house, an on-site carving center. A two-hour motor coach tour (priced at $35) by **Cape Fox Tours** (907–225–5163) includes both Saxman Village and a tour of historic Ketchikan.

The ◆**Tongass Heritage Center,** located at the edge of Ketchikan's city park, a half mile or so from downtown, houses priceless nineteenth-century totems rescued from decay at abandoned Native villages and sites. They are absolutely majestic, with their deeply carved crests and legends from the cultures of Tlingit and Haida peoples. The **Tongass Historical Museum**, downtown at 624 Dock Street, contains exhibits and artifacts from Ketchikan's Native past and its fishing-mining-timbering heritage. You can hear tall tales in "Logger Sam's" rustic bunkhouse and see a scaled-down model of an authentic salmon seiner. Combined admission charge to center and museum is $5.00. For more information, call (907) 225–5600.

If you're a hiker, you'll find Ketchikan a great place to roam from, with lots of ocean, forest, lake, and mountain trails. The 3½-mile **Deer Mountain Trail,** which begins practically downtown

3

and runs to the 3,000-foot summit, provides a particularly grand vista of the city below and nearby islands and ocean waters. Ask for directions to the trailhead at the **Visitor Information Center**, downtown on the Front Street cruise ship dock.

Earlier we mentioned the opportunity to explore waters around Ketchikan by small sightseeing cruiser. Dale Pihlman's **Alaska Cruises** (220 Front Street; 907–225–6044) offers an eleven-and-a-half hour excursion from downtown Ketchikan to ❹**Misty Fjords National Monument**, a wondrous nearby wilderness area of steep-walled fjords, sheltered bays, tiny inlets, islands, isles, mountain trails, lakes, and green, green forests—not to mention whales, seals, bears, and mountain goats. The cost, including three meals, is $140 for adults. If time is limited (or even if it isn't), you may opt for a $185 six-and-a-half-hour fly/cruise version of the trip, which offers a breathtaking aerial perspective.

If you want professionals to organize, equip, and guide you on a Misty Fjord kayaking trip, Betsey Burdett and Geoff Gross offer four- and eight-day excursions within the monument as well as among the Barrier Islands in the South Prince of Wales Island Wilderness area. Their company, **Southeast Exposure** (507 Steadman Street; 907–225–8829), also offers day trips along the Ketchikan waterfront and into semiwilderness waters nearby. Single fiberglass kayaks rent for $35 per day. Guided tours start at $50.

Speaking of camping, this might be a good place to mention an unusual opportunity that many consider the greatest travel bargain in America: a network of **U.S. Forest Service cabins** in the Alaska wilderness. The USFS maintains more than 145 warm and weather-tight cabins beside remote mountain lakes and isolated ocean shores throughout the **Tongass National Forest** that comprises most of Southeast Alaska. An additional forty such units exist in the Chugach National Forest in Alaska's south-central region. You can reserve units for up to a week at a time—at the modest daily rate of $25 *per group*.

Most units have bunks to accommodate up to six and contain either wood- or oil-burning stoves. Don't, however, expect a "Hilton in the wilderness." You bring your own food, sleeping bags, and other supplies. Privies are "down the path." Mostly these are fly-in units, though you can reach a few by boat or hiking trail. For bear protection Alaskans and visitors often carry 30-06 or larger rifles. No permit is required. It's seldom, however, that someone has to use one. Virtually every town in both regions has charter air services that specialize in serving fly-in campers. Rates vary with the distance you need to fly.

For information about Tongass cabins, call the Forest Service Information Center in Juneau at (907) 586–8751. For similar information concerning the Chugach, contact the Alaska Public Lands Information Center in Anchorage, (907) 271–2737.

From Ketchikan a popular fly-in choice is **Patching Lake Cabin**, a wood stove–equipped mountain lake unit with a skiff on-site. You'll find trout in the water for fishing plus the possibility of deer and black bear in the woods for viewing. (Don't, however, even think of feeding these critters or observing them too close.) The local USFS number for information or reservations is (907) 225–2148. A fly-in charter to Patching Lake would be in the neighborhood of $350 for a party of two.

If you're a collector of varied boat rides, here's a chance to add an Indian longboat canoe to your list. **Alaska Travel Adventures' Mountain Lake Experience** begins with a sight-seeing motor coach ride to a large secluded mountain lake. There you board a 37-foot craft based on authentic Southeast Alaska Indian design for a paddle along the forest-rimmed lake. After coming ashore and taking a short hike (you'll view, among other things, carnivorous plants) you're served a snack of Native-style smoked fish, Alaskan sourdough rolls, clam chowder, and beverages. The tour is priced at $69. For information about this or Alaska Travel Adventures' Ketchikan hike experience, call (907) 247–5295.

Ketchikan-based **Taquan Air** (907–225–8800) is Southeast Alaska's largest light-aircraft carrier, but the company has chosen not to seek contracts with the mega–cruise lines to fly massive numbers of passengers from ports of call. Instead it concentrates on independent travelers (as well as bread-and-butter Alaskan clientele) and features such opportunities as wildlife watching on **Eagle Island** and **Smuggler's Cove**, overnight fishing or kayaking trips from Prince of Wales Island, "Canadian Discoverer" flights to **Prince Rupert** in northern British Columbia, and daily 11:00 A.M. flights (except Sundays) to **Metlakatla**, a close-by Tsimshian Native village on Annette Island. Among sites to see and explore in Metlakatla is the village founder **Father Duncan's Cottage**, now a fascinating museum that chronicles the history of Annette Island's formerly Canadian Indian peoples and the lay Anglican priest who brought them to Alaska. The museum is open from 1:00 to 4:00 P.M. Monday through Friday and by appointment on Saturday. One of Taquan's newest tours is a Sunday-only four-hour flight and ground experiences that includes a two-hour tour escorted by U.S. Forest Service naturalists through **El Capitan Cave** on Prince of Wales Island. The flight departs Ketchikan at 7:00 A.M.

Another Ketchikan small-craft carrier, **Ketchikan Air** (907-225-6608), likewise offers airborne bush adventures such as flightseeing over **Misty Fjords National Monument**, and a three-hour trip to the more northerly **Anan Creek Bear Observatory**. For kayakers, the carrier offers air access to a five-hour kayak expedition from **El Capitan Lodge** on Prince of Wales Island.

It's not located off the beaten path, but the smallish, moderately priced **Gilmore Hotel** at 326 Front Street (907–225–9423) is often overlooked. The hotel offers a commanding view of Ketchikan's frantic waterfront, taking in fishermen preparing their nets, luxury cruise liners in port, freighters heaped with cargo, and a constant stream of float planes landing, taking off, or flying down the channel. Built in 1927 of solid concrete, the hotel's forty rooms are modern, clean, have full baths, and color TVs. Rates begin at $66 for a double. It's on the National Historic Register. **Annabelle's Famous Keg and Chowder House** off the hotel lobby offers room service or restaurant dining on the premises. The gorgeous 20-foot mahogany bar at Annabelle's is well worth a look-see, as are the murals that depict Ketchikan's notorious old Creek Street red light district, where Annabelle, in the 1920s, entertained as a favorite "lady of the night."

Speaking of **Creek Street** and its entrepreneurs, do give the lane a stroll, off Stedman Street opposite the big harbor downtown called Thomas Basin. A former brothel called **Dolly's House** (open daily in the summer; admission is $3.00) has been restored as a museum there, as have numerous other "houses," which now contain boutiques, gift shops, and galleries.

Fourteen miles north of Ketchikan the nicely named **Eagle's Roost Bed and Breakfast** (907–247–9187; 410 Knudson Cove Road) perches just above Knudson Cove harbor and marina. A large covered deck allows for taking in the surrounding rain forest, even if it's sprinkling. Rates are $75 to $90 for two.

6

Al and Carol Johnson's **Great Alaska Cedar Works Bed and Breakfast,** 11 miles north of Ketchikan at 1527 Pond Reef Road, is comprised of two cottages, one on the beach, complete with views of passing cruise ships, fishing vessels, eagles, and sea birds. Both have private baths, feather beds, and continental breakfasts featuring home-baked goodies from Carol Johnson's oven. For reservations and information, call (907) 247-8287. Rates start at $55, single or double.

Ketchikan Hostel, housed in the First United Methodist Church at Main and Grant Streets, offers pretty basic accommodations (mattresses on the floor in two "dorm" rooms, limited family accommodations in other rooms), but the people in charge are friendly and the price is certainly right at $7.00 per person. The walk to downtown is short but sort of steep. Reservations are a good idea; call (907) 225-3319.

She will never serve the masses (how many people can a '55 Chevy sedan accommodate?), but for a select few visitors who want really personalized tour attention, the former schoolmarm Lois Munch will introduce you to Ketchikan's Native history, take you to totem parks, tell you about the critters in a saltwater tide pool, explain the flora and fauna of the area, and even show you an occupied eagles' nest. She calls her operation **Classic Tours** (907-225-3091). You can't miss her on the waterfront. The restored Chevy is blazing red, trimmed in white.

It's not quite the biggest island under the American flag (the Big Island of Hawaii and Kodiak Island in Southwest Alaska rank first and second in that category) but ❖**Prince of Wales Island** (POW) is huge, nonetheless: 2,231 square miles of forested mountains, deep U-shaped valleys, lakes, streams, and 900 miles of coastal shores, bays, and inlets. You get to Prince of Wales by state ferry from Ketchikan or by plane. POW is not without controversy: Environmentalists say the island has been overlogged; the timber industry says reforestation is coming along very nicely. You decide for yourself. One thing logging has done is create lots of roads (some gravel, others asphalt) that you can use for exploring and camping. Kayaking or canoeing is superb at lots of freshwater and saltwater access points.

It's definitely remote and accessible only by air, but any reference to roughing it on the island at ❖**Waterfall Resort** would be outrageous. The made-over former fish cannery has been featured on TV's *Lifestyles of the Rich and Famous,* and the resort gives the word *deluxe* a whole new meaning. Take fishing. You don't just check out a skiff and head for the fishing grounds. Instead you're assigned a spiffy cabin cruiser and a personal fishing guide for the length of your stay. The angling is world class for king and silver salmon, halibut, lingcod, and red snapper. Accommodations in rooms, condos, and cottages are "plush rustic" and leave nothing to be wished for. Meals feature a generous choice of fish or other entrees. It's pretty expensive (prices start at $2,530 per person for four days, three nights), but if you can afford the tariff, it's worth every penny. Call (800) 544–5125.

Another fishing lodge in the luxury category is the **Whales Resort** on the northern shores of the island. Here, too, the emphasis is on quality, with guided fishing, deluxe cabin cruisers, and gourmet dining cuisine. For information call (800) 531–9643.

For do-it-yourselfers the **U.S. Forest Service** has five campgrounds and more than twenty $25 rental cabins on lakes and inlets throughout the island. Call (907) 826–3271 in Craig; (907) 828–3304 at Thorne Bay. The **Log Cabin RV Park and Resort** (800–544–2205) offers cabins at $35 per night plus camper facilities, and fishing out of Klawock. The **Fireweed Lodge** (907–755–2930), also in Klawock, offers twenty rooms at $75 for doubles plus meals, rental cars, fishing charters, and access to excellent hiking and canoeing. **McFarland's Floatel** (907–828–3335) provides beachfront log cabins at Thorne Bay. The $140-per-night units will accommodate up to four guests. Jeff and Kelli Larson's **Southeast Retreat** at Thorne Bay (907–755–2994) is accessible only by boat or floatplane, but once you're there, the Larsons will provide you with a 16-foot skiff to facilitate your fishing (and seal, porpoise, or whale watching) or an auto to aid in your search for eagles, black bears, and other "watchable" wildlife. One to four guests share a 1,200-square-foot cedar lodge, fully modern and overlooking forest-rimmed Thorne Bay. Rates start at $150 for one or two guests plus $35 per day per guest for meals.

Sylvia Geraghty has upgraded her **Bear Bight Camps** (at **Tokeen** on El Capitan Island, 80 miles northwest of Ketchikan) from tents to "cute cabins," but her operation, she emphasizes, is still "as far off the beaten path as you can get in Southeast Alaska." Guests can use kayaks, skiffs, and canoes to explore the

8

area. Groceries, liquor, and fishing licenses can be purchased at the site. There's still no telephone, she reports, but you can write to her at: Tokeen, P.O. Box TKI, Ketchikan, AK 99950-0230.

It would be easy to miss ❖**Hyder,** in southernmost South-eastern. In fact, sadly, most travelers do. If you're Alaska-bound, however, and traveling along British Columbia's Yellowhead Highway between Prince George and Prince Rupert, take the 140-mile paved Cassiar Highway north from its junction with the Yellowhead Highway (about 150 miles before Prince Rupert). Then take the access road off the Cassiar to Hyder. This road leads also to Hyder's very close neighbor, **Stewart.** Stewart (population 1,000 or so) sits in British Columbia, Canada, and Hyder (population 75) lies in Alaska. They're separated by 2.3 miles and the U.S.–Canada border. After your visit, if you don't want to retrace your path down the Cassiar, you can board the small Alaska ferry *Aurora* once a week for a direct connection to Ketchikan. Similarly, of course, if you're heading south from Ketchikan, you can take the *Aurora* to Hyder instead of Prince Rupert.

What's to see in and around Hyder? For one thing, you'll find spectacular glaciers to view, including **Salmon Glacier**, the world's fifth largest, only 20 miles north of town. You'll also find abandoned mine sites, late nineteenth-century buildings to photograph, superb fishing, hiking trails and—three miles north of town—a salmon stream and bear observatory where you can see black bears or brownies. Just barely on the Alaska side of the U.S.–Canada border is the **Hyder Museum and Information Center,** which should be your first stop in this part of Alaska. In Stewart, the **Stewart Historical Society Museum** displays wildlife in the Fire Hall as well as bits and pieces of local history.

The **Grandview Inn**, located ¾ mile from the border on Hyder's main road, has ten clean, private rooms, three with kitchenettes, in quiet, woodsy surroundings. The rate is $50 per night, U.S. funds. Call (604) 636–9174.

THE MIDDLE OF THE PANHANDLE

Wrangell is a natural for the visitor who wants an out-of-the-way travel experience in a locale that's still a little rough around the edges. It's clean, neat, and easy to get around, but everything isn't laid out for you. You get there either by a daily Alaska Airlines jet from Juneau, Ketchikan, or Seattle or by the ferries of the Alaska Marine Highway System. The tour company movers of masses have seemingly passed Wrangell by, at least for now. The mega–cruise ships rarely call, and even medium or small vessels stop much less frequently than in Ketchikan, Sitka, and Juneau. The result is that it's a made-to-order destination for travelers who enjoy ferreting out backcountry or backyard jewels in the rough (literally and figuratively)—from semiprecious garnets you can literally collect yourself on a nearby ledge to some of the best and most photogenic totem poles in Alaska. Now for a little background.

Wrangell history goes back possibly 8,000 years, when someone (no one knows who) was here and carved mysterious stick-figure petroglyph etchings in stone along the seashore. More recently, according to Tlingit oral history, the present Native peoples settled the area more than 2,000 years ago, arriving via the Stikine River. Sometime in the 1700s a Tlingit chief named Shakes (the first of several to claim that name) selected the present site of Wrangell as home for his people.

In the early 1800s English, American, and Russian ships came exploring. The Russians established Redoubt St. Dionysius in 1834. The English obtained a lease and occupied the same site, calling it Fort Stikine, in 1840. With the sale of Alaska to the United States in 1867, the community came under American jurisdiction and was called Fort Wrangell. Gold mining, fur trading, fisheries, commerce, and timber have been Wrangell's economic staples since.

Recent years have seen the modest beginnings of tourism, and it's true, there's a lot in and around the community for visitors to experience. A good place to visit early, in order to get oriented, is the **Chamber of Commerce Visitor Information** A-frame building on Outer Drive at Bruger Street, next door to City Hall, on the water (907–874–3901). Another is the ◆ **City of Wrangell Museum**, at 318 Second Street. The previous museum building at Second and McCormack streets is Wrangell's original school-house, from 1906, and is the starting place for a self-guided historic walking tour that includes structures from early in the twentieth century and even the nineteenth. Tour maps are available at the museum. The museum has only recently moved and is being temporarily housed in the basement of the city Community Center between the Presbyterian Church and the high school on

Church Street. The collection is well worth a visit. It includes masterfully carved totemic house posts, believed to date back to 1770–1790, from the Bear Tribal House on Chief Shakes Island. Also on display: artifacts from the Russian and British occupations and from the gold rush era, petroglyphs, bird and natural history exhibits, minerals, and various other items. Hours are 10:00 A.M. to 5:00 P.M. Monday through Friday, 1:00 to 5:00 P.M. Saturday, and 1:00 to 5:00 P.M. Sunday or depending on ferry schedule.

The most notable cultural site in the community is ◈ **Chief Shakes Island,** connected to Wrangell by bridge and located in the middle of Wrangell Harbor. The tribal house and totems there are among the best carved and most colorful in Alaska. Storytellers, presenters of Native plays, and the **Shxat'Kwaan Native dancers** often perform at the site when cruise ships come to port. There is a $1.00 admission charge.

You can see some **petroglyphs** on display at the city museum and library, but most must be sought out at low tide on Wrangell Island's mysterious ◈ **Petroglyph Beach** north of town. The etched figures on the rocks, three dozen or more, seem to depict spirit faces, fish, owls, spirals, and other designs, although no one really knows what the figures really mean or who created them. To reach them, turn left on Evergreen Avenue from the ferry terminal. Walk north on Evergreen about ¾ mile to a boardwalk leading to the beach. Walk down the boardwalk and head right toward the big rock outcropping on the northern high-tide limit of the beach. Don't, under any circumstances, attempt to move these rocks. You may, of course, photograph them.

A moderately difficult hike (due to a rapid ascent) over the **Rainbow Falls Trail** can be short or long, depending on whether or not you extend the distance by also hiking the high country ridges along the 2.7-mile **Institute Creek Trail** that junctions along the way with the Rainbow Falls Trail. The basic route takes you about .75 mile from its start at mile 4.6 on the Zimovia Highway to an observation platform and a great view of picturesque Rainbow Falls, then later to a sweeping view of Chichagof Pass. Another popular hiking choice in town is **Mt. Dewey**, also called Muir Mountain since John Muir climbed it in 1879 and caused a considerable stir among the locals when he lit a huge bonfire at the top. The trail is primitive in places, but the view from the top is considered well worth the effort.

Totem pole on Chief Shakes Island

There are two ways to get one or more of Wrangell's well-known garnets. The easiest is simply to buy one from youngsters you'll find selling them at the docks to cruise ship and ferry passengers. Local kids sell the garnets for $1.00 to $50.00, depending on size. Or you can purchase a $10 daily permit at the Wrangell Museum and chip your own garnets from **Wrangell Garnet Ledge,** located on the mainland near the mouth of the Stikine River, about 7 miles northeast of Wrangell Island. Waterborne sight-seeing tours often stop at the site.

And then there's **Our Collections**. Most visitors overlook it, but shouldn't. Some call it a museum. Others see it and claim it's more of a garage sale that's never happened. What it is, is an incredible display of collectibles that Elva Bigelow and her late husband, Bolly, saved and lovingly preserved over six decades of living in Wrangell. You'll find gold rush paraphernalia from mining days up the Stikine River, old-time logging tools, early day fishing gear, trapping supplies, even hand-crank sewing machines, and clocks, waffle irons, and copper wash kettles. It's the kind of place you can happily rummage around in, wondering why you're doing it, but having the time of your life. You locate Our Collections by walking up the road from the ferry terminal and turning left on Stikine-Evergreen Avenue. It's the same route you take to Petroglyph Beach. Along the way, take the time in June and July to sample tasty salmonberries and thimbleberries growing alongside the road. Before you get to the beach, you'll come to the Bigelows' big metal building on the seaward side of the avenue. Our Collections is open when cruise ships or ferries are in port, or by appointment by calling (907) 874-3646. No admission, but donations are gratefully accepted.

For close-to-town overnight accommodations call Gertude Rooney to reserve a room with private or shared bath at **Rooney's Roost Bed and Breakfast** (907-874-2026), located at 206 McKinnon Street just a block from downtown. Prices start at $55 for units with private baths. Another option, this one close to Chief Shakes Island, is the **Hungry Beaver** (907-874-3005) just behind the restaurant and lounge of the same name at 274 Shakes Street. Four comfortable rooms with kitchenettes run $65 for doubles. For at least one meal partake of the restaurant's locally famous pizza fare. For the economy minded, the **Wrangell Hostel,** operated by the First Presbyterian Church, at

13

220 Church Street, opens mid-May through Labor Day and charges $10 per person a night. Phone (907) 874–3534.

Bruce Harding's **Old Sourdough Lodge**, 1104 Peninsula Avenue, started life some years back as a small bunkhouse for loggers. Today the rustic log lodge offers a wide selection of comfortable accommodations that include the Jacuzzi-equipped Harding River suite that sleeps six as well as standard rooms with bath. Also on-site: a sauna and steam bath, plus the Sourdough Room cocktail lounge. Standard room rates start at $55; bed-and-breakfast accommodations start at $75. Meals cost $8.00 for breakfast or lunch; dinners start at $16. Call (800) 874-3613 for information.

Todd Harding operates **Stikeen Wilderness Adventures**, offering one-day trips through forested wilderness up the Stikine River aboard the twenty-three-passenger *Stikine Princess*, the eighteen-passenger *Iskut Express,* and *The Wild Side.* The latter vessel carries five passengers and offers adrenaline-seekers a "Ride on the Wild Side." All three vessels were specifically designed and built to navigate the Stikine, the fastest flowing navigable river in North America. The company also offers trips south of Wrangell to **Anan Creek Bear Observatory,** the only black bear observatory in Southeast Alaska. The Stikine River and Anan trips cost $135. Excursions up the river to the United States–Canada border run $175. For information, call (800) 874–2085.

Dean and Chris Jaquish own and operate **Alaska Yachting and Fishing**, a service that provides day or overnight cruising, wildlife viewing, or fishing aboard their vessel *Christine,* a 42-foot Hatteras motor yacht. Two smaller tenders take passengers to shore or poke into hard-to-reach places. Day charters cost $145 per person, overnights $255.

Somewhat larger is the 53-foot *Belinda V.*, whose early life was that of a commercial troller and long-liner fishing for halibut and black cod in the rugged waters of the Gulf of Alaska. During adventure tours or fishing excursions, passengers can learn about nautical charts, navigation, radio and radar operation, and other aspects of life on the sea. Rates begin at $175 per person per day. Call **Belinda V. Charters** for details, (800) 543–4269.

The Wyricks—Ken and Toni—wear several visitor-service hats. Toni operates **Harbor House Lodging**, a B&B with accommodations not only on the water but over the water. Rooms are $65 a night for a single or double, $93 for a two-bedroom apartment with complete kitchen and balcony. Ken runs **Harbor House Rentals**, where you can rent 16- or 17-foot aluminum boats for do-it-yourself fishing and sight-seeing. The 16-footers rent for $75 for a half day or $100 for a full day. The larger craft run $125. Ken's **Alaska Star Charters** provide luxury yacht tours for up to six guests to out-of-the-way bays, glaciers, streams, and wildlife viewing areas, starting at $2,895 per person for six days, five nights. For more information, call (907) 874–3084.

Remember those bargain-priced ($25 per night) fly-in **U.S. Forest Service cabins** in the wilderness? Twenty of them are located in the Wrangell Ranger District, including one near the Anan Creek Bear Observatory. Call (907) 874–2323 for vacancies and reservations. If you're a hot-tub buff, ask for information about the **Chief Shakes Hot Springs** tubs (one sheltered, one not) that the USFS has placed along the Stikine River about 22 miles from Wrangell. Ask, too, about summertime ranger-led walks along trails and beaches.

If you're scuba trained, Kevin Kulm of **Alaska Underwater Adventures** (907–874–3015) will help you dive for crab and other shellfish as well as locate kelp beds, shipwrecks, and other sights below the surface. Prices vary. High above the surface, **Sunrise Aviation** (907–874–2319) will take you flight-seeing over the Stikine River and several glaciers, ice-clogged LeConte Bay, and various high-country lakes, for $85. You even get a souvenir T-shirt or cap. On the ground, Mark Galla's **Alaska Peak and Seas** (907–874–2454) will take you into the backcountry for photography or trekking adventures priced from $250 per day plus bush flight or $300 plus air charter for backcountry fishing.

Back in 1897, when the rest of the world went crazy over gold in the Klondike, Norwegian-born Peter Buschmann came north too, but only as far as Mitkof Island in Southeast Alaska. He settled there to fish and eventually build a salmon cannery and sawmill. Other Norwegians, noting the great fisheries of the region, the abundant ice from nearby LeConte Glacier, and the majestic surroundings, joined Buschmann and his family and named their community **Petersburg.**

Today, Peter's *burg* thrives as one of the most active fishing ports in the United States. Fishermen seine, troll, and gillnet for salmon in the summer, seek halibut into the fall, fish for herring in the spring, go after crab in the winter, and harvest shrimp year-round. Sport fishing for salmon and halibut is especially rewarding.

About 3,700 Alaskans call Petersburg home. Most of them fish or work in the fisheries industry or in businesses that service the fishermen. In the summer, one of the pleasantest no-cost "tours" you can take is simply to wander in Petersburg's three **public harbors** along 2½ miles of floats, taking in the 1,200 or so commercial fishing vessels that may be in port at any one time. Tourism is a rapidly growing but not yet dominant industry in Petersburg, and thereby—as in Wrangell—lies much of the community's charm. The town is "real." And it's clean, neat, well laid out, and noticeably Norwegian, with its Scandinavian rosemaling floral designs on buildings and homes, its huge, white 1912 **Sons of Norway Hall** downtown (complete with a **Viking sailing vessel** ready to put to sea). If you're lucky you'll find Norwegian seafood specialties on menus at local restaurants. (Beer batter halibut is a particular pleaser. So is the tiny succulent, popcorn-sized shrimp for which the community is known.) The town, no surprise, is nicknamed Little Norway, and its biggest celebration is the **Little Norway Festival,** timed each May to celebrate Norwegian Independence Day.

A good place to start your visit to Petersburg is the **Visitor Information Center** at First and Fram streets. Office hours are 8:00 A.M. to 4:30 P.M. in the summer. Phone (907) 772–4636 for information.

The community's biggest visitor attraction is nearby ◈**LeConte Glacier**, one of the most active in North America, with a constant succession of icebergs calving and crashing explosively from its wide face into the frigid waters of **LeConte Bay**. Many days the big and little bergs literally carpet bay waters from shore to shore, and sight-seeing boats must gently push the ice aside as they cruise in front of the glacier.

The waters of North Frederick Sound, also near Petersburg, provide superb viewing of another major visitor attraction: great **humpback whales.** Large numbers of these gentle giants feed here in the summer months, to the considerable delight of visitors as well as locals. Several charter operators offer LeConte glacier and whale-watching excursions, among them Steve Berry's **Sights Southeast** with whom you can arrange cruises through

Viking Travel (800–327–2571). Berry will not only show you the whales, he'll let you listen to them via onboard hydrophones. A four-hour glacier cruise costs $85 per person and a six-hour whale-watching trip runs $135. A combination package allows you to book both segments (on the same or different days) for $185.

Viking Travel, incidentally, provides handy one-stop shopping for several tours including guided half-day land excursions around Mitkof Island by **SeeAlaska** for $20, and five-hour sea kayaking trips with **Tongass Kayak** for $45. Viking will also arrange independent travel throughout Alaska.

For a bird's-eye view of LeConte Glacier, you can book a flight-seeing excursion with **Pacific Wing,** (907) 772–4258. A 45-minute flight costs $195 for up to three passengers.

Here's a really innovative tour available from **Northern Bikes** and **Alaskan Scenic Waterways**: It's a five-day **Mountain Bike Adventure** over remote, virtually nonmotorized former logging roads. The locale is accessed by jet boat. Two guides are on hand to interpret plants and wildlife and a camp manager in an all-terrain vehicle travels well ahead of the party to set up camp each night. The cost is $985 per person, with a six-person maximum per trip. Ron Compton's Alaskan Scenic Waterways also packages birding expeditions on and around the 27,000-acre Stikine River delta in the spring ($985 for five days), seven-day Stikine River boating and camping adventures along the fastest flowing river in North America in the summer (priced at $1,925), and remote fishing in the summer and fall for $250 per person per day. Call (800) 279–1176 for more information.

For the visitor who enjoys walking tours, the tabloid-sized Viking Visitor Guide, available at the Visitor Information Center, provides an easy-to-follow walking tour map covering more than 30 points of interest, from major fish processing plants along the waterfront to **Eagle's Roost Park** off Nordic Drive just a few minutes walk from downtown. One or two eagles are almost always in residence to pose for pictures on their craggy perches.

You'll know you've arrived at the ◆**Clausen Memorial Museum**, located at Second and Fram Streets, when you see the large bronze sculpture called *Fisk* (Norwegian for "fish"), which displays the many species of fish to be found in these waters. Inside, exhibits vary from an old-time fish-gutting machine (called an iron chink) to the re-created office of a pioneer cannery

17

owner. There are also fur farming exhibits, Native artifacts, including an old Indian canoe, and early-day community photographs. Don't miss the two huge wall-mounted salmon, one of them the largest king ever caught (126.5 pounds) and the other the world's largest chum (a 36 pounder).

Tongass Traveler is a sight-seeing service that tours a seafood cannery, a salmon smokery, and other sights during a two-hour van trip. Shrimp cocktail and beverage are included in the $25 charge. Call (907) 772–4837.

The U.S. Forest Service rents numerous cabins in the National Forest around Petersburg, including **Ravens Roost**, one of the relatively few USFS shelters you can hike to. It's located on the mountain behind Petersburg Airport, nearly 4 miles by trail or 3 by helicopter. The Raven Trail begins near the orange and white tank south of the airport with 1 mile of boardwalk through muskeg (spongy bog) before the trail's ascent begins. The middle section is relatively steep, then flattens along the ridge top. The easy way to enjoy the experience is to fly in by helicopter, then hike out downhill. Like others, the cabin rents for $25 per night per party. For details from the USFS Petersburg Ranger District, call (907) 772–3871. Temsco Helicopters will drop you off at the cabin for around $100. Call (907) 772–4780 for more information.

When Petersburg folk talk of driving "out the road," they're referring to the 34-mile **Mitkof Highway**, along which you can visit the **Falls Creek Fish Ladder** near mile 11, and the **Crystal Lake Fish Hatchery** and **Blind Slough recreation area** at mile 17.5. Birders visiting in the wintertime will especially enjoy the **Trumpeter Swan Observatory** at mile 16.

One of Alaska's rarer boating experiences is a three-hour outing aboard a genuine workboat, **Syd Wright's *Chan IV*.** Wright, a retired educator, is a walking, talking, entertaining encyclopedia of things Alaskan. One of the highlights of the trip will be a sampling of crab, shrimp, or other seafood delicacies. The fee is $85; call (907) 772–4859 for more information. For the fisherman, **LeConte Outfitters** offers quality fishing and sight-seeing trips through the island-studded waters of the area. The cost is $200 per day per person, multiple-day trips only. For more information call (907) 772–4790.

If you're looking for a downtown lodging location call the **Tides Inn** (907–772–4288; First and Dolphin streets). Ask for a room overlooking the harbor. Owner Gloria Ohmer was born and raised in Petersburg, and she's an absolute fount of knowledge about things to see and do. Rates start at $85, including complimentary continental breakfast. **Nordic House Bed and Breakfast,** three blocks north of the ferry terminal (806 Nordic Drive; 907-772-3620), offers a view of Wrangell Narrows, boats, planes, sometimes even wildlife. Rates are $70 for a double with shared bath. The **Rocky Point Resort,** 11 miles south of town on Wrangell Narrows, offers saltwater fishing for salmon, halibut, trout, crab, and shrimp in protected waters. The $250 rate per person per night includes a cabin, a skiff with motor, meals, fishing gear, and freezing facilities so you can take your catch home. Call (907) 772-4420 for reservations and information.

For one of life's memorable seafood dining experiences, plan at least one dinner at the **Viking Room** of the **Beachcomber Inn** (907-772-3888), located about mile 4 on the Mitkof Highway. Steaks are available as well. You can enjoy cocktails in the Cannery Lounge. Dinners are priced $6.00 to $22.00. The inn is actually a converted cannery offering quiet, cozy accommodations, priced from $60 to $70.

Many Alaskans and most visitors rank **Sitka** the most visually beautiful community in the state. Perched at the base of majestic mountains on Baranof Island, the community looks westerly toward Pacific Ocean waters upon hundreds of big and little, near and distant isles, mountains, and a massive volcano. Native Alaskan and Russian history abounds in this community. It was the hub and headquarters of Russian America and the czars' vast fur seal gathering and trading empire until the United States purchased Alaska in 1867. Sitka served as the territory of Alaska's capital until the early years of the twentieth century. It is, today, a forestry, fishing, travel, and education center.

Collectors of trivia take note: When you visit Sitka you visit the largest city, in size, in the Western Hemisphere. It's the second largest in the world. There are 4,710 square miles within the unified city and borough municipal borders. (Juneau, at 3,108 square miles, comes in third; Kiruna, Sweden, with 5,458 square miles ranks as the world's largest city.)

If one of your goals is to save money, consider overnighting in the student apartments at **Sheldon Jackson College** on Lincoln Street between Jeff Davis Street and College Drive. The rooms are spartan and showers and toilets are down the hall (so is a lounge with TV), but you'll find everything clean and everybody friendly. The price is right: $30 for a double in an older building and $50 in newer quarters. (Incidentally, first priority for rooms goes to visitors attending college conferences.) The surrounding campus is woodsy, tranquil, historic, and allows a spectacular view of the sea. Downtown Sitka lies only a seven-minute stroll away. For reservations or information, call (907) 747–5203. You can take cafeteria meals on campus as well: $4.50 for breakfast, $5.50 for lunch, and $8.00 for dinner.

Whether or not you opt to house on campus, don't fail to visit the ◈ **Sheldon Jackson Museum**, at 104 College Drive on the campus. Actually, the octagonal-shaped building itself ranks as something of an artifact, having been constructed in 1895 as the first concrete structure in Alaska. It's named for the nineteenth-century Presbyterian missionary and educator who supplied a large portion of the collection. The museum is small and sometimes overlooked, but most visitors find it well worthwhile. The well-presented collection emphasizes the Native peoples of Alaska—Tlingit and Haida Indians of the Southeast, Athabascan Indians of the interior, Aleuts from the Southwest, and Eskimos of the far north. You'll never get a better, closer look at a Tlingit dugout canoe, an Athabascan birch-bark canoe, an ancient two-passenger Aleut baidarka (kayak), and two Eskimo kayaks. You'll see Indian battle armor as well as exquisite Eskimo fur parkas. Also on display: three "mystery balls"—big perfectly round balls of stone, two of them around 10 inches in diameter and one perhaps 16 inches. A museum sign asks, presumably with tongue in cheek, could they be "whale kidney stones, petrified pterodactyl eggs or giant cannon balls"? The museum operates 8:00 A.M. to 5:00 P.M. daily in summer; 10:00 A.M. to 4:00 P.M Tuesday through Saturday in winter. Admission is $3.00.

For visitors with RVs or tents, the campgrounds of choice in Sitka are clearly the two **U.S. Forest Service campgrounds at Starrigavan Bay,** close to 8 miles north of town on Halibut Point Road. Both feature separated, private campsites surrounded by thick, towering trees. Near the entrance to the upper campground you'll also find one of Alaska's easiest walking trails. The **Starrigavan Estuary** wheelchair accessible trail, a .5-mile elevated boardwalk, takes you beside open wetlands and into deep and dark woods of spruce, hemlock, and alder trees.

Another short and gentle hike, this one at the south end of Lincoln Street on the shores of Sitka Sound, lies within **Sitka National Historical Park**. Actually you can enjoy two trails there—one a 1.5-mile stroll back into Alaska history on the site of the bloodiest battle fought between Tlingit Indians and nineteenth-century Russians, the other (less frequented by visitors) a .75-mile jogging course.

If your tastes run far off the beaten path, you may consider chartering a boat for a drop-off at the sea level trailhead of the **Mt. Edgecumbe National Recreation Trail** on Kruzof Island, about 10 miles west of Sitka. The 6.7-mile trail up the side of this volcanic crater (a look-alike for Japan's Mt. Fuji) is steep and usually takes about eight hours. The view from the summit of ocean waters and myriad islands is a mind-boggler.

If you've never experienced the fun of a kayak ride, here's a good place to start. **Alaska Travel Adventures** offers a three-hour **Sitka Sea Kayaking Adventure**, led by experienced guides through protected island waterways. The $69 tour often includes views of deer, brown bears, seals, and (always) eagles. For advance reservations or more information call (907) 789–0052 (in Juneau). **Bidarka Boats** (907–747–8996) will likewise outfit you with single or double-seat kayaks for half day ($25 and $35, respectively), full day ($35 and $45) or longer trips in Sitka Sound and environs.

Sitkan Jane Eidler arranges fascinating ninety-minute historic **walking tours** of downtown Sitka taking in a lofty view of ocean and islands from **Castle Hill** (where "Russian America" officially became "Alaska, U.S.A." in 1867), a re-created **Russian blockhouse**, the old Russian cemetery, the Lutheran Cemetery where, interestingly, Russian Princess Maksoutoff lies buried, historic houses, the **Saint Michael's Russian Orthodox Cathedral,** the **Russian Bishop's House** (part of Sitka National Historical Park), and more. Primarily these are group tours, but you can call (907) 747–5354 to see if there's a group scheduled with which you can tag along.

There's a new and different motor-coach tour on the scene in Sitka. On days when cruise ships are in port—which is almost every day in the summer—the **Sitka Tribe of Alaska** offers a

21

tour from the perspective of the Indian people who lived here before, during, and after the Russians. The narrated, two-and-a-half hour excursion, priced at $18, takes in **Sitka National Historical Park**, **Sheldon Jackson Museum**, a narrative drive through **Sitka's native village**, and a Native dance performance featuring the **Gajaa Heen Dancers**. For details, call (907) 747–7290.

The USFS lists twenty-one fly-in or boat-in cabins accessible from Sitka. Probably the most exotic in all of Alaska is the ◆ **White Sulphur Springs cabin**, on nearby Chichagof Island. It features a weather-tight log cabin with large windows facing out from a picturesque rocky beach onto the broad Pacific—plus an adjacent structure containing an oversize hot springs bath (almost a pool) with the same awesome ocean view. Getting to this cabin is costlier than most because you have to helicopter in, but if you can afford the tariff the trip itself will rank as one of your vacation highlights of a lifetime. The local USFS number in Sitka is (907) 747–6671.

Surely one of Alaska's premiere wildlife viewing excursions is the 50-mile, three-and-a-half hour sight-seeing boat trip from Sitka to Salisbury Sound. Priced at $80 and called the ◆ **Sea Otter and Wildlife Quest**, the cruise takes you through great bays and narrow passages past countless thick-forested islands in your quest for sea otters, three species of whales (humpback, killer, and minke), brown bears, deer, seals, and eagles. Although you can't really score a view of all these critters on any one cruise, I recently took the trip and saw a huge humpback (doing spectacular dives with tail held high), Sitka black-tailed deer on three different beaches, eagles and mammoth eagle nests, harbor seals by the dozen, and sea otters by the score. To avoid hordes of cruise-ship passengers, call Allen Marine, operators of the trip, and ask about their afternoon tours (not offered daily), for locals and non-cruise ship visitors. These tours, priced at $80, are far less crowded, and if no one has a time crunch the skipper may extend the trip to extra inlets and islands. For details, call (907) 747–8100.

Here's another quality wildlife viewing excursion by water: **Sitka's Secrets** (907–747–5089) offers four-hour trips for $80 on the 26-foot vessel *Sitka Secret* to **St. Lazaria National Wildlife Refuge** for a view that sets birders cackling. St.

Lazaria, a 65-acre island some 15 miles west of Sitka, contains the nests of an estimated 2,000 rhinoceros auklets, 5,000 common and thick-billed murres, 11,000 tufted puffins (comical little creatures sometimes called sea parrots or flying footballs), 450,000 fork-tailed and Leache's storm petrels, plus eagles and other winged species. En route there's a good possibility you'll view whales, seals, sea lions, and sea otters.

John Yerkes' **Sitka Sportfishing** (907–747–5660) provides more than the name implies. From his 38-foot modern motor yacht, *Sea Food,* Yerkes arranges outer coast hikes, beachcombing, kayaking, hot tubbing, whale watching, and exploring. Half-day sight-seeing trips start at $85, three-guest minimum.

The primary goal of the **Alaska Raptor Rehabilitation Center**, at 1101 Sawmill Creek Road, is healing injured birds of prey, especially eagles, but the center also has a worthy program for two-legged human types as well—a fascinating narrated tour of their grounds. There are always several eagle "patients" in residence. Call (907) 747–8662 for daily tour schedules.

If you're into two-wheel tripping, **J&B Bike Rentals** (907–747–8279; 203 Lincoln Street) downtown, will rent bikes by the hour or day.

Sitka contains a bevy of B&Bs, virtually every one of them more than adequate; several are outstanding. Among the latter: **Alaska Ocean View Bed and Breakfast**, run by Carole Denkinger, provides gourmet breakfasts at times convenient to her guests plus snacks in the afternoon. These latter munchies are best enjoyed while basking in an outdoor spa on her red cedar executive-home patio. As the name implies, the view takes in ocean, islands, and mountains, yet it's close by harbors, shopping, and restaurants. Rates for doubles range from $69 to $109 for a suite. For information, call (907) 747–8310.

Burgess Bauder's Lighthouse is, well, different. It's not exactly a B&B, since the host doesn't reside in or near the premises. But it certainly isn't your usual lodge or inn, either. What it is, is a real lighthouse that Bauder constructed and located on an island a few minutes by boat from downtown Sitka. Bauder provides you with a skiff for comings and goings, though you may not wish to stray far from the tranquil surroundings. Small wooden hot tubs offer relaxing moments in the evening.The Lighthouse will sleep eight. The two bedrooms located in the tower offer particularly commanding views. You do your own cooking. Rates start at $125. Call (907) 747–3056.

Members of the United Methodist Church in Sitka operate the **Sitka Hostel** in the basement of the church, at 303 Kimshan Street, about a mile from downtown. Basically it's a dorm situation although arrangements can be made for families. No king- or queen-sized beds here; you sleep on cots. But the atmosphere is friendly and the nightly cost is only $7.00. Call (907) 747–8356.

And finally, this bit of intelligence: For Sitka's best photos of American bald eagles, take a short drive or longish walk to **McDonald's**, north of downtown at 913 Halibut Point Road. From your sea-view window in the restaurant or from the parking lot, you can almost always see several of the great birds soaring and swooping into the water across the street for their own fast "McFish" meals.

Port Alexander is one of those small, isolated communities that infrequent visitors end up raving about. Located at the southern tip of Baranof Island, the town once boasted 2,000 residents. Today there are about 125, among them Paul and Gayle Young, who operate **Rainforest Retreat Bed and Breakfast,** a private beachside cabin that's fully modern and clean with oil heat, running water, and a picture-window view of the inner bay and Sawtooth Ridge. They have additional accommodations in the main house. Guests hike into old-growth forests, muskeg meadows, alpine country, or along intertidal beaches. They climb locally renowned No Name Peak, visit fish buying scows, pick berries, catch shrimp, or dig for clams and—most pleasant of all—meet local characters who spin colorful stories (some of them Alaska-sized whoppers!). Daily rate is $80 per person. Air access (for about $90 one way) is via Sitka, 65 miles north. For information, call (907) 568–2229.

THE UPPER PANHANDLE

I once wrote a guidebook about **Juneau** called *This is Juneau, the Nation's Most Scenic Capital City.* Wordy perhaps, but the description is apt. The most populated portion of town sits on the shores of Gastineau Channel, backed up by awesomely steep Mt. Juneau, Mt. Roberts, and various other peaks in the 3,000-foot-

and-higher class. Within Juneau's 3,108 square miles you'll find big bays, tiny inlets, thickly vegetated islands, and numerous glaciers (including **Mendenhall Glacier**, the second most visited river of ice in Alaska). The town also contains large portions of the Juneau Icefield, a 1,500-square-mile, high-altitude desert of hard-packed ice and snow that extends from behind the city to beyond the Canadian border. It's from the overflow of this ice field that Mendenhall, Taku, and other great glaciers descend. Juneau had its start in 1880 as a miners' camp after a local Indian chief, Kowee, led prospectors Joe Juneau and Dick Harris over Snowslide Gulch into Silverbow Basin. They found, according to Harris's account, gold "in streaks running through the rock and little lumps as large as peas or beans."

You can see exhibits of the community's gold mining history in the small, often overlooked **Juneau–Douglas City Museum** at Fourth and Main streets, open 9:00 A.M. until 5:00 P.M. weekdays, 10:00 A.M. to 5:00 P.M. weekends. Admission is $1.00. You can view more history (including native Eskimo, Indian, and Aleut displays) and wild animal dioramas (including a spectacular multistoried eagle's nest tree) in the **Alaska State Museum**, 395 Whittier Street, a couple of blocks from downtown. If you're traveling with young children don't miss the Discovery Room on the second floor where kids can climb aboard a playlike copy of Captain James Cook's eighteenth century vessel *Discovery*, stroke wild animal pelts, and dress in period costumes. Museum admission is $3.00. Hours are 9:00 A.M. to 6:00 P.M. weekdays, 10:00 A.M. to 6:00 P.M. weekends.

Also often passed by—but for history buffs well worth the effort of a few blocks' climb to Chicken Ridge from downtown—is ◆**Wickersham House**, the restored Victorian home of Judge James Wickersham, a pioneer jurist and Alaska territorial (nonvoting) delegate to Congress. You can see the judge's diaries, his artifact collection and period furniture as well as interpretive displays and a grand hilltop view of the city's business district. If you don't want to climb the steep streets and walkways to this state historic site, take a cab to 213 Seventh Street. Phone (907) 586–9001. Admission is $2.00. Hours are 10:00 A.M. to 4:00 P.M. Thursday through Sunday, 10:00 A.M. to 6:00 P.M. Monday.

Juneau is blessed with an incredible number of hiking trails, many of them remnants of old mining roads dating back to the

1920s and even earlier. If you lack wheels, you can easily reach several from downtown Juneau, including the **Mt. Roberts Trail** (2⁷/₁₀ miles one way), which begins at the end of Sixth Street; **Perseverance Trail** (3.5 miles one way), which you access by walking up Gold Street to Basin Road; and the **Mt. Juneau Trail** (2 steep miles one way), which begins as a side trail about .5 mile along the Perseverance Trail. The Mt. Roberts and Mt. Juneau treks meander through thick forests until they break out, finally, above timberline for awesome aerial views of green forests, Gastineau Channel, and Douglas Island, across the water.

Near **Mendenhall Glacier**, 13 miles north of downtown, the **West Glacier Trail** (3½ miles one way) takes you from the parking lot on the west side of Mendenhall Lake through alder and willow forests for a mostly gradual climb up the side of Mt. McGinnis. Your destination is a 1,300-foot vantage point, where you can look down on the rolling white expanse of the glacier. If you want knowledgeable local expertise while you're trekking in the area, **Gastineau Guiding** (907–586–2666) offers daily three-and-four-hour escorted hikes along forest trails to saltwater shores and alongside historic remains and relics of the community's gold producing heyday. The cost is $40.

Beer aficionados take note: **Alaskan Brewing Company**'s amber beer and pale ale brews have taken gold medals and blue ribbons in tasting competitions across the country. You can tour Alaska's pioneer microbrewery on Shaune Drive off Old Glacier Highway, about 4 miles from downtown. The company offers tours and tastings 11:00 A.M. to 4:30 P.M. Tuesday through Saturday in the summer, but it's the most fun on bottling days. Call (907) 780–5866 for bottling days and times. Speaking of tasting brews, Alaska's best-known saloon, the **Red Dog**, is located downtown at 278 South Franklin Street, but don't overlook the saloon in the **Alaskan Hotel and Bar,** at 167 South Franklin. The big, ornate back bar there is worth a look-see, whether or not you imbibe. The hotel, incidentally, was built in 1913 and offers refurbished rooms with private and shared baths. The rates are $77.70 with bath, to $88.80 for a suite. Phone (800) 327–9347.

About dining in Juneau: The opportunities are mouthwateringly wide, from Mexican and Tex-Mex cuisine downtown at **El Sombrero** (157 South Franklin; 907-586-6770) and the **Armadillo Cafe** (413 South Franklin; 907–586–1880) to arguably

Alaska's best Friday clam chowder at the old-fashioned **Douglas Cafe** (907–364–3307) across the bridge at 918 Third Street, in the community of Douglas. Virtually unknown to the tourist trade is the tiny **Hot Bite,** open summers only on the dock at Auke Bay, 13 miles north of downtown. There the proprietors have raised the creation of hamburgers to an art form. Off the usual tourist track but probably Juneau's favorite restaurant, for good reason, is the **Fiddlehead Restaurant and Bakery** (429 West Willoughby; 907–586–3150), a short drive or a longish walk from city center. The menu varies from the likes of a modestly priced meal of black beans and rice to more expensive full-dinner offerings of fresh-caught salmon, halibut, crab, or beef. If you can, time your luncheon visit to avoid the noon-hour crowd of state workers.

Gourmet diners and history buffs will enjoy the atmosphere and the food at the historic **Summit** restaurant in the **Inn at the Waterfront** (455 South Franklin; 907–586–2050) or the equally long-lived **Silverbow Inn** (120 Second Street; 907–586–4146). Both enterprises also offer a small number of hotel accommodations, and both structures, although thoroughly modern, date back to the late nineteenth century.

If you're a Friday visitor, plan to pick up a sack lunch at any of several downtown sidewalk vendors and head for the State Office Building, **the S.O.B.,** in local parlance. There in the structure's great atrium, local and visiting organists perform each week on a grand and lusty old Kimball theater pipe organ, to the considerable delight of scores of brown-bag lunch consumers perched on benches and ledges.

You can reach more than two dozen **U.S. Forest Service cabins** in the wilderness by air (and even by boat or trail) from Juneau. Two of the closer (and therefore less costly to reach by plane) lakeside cabins are the ◆**East Turner Lake** and **West Turner Lake** units up Taku Inlet, south of the city. Trout and char fishing can be productive from either end of the lake, and wildlife watching can include brown bears (from a distance, please!), deer, mountain goats, and waterfowl. Reserve these or other cabins for $25 a night at the U.S. Forest Service Information Center in the Centennial Building, downtown at 101 Egan Drive, phone (907) 586–8751.

Alaska Discovery (800–586–1911) is one of the state's longtime and very special practitioners of the outdoor guiding art. Whether you're shopping for a day's sea kayaking adventure in protected waters north of Juneau or a week's canoe or float trip in the Arctic wilderness, Alaska Discovery has a trip tailored to your skills, budget, and inclinations. From Juneau, two one-day options are outstanding: Their **Juneau Sea Kayaking** excursion includes instruction for the uninitiated, five hours of paddling along forested beaches and coastal islands, plus lunch and beverage. Wildlife commonly seen includes seals, sea lions (possibly hundreds ashore on an island rookery), bald eagles, and—if you're really lucky—humpback or orca (killer) whales. Alaska Discovery offers similar excursions in Glacier Bay. The trip is priced at $95.

Their **Admiralty Island Canoeing** trip takes you by air to the nearby island that Tlingit Indians called *Kootz-na-hoo*, or "Fortress of the Bears." This trip offers an almost unparalleled opportunity to view brown (grizzly) bears in their natural forest habitat at and near ◆ **Pack Creek**, where the U.S. Forest Service has constructed an elevated observation platform. The 7:00 A.M. to 5:30 P.M. trip is fully guided. It includes float plane transportation from Juneau, a ¼-mile canoe paddle in protected waters, ample time ashore for hiking and bear viewing, rubber boots and gear, plus lunch and beverages. Participants must be twelve years or older. The cost is $295.

Alaska Discovery and **Wilderness Swift Charters** have combined their respective resources to offer customized trips in fully enclosed motorized vessels through some of Southeast Alaska's most spectacular glacier/forest/wildlife country in a relatively short time. Destinations can range from Sawyer Glaciers in Tracy Arm to Admiralty Island's Pack Creek bear sanctuary and Stephens Passage. Because they are customized, trips can vary from three to four days; the rate is $225 per person per day, with a four-person minimum and twelve-person maximum.

Here's another Pack Creek option: Among a variety of fishing and wildlife viewing excursions packaged by **Alaska Fly 'n' Fish Charters** (907–790–2120) is a one-day guided floatplane visit to the bear sanctuary. Like Alaska Discovery, the company is one of several allowed to guide a limited number of visitors at this truly world-class viewing site, but in addition to the guided visit, the firm offers drop-off and pickup flights for persons who have obtained their own $10 permits for unguided visits. An Alaska Fly 'n' Fish guided trip to Pack Creek runs $250 per person, and from $140 to $200 for air only depending on the number of passengers. For more information from the USFS, including a list of approved guiding companies and procedures for getting an unguided visit permit, call (907) 586–8751. You can get this information in person at Centennial Hall in downtown Juneau, but travelers who wait until they get here usually find the limited number of permits are long gone.

In Juneau, **Alaska Travel Adventures** offers three-and-a-half-hour splashy **Mendenhall Glacier Float Trips** down almost whitewater on the Mendenhall River for $83, a **Gold Panning and Gold History Tour** in the shadow of the old AJ mine for $30, **Auke Bay Kayaking** through protected waters north of town, priced at $65, and the outdoor **Gold Creek Salmon Bake**, now located on Salmon Creek near the hospital, for $22. This, incidentally, is Alaska's longest-running salmon bake. The Millers feel it's the North Country's best. The menu includes not only fresh king salmon steaks (grilled on an open pit over alder coals and glazed with a brown sugar and butter sauce) but barbecued ribs, baked beans, lots of other trimmin's, plus your choice of complimentary wine, beer, coffee, or soft drink. All this in sheltered surroundings alongside a sparkling stream and waterfall at the site of old mine diggings. To avoid a cast of thousands, call ahead (907–789–0052), ask when the busloads of cruise ship passengers are expected, then plan your own arrival earlier or later. Also on-site: the **Juneau Raptor Center,** where you'll find live eagles and other birds of prey plus exhibits you can enjoy and learn from. There's no charge for viewing the birds.

Still another sea kayak rental firm, **Alaska Serenity Kayak Company** (907–789–2655) will provide quality single and double kayaks for a day, a week, or longer. Their suggested paddling destinations range from in-town off the shores of Sandy Beach and the ruins of old gold mines to more distant pristine wilderness areas such as the Tracy Arm Fjord and glaciers area.

If skiing's your thing and you're in Juneau during the winter months, **Eaglecrest Ski Area**, about twenty minutes from downtown off North Douglas Highway, offers slopes (and two double chairlifts) for everyone from beginner to expert. For information in season call (907) 586–5330 for recorded snow conditions.

You'll find numerous ways to see glaciers around Juneau—on motor-coach tours, from boats, during hikes, and looking down from airplanes. The best way of all, in the Millers' estimation, is by helicopter. You not only fly over one or more rivers of ice, you touch down and disembark from your chopper for twenty minutes or so of frolicking on the hard-packed ice. Among experienced Alaska firms providing glacier helicopter tours: **Temsco Helicopters** (907–789–9501) and **ERA Helicopters** (800–843–1947). Fares range from $150 to $200-plus. Temsco, which originated these excursions in the Juneau area, has recently inaugurated two-hour heli-hiking options on nearby mountain ridge tops.

The longest-running operator of day cruises from downtown docks to spectacular ◆**Tracy Arm Fjord** and twin Sawyer glaciers, **Glacier Bay Tours and Cruises**, offers all-day options for $131.60 aboard the *Glacier Spirit* as well as half-day cruise/fly excursions priced at $210.13. Tracy Arm is a long, deep, meandering fjord whose steep walls rise dramatically for thousands of feet. Whales, seals, mountain goats, deer, and bears are among the wildlife viewing possibilities. Call (907) 463–5510 for information.

The Alaska traveler seeking a *really* offbeat challenge should contact Bruce Grigg's **Out of Bounds, Inc.** This Juneau-based outfit packages not-so-soft adventure as diverse as heli-skiing or snowboarding in the snow-capped Chilkat Mountain Range, glacier hikes and climbs on Mendenhall Glacier, para-gliding off Thunder Mountain in Juneau's Mendenhall Valley, mountain biking for 1,000 miles beside the Alaska Pipeline from Valdez to Prudhoe Bay, surfing remote beaches below 18,000-foot Mt. Saint Elias near Yakutat, plus (somewhat tamer) shore fishing, charter fishing, and sea kayak trips. For details, call (907) 789–7008.

You can charter Andrew Spear's 30-ton, 50-foot, three-stateroom Down East sailing cutter *Adventuress* under three options: full service (Andy provides everything, including wine with gourmet meals), crew assisted (well, you have to make your own bed, buy your own food, and do the cooking) or bare boat (for completely knowledgeable sailors). Call (907) 789–0919 for brochures and information.

Your Wilderness Connection (907–463–6788) tours include a floatplane trip over glaciers, icebergs, and forested river valleys to Taku Wilderness Lodge, then a day of rafting and sightseeing in some of the most spectacular wilderness in the Southeast panhandle. Price runs $338. If your preferences run to speedier craft, the company also offers a jet boat tour through

A small cruise vessel in Tracy Arm Fjord

iceberg-filled lakes and a close-up view of glaciers. You can also overnight at the lodge or at their Tulsequah Camp near the Alaska–British Columbia border.

Francis and Linda Kadrlik's **Adventures Afloat** (800–3AFLOAT) will likewise introduce you to the wilderness of Southeast Alaska with a flight-seeing arrival at their base of operations. In this case the base is the elegant 106-foot classic yacht *M.V. Valkyrie,* your floating home for two-, three-, or six-day eco-tours that include wildlife watching, exploring, and fishing from the smaller (32-foot) *High Roller.* Prices start at $775.

You'll find a number of good value B&B accommodations in and around Juneau. Here are two B&Bs about 11 miles from downtown and close to Juneau's number one visitor attraction,

Mendenhall Glacier. Guests at **Pearson's Pond Luxury Inn** enjoy private or shared baths, queen beds, private entries and decks, robes, slippers, and self-serve continental breakfasts plus the use of the spa, kitchens, barbecue, rowboat, and bikes. Rates are $129 and $149 for double rooms with private baths. For details, call (907) 789–3772. **Sepal Hollow Bed and Breakfast**, 10901 Mendenhall Loop Road, offers a home of California contemporary design adapted to a vintage Alaskan backwoodsy setting. The B&B offers queen-sized beds, hearty breakfasts, an enormous deck (from which to observe eagles, porcupines, and squirrels), and Georgia Sepal's enthusiastic hospitality and local knowledge. Rates are $65 or $70 for two. For more details, call (907) 789–5220.

If these accommodations don't seem right or if they're booked, one of the best sources of B&B information in Juneau, Southeast Alaska, and even statewide is the **Alaska Bed & Breakfast Association**. The same mother-daughter team that operates this company also runs **Alaska Rainforest Tours**. Their $5.00 catalog lists overnight accommodations plus tours that vary from offbeat ferry trips from Ketchikan in Southeastern to sharing a fishing camp with Inupiat Eskimos in Arctic Kotzebue. Call (907) 586–2959 for B&B reservations, (907) 463–3466 regarding tours, or either number to order a catalog.

The **Juneau International Hostel**, located at 614 Harris Street, is a particular pleasure for fans of hosteling. It's located in a large, historic, rambling house on the side of a hill called Chicken Ridge. Clean, spacious, and handicapped accessible, it's just a few blocks above downtown Juneau. In spite of its relatively large capacity (forty-eight beds, sitting room with fireplace and library, laundry) it's filled almost all the time in the summer. Reservations are a must. The cost is $10 for adults. Call (907) 586–9559.

If your plans call for a trip between Juneau and Sitka, one of the pleasantest ways to travel between the two ports is via the **Alaska Marine Highway ferry *LeConte*.** The advantage of sailing on this vessel, as opposed to one of the larger ships of the fleet, is that the *LeConte* stops along the way at **Hoonah, Tenakee Springs** (most trips), and **Angoon.** Of course, you don't have to be heading to Sitka to visit these small communities; you can, if you like, simply take a round-trip from Juneau to one or all three, then return by ferry or small plane to Juneau. Call (800) 458–3579 for information or reservations.

Located on the northeast shore of Chichagof Island, about 40 miles and three ferry hours north of Juneau, lies **Hoonah,** a thriving village of mostly Tlingit Indian people. If you're not laying over, check with your ship's purser and see if you have time to mosey into the village (about a fifteen-minute walk). If you don't, at least take the time to visit the graveyard right across the highway from the ferry dock. You'll find some graves there that are quite old, others new, some traditional with angel figures, others marked with the distinctive Russian Orthodox Church's cross with two cross beams, and still others with cast figures from the Tlingit Indian totemic tradition.

In town you'll find several restaurants plus lodging, grocery, gift, and general merchandise establishments. Overnighters will find **Hubbard's Bed and Breakfast** (in the woods but only a mile from downtown) clean and pleasant. Rates are $75 for a double; call (907) 945-3414 for reservations. Want to see a genuine brown (grizzly) bear while you're in the area? Check out the village garbage dump (honest), about 2 miles from town. But do not walk to the site. Get someone to drive you, or hire a cab. These critters are big and wild. If you want to combine a Hoonah visit with cruising or fishing, skipper Mark Quam's **Galatea Charters** offers trips aboard the 38-foot *M.V. Galatea* to Elfin Cove, Point Sophia, Idaho Inlet, and other scenic points. Rates start at $300 for a half-day boat charter which covers one to six passengers. For details call (907) 945–3525. The ferry to Hoonah from Juneau costs $20 one way. Airfare is $40.

Between Hoonah and Sitka the ferry *LeConte* stops most trips at ❖ **Tenakee Springs,** long enough sometimes for passengers to run with towel in hand to the community's hot springs for a quick, relaxing soak. The springs, incidentally, provided one of the principal reasons for the community's founding back in 1899. Miners would journey to the site every winter when cold weather shut down their "diggin's" and they'd stay for weeks or months. The tradition continues, sort of. Lots of Juneauites, Sitkans, and other Southeast Alaska residents still come to take the waters, both winter and summer. Interestingly, there are posted hours for men's bathing and other hours for women. But never the twain meet, at least in the 5-by-9 foot bathing pool. You'll find several overnight options in Tenakee Springs, including furnished cabins for rent from longtime Alaskans Elsie and

Don Pegues' **Snyder Mercantile Company** (907–736–2205). Rates are $30 per night for a one-room cottage and $60 for a deluxe, two-bedroom mini-lodge. Bring your own sleeping bag. Another option is to book a sportfishing package from **Tenakee Hot Springs Lodge** (907–736–2400). Rates start at $2,390 for five days and nights including air from Juneau, fishing boat charter, and home-cooked meals as well as lodging. The **Blue Moon Cafe** is yet another dining choice. Fishing in the area is first rate; beachcombing and hiking are likewise, and chances are you'll see sea life in the water—humpback whales, seals, sea lions, and otters. The one-way ferry trip from Juneau to Tenakee Springs costs $22. Airfare is approximately $65.

The Tlingit village of **Angoon** offers yet another offbeat destination from Juneau. Located on the northwest coast of Admiralty Island, the community is accessible by ferry and by air from Juneau, which is 95 miles away. Two very comfortable lodges at Angoon—the **Favorite Bay Inn** and the **Whalers Cove Sportfishing Lodge**—provide all the comforts with easy access to sportfishing, kayaking, canoeing, and simple sight-seeing. Worth a visit: nearby Killisnoo Indian graveyards. The islands and waters of Kootznahoo Inlet and Mitchell Bay are prime kayaking locales. To contact either lodge call (800) 423–3123. The rates start at $109 for bed and breakfast accommodations. Call for sportfishing package rates. A one-way-trip from Juneau to Angoon costs $24; airfare is $70.

Here's one of the most economical day cruises you can experience in Alaska. Early every Sunday morning the smaller ferry *LeConte* departs from Auke Bay terminal (about 14 miles north of Juneau) for the picturesque fishing village of **Pelican,** on the northwest corner of Chichagof Island. The route takes you through Icy Straits, past prime whale-watching waters off Point Adolphus. Along the way you may view sea lions, seals, bears, deer, eagles, and other wildlife. Arrival at Pelican is at midday, and you have an hour and a half to walk along the town boardwalks, stroll around the commercial fishing docks, and watch as commercial fishers unload halibut, salmon, crab, and black cod at the cold storage plant. You can have lunch at the local cafe or your choice of two bar and grill establishments, including **Rosie's,** sort of a Southeast Alaska institution among fishermen. The return ferry departs midafternoon and arrives seven hours later in Juneau. If that's too much time afloat, you can fly back on **Glacier Bay Airways** (907–789–9009) or **Wings of Alaska** (907–789–0790). Call the Alaska Marine Highway System (800–458–3579) for latest scheduling information. The one-way ferry trip costs $32; one-way air is $75. If you lay over, the **Otter Cove Bed & Breakfast** (907–735–2259) offers beach and streamside privacy within a few minutes' walk on the boardwalk to "downtown." The rate is $65.

The people of **Haines** will tell you, perhaps with some justification, that their community has the best summer weather in Southeast Alaska. The warmer, drier air of the Yukon interior regions, they say, flows over Chilkat Pass into the Chilkat Valley and brings with it more sunshine and less rainfall than other panhandle communities experience. Whatever the reason, Haines and vicinity does offer the visitor a pleasurable place to perch for a day or a few days.

Sadly, many visitors pass Haines by. They're in such a toot to get off the ferry and rush north to the main body of Alaska, they miss many of Haines's considerable pleasures; pleasures like the Tlingit Indian dancing and cultural exhibits at old Fort William Henry Seward. Like the old fort itself (now a National Historic Landmark), with its rows of elegant officers' homes and its traditional military parade ground. Like a nightly mouthwatering salmon bake, a fascinating museum of Southeastern Alaskana, and a state park that many rank among America's most pleasurable.

You get to Haines aboard the ferries of the Alaska Marine Highway System, either from Skagway, a quarter of an hour's sailing from the north, or from Juneau, about four and a half hours from the south. There's also a passengers-only water taxi that makes two round-trips daily (fifteen minutes each way) between Haines and Skagway. Or you can drive to Haines over the 151-mile Haines Highway, which junctions with the Alaska Highway at Haines Junction, Yukon Territory, Canada. You can also fly to Haines. Several excellent small-plane carriers provide frequent scheduled flights from Juneau. Rugged coastlines, thickly forested islands, high-rising mountains, and Davidson and Rainbow glaciers are only a few of the sights you encounter along the way.

Once in Haines, a good place to stop for advice, a map, and literature is the **visitor center** on Second Avenue, about halfway between the Haines downtown business district and Fort Seward. Only a few minutes' walk from the visitor center

is the ◆Sheldon Museum and Cultural Center
(907–766–2366), on the harbor end of Main Street. This museum
literally had its start in 1893, when Steve Sheldon, at the ripe
old age of eight, purchased a piece of the original transatlantic
cable and began a lifetime of collecting. He arrived in Haines
from his native Ohio in 1911 and met and married a woman
from Pennsylvania, also an avid collector. Their family hobby
has resulted in what is now the Sheldon Museum, a collection
that encompasses Tlingit basketry and totemic art (including a
rare, unfinished Chilkat ceremonial blanket), mementos of Fort
Seward (later called Chilkoot Barracks when it housed the only
U.S. troops in Alaska), photos of colorful Jack Dalton, plus pack
saddles and other gear Dalton used to clear the Dalton Trail toll
road to the Klondike. You can also see the shotgun he kept
loaded behind the bar of his saloon. The museum is open 1:00
P.M. to 5:00 P.M. daily, plus mornings and evenings when cruise
ships are in port. Admission is $2.50.

Haines's premier attraction is unquestionably ◆Fort
William Henry Seward, established in 1904, renamed
Chilkoot Barracks in 1922, and deactivated in 1946.The government sold the entire fort to a group of World War II veterans in
1947, and although their plans to create a business cooperative
did not fully work out, the fort's picturesque buildings have been
largely preserved. You can, in fact, sleep and dine in any of several grand old officers' quarters, which now serve as hotels,
motels, or B&Bs. Other old structures still at the fort include
warehouses, the cable office, and barracks. One large building
now houses the Chilkat Center for the Arts, where some
nights you can watch the award-winning, nationally recognized
Chilkat Indian Dancers during evening performances. For a
schedule of performances call (907) 766–2160. In still other fort
buildings you can see contemporary Tlingit craftsmen of Alaska
Indian Arts (AIA) fashion large and small works of traditional
totemic art from wood, silver, fabric, and soapstone. Totem poles
carved and created by AIA on the fort grounds can be seen all
over Alaska and, indeed, the world. You'll see totemic art, too, at
the Totem Village Tribal House, also on the fort parade
grounds. Adjacent to the structure is a traditional trapper's log
cabin of the kind you might find in Alaska's bush country. From

5:00 to 7:00 P.M. nightly at the totem house, the highly acclaimed chefs of the **Halsingland Hotel** offer up choice salmon filets and all the trimmin's at an outdoor **salmon bake** (907–766–2000). "All you can eat" for $20 makes this one of Alaska's better bargains.

Adjacent to the fairgrounds at the northern edge of the city (Haines is home to the **Southeast Alaska State Fair** each August), you'll come to some gold-rush era buildings that may seem vaguely familiar. These buildings, now called **Dalton City,** served as the set for the Walt Disney movie *White Fang,* based on Jack London's novel. When the moviemaking ended, the Disney company donated the set to the community. The buildings may be of recent origin, but they present an authentic picture of a gold-rush community during the tumultuous time of the Klondike gold stampede. The picture-taking opportunities are many.

A site often overlooked by visitors is ❖ **Chilkat State Park,** about 8 miles south of town on the Mud Bay Road. This is one of the Millers' favorite camping places, but you don't have to be a camper to enjoy this forested area on the Chilkat Peninsula. There are, for visitors seeking just an afternoon outing, ample trails, saltwater beach walks, and gorgeous views of Davidson and Rainbow glaciers. The state charges $6.00 for camping here.

In the late fall and early winter, throngs of eager birders arrive to visit the ❖ **Alaska Chilkat Bald Eagle Preserve,** just a few minutes' drive from the city. There, 3,500 to 4,500 American bald eagles gather each year to feast on a late run of Chilkat River salmon. This is the world's largest concentration of bald eagles, and the spectacle is easily seen from turnoffs alongside the highway. A number of eagles and many other bird species can be seen there year-round, and other wildlife is frequently spotted, especially during summer float trips down the stream.

Chilkat Guides, Ltd. offers daily **Bald Eagle Preserve Raft Trips** through some of the most spectacular portions of the Chilkat River and the preserve. This is a gentle float in spacious 18-foot rubber rafts. Eagles, bears, moose, even wolves, if you're lucky, may be seen during the four-hour trip. The tour begins with a van pickup near the old army dock, and includes a 30-mile drive to the preserve. Then comes the float downriver to a haul-out spot near the Indian village of Klukwan. The price is $70 for adults. Another Chilkat Guides offering takes clients up the

Tsirku River and Leblondeau Glacier for a two-day camp-out in a land of blue ice, waterfalls, wildlife, jagged peaks, and remote wilderness solitude. The tour is a combination of a scenic fly-in, walking literally on a glacier, wilderness camping, and rafting-out. It costs $325 per person. For more details, call (907) 766–2491.

Both **Chilkat Guides** and Juneau-based **Alaska Discovery** package float trips down the magnificent **Alsek and Tatshenshini Rivers,** which flow out of the Canadian interior. These trips (which Chilkat Guides does in ten and thirteen days, respectively, and which Alaska Discovery schedules for ten and twelve days) open up some of the world's most awesome mountain/glacier/wild river country. Exciting whitewater, relaxing floats, abundant wildlife, and wild country treks are only a few of the features of these premier experiences, which begin in Haines and end at Yakutat, for a jet flight back to Juneau. Prices for the Tatshenshini trip varies from $1,850 to $1,875, for the Alsek from $2,250 to $2,450. Contact Chilkat Guides at the number above; Alaska Discovery can be reached at (800) 586–1911.

Don and Karen Hess's **River Adventures** combines van (or bus) touring with a jet boat ride. The result is a half-day, four-hour outing 25 miles up the Haines Highway through the Chilkat Bald Eagle Preserve to a boat dock, where passengers transfer to river craft for 44 miles of wilderness, wildlife, and birdlife watching. Moose and bear are often seen, and during a smoked salmon snack break there's time to use a high-powered spotting scope to view game on nearby mountainsides. The cost is $70 for morning and afternoon trips, $55 for special three-hour evening tours. Call (907) 766–2050 for more details.

You'll seldom find a city tour more modestly priced than the forty-five-minute **Haines Shuttle and Tours** excursion. For $5.00, Carl Dixon's company will guide you around town, through Fort Seward and the totem carving site, the boat harbor, a Native cemetery, and Dalton City. Longer excursions include Chilkat State Park and the opportunity to photograph Rainbow and Davidson Glaciers. A three-hour tour costs $29. Another three-hour offering includes the town tour and a drive to Chilkoot Lake, where you just may view brown bears feeding. The company's most ambitious tour is a six-hour excursion to the summit of Haines Highway in British Columbia and includes side trips and stops at **Mosquito Lake,** salmon spawning beds, the

Chilkat Eagle Preserve, and the historic old **33-Mile Road-house.** Call (907) 766–3138 for more information.

Bicyclists can join other pedalers on day rides or longer tours through **Sockeye Cycle** of both Haines and Skagway. In Haines they're located on Portage Street uphill from the dock in Fort Seward. Their excursions include an exploration of the abandoned old gold rush town site of Porcupine ($95 for one day, $160 overnight with two meals) and a ride on challenging roads along the shores of Chilkoot Lake to see vast schools of spawning salmon and perhaps brown bears who gather to feed on the fish ($60). Even more challenging is a 350-mile nine-day **Golden Circle Tour** north from Haines up the Haines Highway to Canada's Yukon, east to Whitehorse in the Yukon Territory on the Alaska Highway, then south on the Klondike Highway to Skagway. The trip costs $1,400. Rentals are $6.00 for an hour, $20.00 for a half day, and $30.00 for a full day. For details about these and other trips, call (907) 766–2869 in Haines, (907) 983–2851 in Skagway.

Janis Horton's **Chilkoot Lake Tours** (800–354–6009) offers easygoing, quiet tours and fishing excursions that take in some of Southeast's most scenic lake and wildlife-viewing country. Two hours of sight-seeing costs $40 per person; a three-hour fishing trip for Dolly Varden and sockeye salmon runs $50. She also operates Eagle's Nest Motel, near the center of town, and **Eagle's Nest Car Rental.** Doubles at the motel cost $70; auto rentals start at $45 a day.

According to Craig Loomis of **First Out, Last In Fishing Charters,** "May is a great month to go to Sea Lion Rock to view hundreds of sea lions basking in the sun." June, he says, is "dynamite king salmon fishing," while July and August "are for reeling in halibut" in the 15- to 250-pound class. For details, call (907) 766–2854.

It's pleasant simply to stroll by the **Chilkat Restaurant and Bakery** (907–766–2920), on Fifth Avenue between Main and Dalton streets, just to savor the smells of baked goods and cooking that wafts from within. It's pleasanter still to stop in for a breakfast of waffles, omelettes, or sausage gravy and hot biscuits. Lunch can be as light as soup and a burger, or it can be a full meal. Among dinner specialties: halibut, salmon, and Klondike stew and biscuits. Roberta Lane describes this as a family restaurant (no smoking) and a "from-scratch bakery," featuring Alaska sourdough and farm breads. Breakfasts cost from $4.50, lunches from $5.00, and dinners somewhat higher, though the luncheon menu is available through the dinner hour.

The historic building that houses the **Fort Seward Lodge, Restaurant, and Saloon** was constructed in the early 1900s as the fort's post exchange. In those days it included a gym, movie house, library, and two-lane bowling alley as well as a soda fountain. The latter was a popular place with tourists, who enjoyed watching the soldiers' pet bear (named Three Per, for three percent beer), who would beg for ice cream cones when she couldn't entice the soldiers to give her beer. Three Per has long since gone to bear heaven, but the building is still popular with visitors, who can enjoy all-you-can-eat crab dinners in season, rent rooms with private or shared baths, and savor a favorite libation in the bar. Rooms start at $45, meals and saloon charges are in the moderate range. For more information, phone (907) 766–2009.

Also on fort grounds: Norman and Suzanne Smith's **Fort Seward Bed and Breakfast,** house number 1 on Officer's Row, features stately Jeffersonian rooms with fireplaces, cable TV, and awesome views of Lynn Canal. Full sourdough pancake breakfasts are included in the $82 rate for two. For information, phone (907) 766–2856. Also on the parade grounds in Officers' Row are **Fort Seward Condos,** owned and operated by Ted and Mimi Gregg. These completely furnished bedroom apartments come with fully equipped kitchens. The Greggs were among the original purchasers of the fort back in the forties and have a wealth of memories and history to share. Rates start at $85 per night. Call (907) 766–2425. Dave and Donna Nanney's **Chilkat Eagle Bed and Breakfast** sits next to the Chilkat Center for the Arts. It's small, intimate, and was built in 1904 as NCO quarters. Hospitality is practiced here in four languages: English, Spanish, French, and Japanese. The rate is $65 for a double. Call (907) 766–2763.

Mary Rietze's **Cathedral Peaks Bed and Breakfast,** at mile 7.5 on the Haines Highway, has a grand view of the sky-piercing Cathedral Peaks in the Chilkat Range and cathedral ceilings in her B&B from which to enjoy them. On the walls are mounts of big game animals native to Alaska. For breakfast, she serves sourdough waffles topped with locally made Alaska birch syrup. Doubles cost $75; call (907) 766–2763.

At mile 8.5 on the Haines Highway, situated on a cliff that overlooks the Chilkat River and the Chilkat Mountains, the **Chilkat Valley Inn** offers a wilderness and wildlife-viewing setting only minutes from town. Lois Gammill and Don Quan heat their units with cozy wood stoves, as many Alaskans do. Call (907) 766–3331. The rate is $80 per night.

Bear Creek Camp and International Hostel (907–766–2259) offers a lot of options—regular cabins, cabins with bunk beds, campsites, plus a separate shower house and bathrooms. There's also a kitchen for guests' use in another cabin. The camp and hostel is situated among trees and mountains about 2 miles from downtown. If you don't have wheels, call managers Alan and Lucy Miller and they'll come and pick you up. The nightly fee is $10.00 for a bunk in the hostel, $30.00 for a cabin, or $3.25 for a campsite. To get there head out Mud Bay Road. When you come to Small Tract Road, turn left and drive for about a mile. It's around a corner and on the left.

You can reach the **Weeping Trout Retreat and Golf Course,** on the shores of Chilkat Lake north of Haines, only by boat, but it's probably well worth the effort for travelers looking for rejuvenation in quiet surroundings or golf in the most unlikely of places. Accommodations are modest but more than adequate, with rooms available in the main lodge or in cabins. Boats, rafts, and canoes are available for exploring, but the most intriguing feature of the place is the par-three, nine-hole golf course, whose fairways boast such names as Devils Club (154 yards), Cut Throat Cut (181 yards), and minuscule Lake Lob (45 yards). The charge for a three-day stay is $500 per person, $900 for party of two. Call (907) 766–2827.

Deishu Expeditions rents kayaks and organizes tours ranging from half-day local paddling to six days between Juneau and Haines. Their shoreline trip beside **Chilkat State Park** is a particular delight, especially in June when kayakers can paddle out to **Strawberry Island** for berry picking and poking around the old homestead there. Rentals for single kayaks are $25 a half day, $35 a full day; guided tours are $65 for a half day, $95 for a full day. Lots of tours to choose from. Call (800) 552–9257 for more information.

Glacier flight-seeing excursions are popular from many communities, but Haines's location makes it a particularly good base from which to launch an airborne look at Glacier Bay via **L.A.B. Flying Service.** L.A.B., one of the grand old names in Southeastern aviation, offers seventy-minute air tours over Glacier Bay National Park for views of massive ice rivers, steep-walled fjords, bays, forests, and rivers. For details about these and other flights from Haines, Skagway and Juneau call (907) 766–2222.

Pardon the bad play on words, but this outfit is for the dogs. Sled dogs, that is. **Chilkoot Sled Dog Adventures** features Southeast Alaska's only live presentation about mushing, plus a daily drawing which awards one visitor a summer dogsled ride on wheels. Admission is $5.00. A shuttle to the site leaves the downtown visitors center Monday, Wednesday, and Friday at 1:00 P.M. Call (907) 766–3242 for details.

When you're ready to leave town, if you're Skagway-bound and don't have a car, you should consider the Haines–Skagway **Water Taxi and Scenic Cruise**, a one-hour narrated boat excursion that features more than twenty waterfalls plus the possibility of viewing seals, sea lions, porpoises, bald eagles, and other creatures. The "taxi" is the eighty-passenger, 50-foot *Sea Venture II*, which operates between the two cities twice daily. The fare is $20 one way, $35 round-trip. In Haines call (907) 766–3395 for information and reservations. In Skagway call (907) 983–2083.

In the annals of the nineteenth-century American frontier, no town had a more frantic, frenzied, fascinating history than **Skagway**. This city at the northern end of Lynn Canal, some 90 miles north of Juneau, was jam-packed to overflowing during the "Days of '98," when thousands of would-be gold seekers poured into the community to outfit themselves for treks to the Klondike gold fields. It was one of the most lawless towns under the American flag. Jefferson "Soapy" Smith and his gang of toughs and con men controlled the city, prompting the superintendent of the Canadian North West Mounted Police across the border to call it "little better than hell on earth." Amazingly well preserved, with many structures from late in the last century and early in this one still standing and in use, much of the town today comprises the ◆**Klondike Gold Rush National Historical Park**. And there's still a lot of violence in this town... but it's all make believe, a nightly reenactment of the July 8, 1898, shoot-out between "good guy" citizen Frank Reid and "bad guy" desperado Soapy Smith. (Both men died in the encounter.)

There's more to Skagway than gold rush structures and shoot-outs, though. There is, for instance, the ◆ **White Pass & Yukon Route**. Declared an International Historic Civil Engineering Landmark by the American Society of Civil Engineers, a designation achieved by only fourteen other projects, including the Eiffel Tower in Paris and the Statue of Liberty in New York, the narrow-gauge railway provides one of North America's premier rail experiences. Construction of the line between Skagway and Whitehorse, Yukon, began, against horrendous grades and incredible natural obstacles, in 1898. The builders clawed and blasted their way to the 2,885-foot White Pass in 1899 and to Whitehorse the following year. The WP&YR today carries visitors from Skagway, at sea level, to the pass in the incredibly short distance of only 20 miles. Riders have three options: a three-hour round-trip, taking in the most spectacular of the cliff-hanging mountain and lush valley sights as far as the summit; a 28-mile trip to Fraser on the Klondike Highway, where Whitehorse-bound travelers transfer to motor coaches; or a five-and-a-half-hour round-trip excursion to Lake Bennett, where some 20,000 stampeders camped during the winter of 1898 after climbing and crossing the Chilkoot Pass. (They then proceeded by boat and raft through additional lakes, rapids, and riverways to the Klondike.) WP&YR round-trip fares start at $75. For reservations or information call (800) 343–7373.

And speaking of the railroad, the headquarters and information center of the **Klondike Gold Rush National Historical Park** is located in the restored old **WP&YR Depot**, at Second Avenue and Broadway. You'll find historical photos, artifacts, and film showings there plus visitor information about the town and current conditions on the Chilkoot Trail. Walks through the downtown historic district guided by Park Service rangers leave from the center several times daily. The National Park Service, at substantial effort, has restored a number of Skagway's most historic buildings, including the **Mascot Saloon**, Third Avenue and Broadway, built in 1898, and the **Trail Inn and Pack Train Saloon**, Fourth Avenue and Broadway, constructed in 1908. **Captain Benjamin Moore's cabin**, a half-block west of Broadway

43

between Fifth and Sixth Avenues, goes back all the way to 1887; the good captain was there, waiting for the gold rush to start, when the first stampeders clambered ashore a decade later. Call (907) 983–2921 for walking tour schedules. The tours are free of charge.

Other worthwhile stops in Skagway include: the **Corrington Museum of Alaska History**, at Fifth Avenue and Broadway, with exhibits from prehistory to modern-day Alaska; the ruins of the old **Pullen House** hotel adjacent to City Hall, built by "Ma" Pullen during the Days of '98; and **Gold Rush Cemetery**, about 1.5 miles north from downtown, where Frank Reid and Soapy Smith lie buried.

The **Arctic Brotherhood Hall**, at Second Avenue and Broadway, has at least three claims to fame: It's old, having been built in 1899 to house "Camp Skagway Number 1" of a once thriving Alaska–Yukon fraternal organization of gold seekers. It now houses the city's visitor information center and therefore provides a good source of information about Skagway and environs. And its curious, false-fronted facade is covered with more than 20,000 (count 'em, 20,000) individual pieces of big and little rounded pieces of driftwood.

During the Klondike gold rush, Skagway was the jumping-off place for the White Pass "Trail of '98" horse and wagon route to the Yukon. For stampeders who couldn't afford either pack horses or wagons, the nearby community of Dyea (pronounced Dy-EE) was the starting point for the famous **Chilkoot Trail** to the gold fields. The trail today is part of the Klondike Gold Rush National Historical Park and, like trekkers of old, you too can hike from Dyea (accessible by gravel road, 9 miles north of Skagway) to Lake Bennett. It's a three- to six-day walk, with some shelters along the way. For details from the park superintendent's office, call (907) 983–2921.

Although the Chilkoot Trail is the best known trail in the area, the hiker with limited time can enjoy several other hiking options, including the easy, woodsy **Lower Dewey Trail**, less than a mile in length. You'll find the **Skyline Trail and A.B. Mountain** longer (more than 3 miles to the summit), more strenuous, but greatly rewarding. ("A. B.," incidentally, stands for Arctic Brotherhood, a gold rush fraternal organization.) Trail maps are available at visitor centers.

The ◆ **Trail of '98 Museum**, at Seventh Avenue and Spring Street on the edge of the downtown district, is an outstanding

44

small museum. It's located in Skagway's **City Hall**, built by the Methodist Church between 1898 and 1899 to serve as a college. Later it housed the U.S. District Court (the judge's bench and chair are still there), and since 1961 it has contained the current Trail of '98 collection, including Frank Reid's will (he's the good guy who shot bad man "Soapy" Smith), the tie Soapy was wearing at the shoot-out, an Eskimo kayak and Indian canoe, an authentic Chilkat Indian blanket, a Faro gaming table and other gambling paraphernalia, plus all manner of prospecting gear. Outside, an old Baldwin steam locomotive makes a perfect photo backdrop. Admission is $2.00. For further information, call (907) 983–2420.

Even if you're lodging elsewhere, take the time to stroll through the lobby of the grand old **Golden North Hotel,** on Broadway. It's one of Alaska's oldest hotels (circa 1898) and its decor reflects the turn of the century era. Rooms have been lovingly furnished with period pieces contributed by pioneer Skagway families, whose stories are printed and framed in each room. Rates start at $60 for a double. Call (907) 983–2451.

Historic **Skagway Inn Bed and Breakfast**, at Seventh and Broadway, traces its origins to 1897 and its days as a brothel providing "services" for lonely gold stampeders. Today the inn contains twelve rooms restored to Victorian charm. Baths are shared. Innkeepers Don and Sioux Plummer offer full breakfasts, home baked muffins, fresh ground coffee, piping hot tea, courtesy van service (including transportation for hikers to the start of the Chilkoot Trail), and Alaskan expertise to share. Rates start at $55 for a single. Call (907) 983–2289. In the evening, incidentally, you can purchase dinner at the restaurant there called **Lorna's at the Skagway Inn**. Be prepared to be impressed with French cuisine prepared by a Paris-trained chef.

Skagway Hostel, at 456 Third Avenue, is the home of Frank Wasmer and Nancy Schave and accommodates up to twelve hostelers in beds in the main house. There's additional space in a backyard bunkhouse, and even more overnighters can be accommodated in a nearby church. The charge is $12.00; for an additional $5.00 you can join Frank and Nancy and other hostelers for a family dinner that features fresh veggies from Nancy's garden.

Perhaps the strangest "cabin" in the U.S. Forest Service wilderness cabin network is the retired **White Pass & Yukon Route Caboose**, located 5½ miles north of Skagway. The view, a stunner, takes in the Skagway River and the Sawtooth Mountains. Visitors may rent this unit for $25 a night, just like any other in the system, but instead of flying, hiking, or boating in you reach the caboose by—you guessed it—taking the train! For information and reservations forms from the U.S. Forest Service in Juneau, call (907) 586–8751.

For bicyclists, **Sockeye Cycle**, of Skagway and Haines, offers a **Klondike Summit to Sea Cruise**, a tour that provides a van ride to the 3,292-foot summit of the White Pass, then a 15-mile guided coast downhill to town with jagged mountains, forests, and glacier views along the way. The price is $60. For information, call (907) 983–2851 in Skagway, (907) 766–2869 in Haines.

Skagway is the southern terminus of the **Klondike Highway,** which extends into British Columbia and Canada's Yukon Territory. Each fall, on a designated weekend in September, the highway becomes less a highway and more a race course as hundreds of running teams from all over the United States and Canada arrive to race in stages all the way to Whitehorse, 108 miles away. For dates and information about the **Klondike Trail of '98 Road Relay**, contact the Skagway Convention and Visitors Bureau at (907) 983–2854.

GLACIER BAY NATIONAL PARK AND
THE COMMUNITY OF GUSTAVUS

No question about it. ◆ **Glacier Bay National Park and Preserve** is one of the extraordinary parks of the nation. Home to sixteen massive, glistening saltwater glaciers and the site of hundreds of huge and little valley and mountaintop ice masses, Glacier Bay National Park is, in fact, all about the power of ice in shaping a land. It's a place where the relentless grinding force of glaciers has carved deep, steep-walled saltwater fjords and U-shaped mountain valleys, and it's a place of stark, barren, rocky expanses where glaciers have only recently receded. It's also a land of mature, lush spruce and hemlock forests, where the ice receded decades ago. It's a place where the word *awesome* comes frequently to mind.

Glacier Bay National Park lies some 60 miles west of Juneau, accessible by cruise ship, yacht, jet, or light aircraft. Visits can be as short as a day trip out of Juneau or as long as a week or more. The community of **Gustavus**, easily reached by air, abuts the park and provides a rich variety of guiding, fishing, lodging, and supply services.

If you want lodging accommodations within the park boundaries, your only choice (though highly pleasurable) is **Glacier Bay Lodge** on the shores of Bartlett Cove. The lodge is a fifty-six-room resort located 10 miles from the community of Gustavus. It contains fully modern guests rooms, a dining room, cocktail lounge, small gift shop, and the **National Park Service Glacier Bay Visitor Center.** Double rooms begin at $153 per night. If that's too rich for your budget, you may want to consider men's or women's dorm rooms with beds, which can be rented for $28 per night. For a brochure or reservations, call (800) 451-5952.

The sight-seeing yacht ◆*Spirit of Adventure* departs Bartlett Cove daily for a full day, which includes close-up looks at glaciers, thousands of birds, and good prospects of viewing brown bears and mountain goats on land plus whales, porpoises, and seals in the water. Park Service naturalists accompany each sailing. The fare, including lunch onboard, is $153.50. Package tours are available that include one or two nights at the lodge. Bartlett Cove is also base for the Glacier Bay Tours and Cruises vessel *Wilderness Explorer,* which serves as a floating camp for kayakers on overnight tours within the park and elsewhere. Prices for three days start at $469 from Juneau. For information about both vessels, call (800) 451-5952.

Now about **Gustavus,** next door to the park. Funny place this town. Except it's not a town because the 200 strong-willed, individualistic citizens who live there have voted repeatedly not to become any sort of official city with trappings like mayors or government. But Gustavus is a definable community because these same people—as friendly and sharing and helpful as they are fiercely independent—manage to provide everything that they need in order to happily reside there. They're equally prepared to provide travelers with everything they need to happily visit for a few days or a season. The setting is awesome, bounded on three sides by the snow-capped peaks of the Chilkat Range and the Fairweather Mountains and on the fourth by smooth, sandy, saltwater beaches. The community spreads itself sparsely

47

over miles of flat countryside and includes boundless opportunities for berry picking, hiking, bicycle riding, freshwater and saltwater angling, beachcombing, birding, and just gawking.

In the late sixties, the Miller clan traveled from Juneau to Gustavus to spend a long weekend at the **Gustavus Inn.** The inn was a converted rural homestead house originally constructed by a hardy couple in 1928 for their family of nine children. In 1965 new owners Jack and Sally Lesh converted it to an inn. Three memories of that weekend still linger: The homestead was comfortable and charming. Our innkeeper hosts were gracious and hospitable. And Sally Lesh's food . . . well, the food was just out of this world. Fresh-caught seafood such as salmon, halibut, and crab was the specialty, and bountiful was the measure. We fished from the shores of the nearby Salmon River, borrowed bicycles to explore ample back roads and trails, and gorged ourselves during hikes on tiny, succulent, abundant berries. Today, three decades and one Lesh family generation later, David and JoAnn Lesh carry on. The food continues in Sally Lesh's gourmet tradition, and there are ample things to do and places to explore to fill whatever time you have to spend there. Rates start at $130 per adult, $65 per child, including all meals. For more information, call (907) 697–2254 May to September and (913) 649–5220 October to April.

Gustavus's other inn, the **Glacier Bay Country Inn,** likewise offers a very Alaskan, high quality experience in a setting of verdant forests and majestic mountains. Here, too—in a distinctive structure with multiangled roofs, dormers, decks, and log-beamed ceilings—informally gracious living and fine dining are trademarks. The charge is $149 for a single, $238 for a double, including meals. The owners of the inn, Al and Annie Unrein, also book stays at the **Whalesong Lodge,** near the airport and about 4 miles from their inn. The Whalesong, which features two three-bedroom condos, is a good choice for large families or groups as well as for smaller parties. The condos rent for $250 to $300 per day, depending on length of stay; smaller units go for $160 for a double, or $218 with all meals. Another Unrein enterprise, **Grand Pacific Charters,** features overnight trips on sightseeing vessels plus fishing and whale-watching options. For information about lodgings and charters, call (907) 697–2288 May to September and (801) 673–8480 October to April.

If you're looking for economy in comfortable surroundings, Sandy Burd has two options for you. The **Good Riverbed and Breakfast** is located in an elegant, spacious log home with comfy beds, patchwork quilts, and an atmosphere that is rural, yet sophisticated. Hearty breakfasts include the likes of fresh home-baked breads, wild berry jams, locally smoked salmon, and much more. The rate for two is $75. Even more reasonable is **Sandy's Beyond Good River,** a secluded, handcrafted log cabin on the edge of the rainforest. It's available by the day for $50 for two without breakfast, $60 with breakfast, or at lower rates by the week or month. For more details about either place, phone (907) 697–2241.

A Puffin's Bed and Breakfast—among several travel services offered by Chuck and Sandy Schroth's Puffin Travel, Inc.— is centrally located within walking distance of a grocery, cafe, and shops. Each cabin has its own private bath or shower, but you walk down a lighted path to get to all but two of them. Bikes and full breakfast are included in rates that start at $70 for a double. The Schroths also book a wide variety of fishing and sight-seeing tours. Call (907) 697–2260 for more information.

Still another option is **Aimee's Guest House.** A "peaceful old house with all the comforts" is how Aimee Youmans describes it. It's an entire two-bedroom home you can rent for $70 single or double. Aimee Youmans also operates the **Salmon River Smokehouse,** which specializes in smoking all five species of wild Alaska salmon plus halibut. The enterprise, which grew from a homestead occupation, specializes in hot-smoked filets using a special family brine recipe. Phone (907) 697–2330 for both enterprises.

Glacier Bay, with its protected arms and inlets, provides ideal kayaking waters for sight-seeing at sea level. **Glacier Bay Sea Kayaks,** operated by longtime Alaskans Bonnie Kaden and Kara Berg, has been renting these craft to visitors for many years, by the day for short exposures around Gustavus or for taking aboard larger vessels for drop-off at camping locales in the national park. Prices start as low as $35 a day. Call (907) 697–2257 for information.

Award-winning **Alaska Discovery** operates water and hiking tours in the park, catering to both one-day visitors with or without outdoor experience and to knowledgeable kayakers, rafters, and backpackers who seek a more rigorous wilderness adventure. Call (800) 586–1911 for more details.

Another sea kayaking option is John "Rusty" Owens's **Gusto Tours and Charters'** daylong whale-watching expeditions off Point Adolphus. Gusto transports you to the whale-watching waters in a larger support craft, after which you launch kayaks for eye-level looking at the great denizens. You can even hear the creatures on hydrophones supplied for your listening enjoyment. The $200 fee includes lunch on the support vessel. Gusto also offers sight-seeing and fishing options. For details, call (907) 697–2416.

Spirit Walker Expeditions offers a variety of tours from a one- or two-day trip by kayak to nearby (and aptly named) Pleasant Island to their eight-day expedition among the (also aptly named) Myriad Islands, where hundreds of tiny isles make up a miniature inside passage. Prices for these trips range from $100 for one day to $2,000-plus including bush plane airlift from Gustavus to the Myriads. The outfitter's newest offering (at $2,354 for eight days) originates from Yakutat at the top of the Alaska panhandle and takes kayakers to remote and isolated **Russel Fjord** and **Hubbard Glacier,** the largest tidewater glacier in North America. It's 6 miles wide where it meets the ocean. Call (800) KAYAKER for more details.

The 70-foot *Steller,* formerly a state research vessel, provides a floating base for kayakers and motor skiff sight-seers on **Glacier Bay Adventures'** four-day trips. The main search is for humpback whales, but the vessel frequently encounters Steller sea lions, sea otters, porpoises, seals, and minke whales. Visitors usually spend one day in Dundas Bay, where a shore visit allows anglers to sample freshwater fishing in the Dundas River. For more details, call Dan Foley at (907) 697–2442. The inclusive rate is $1,500 per person, including air from Juneau.

Experienced boaters can bare-boat charter the 32-foot Nordic Tug *Morning Wings* from John and Lois Nixon's **Glacier Bay Tug Charters** and see the bay on their own. The rate is $375 a day. Call (907) 697–2205. Jim Kearns's **Fairweather Adventures** offers lodging and marine wildlife tours at the mouth of Glacier Bay, on the banks of the Salmon River. Kayak trips, sport-fishing, beach excursions, and exploring are all available. The cost runs approximately $2,000 for an inclusive full week's adventure. Phone (907) 697–2334 for details.

For decades **Glacier Bay Airways** has provided dependable scheduled air service between Juneau and Gustavus (and, for that matter, Pelican, Haines, and Skagway). The small carrier also offers Juneau Icefield and Glacier Bay flight-seeing plus back-country drop-offs for campers. The fare from Juneau to Gustavus is $60 one way; one-hour flight-seeing from Gustavus costs $120. Call (907) 697–2269 for details.

CANADA'S YUKON

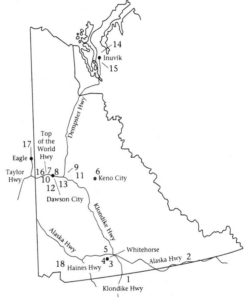

14
● Inuvik
15

Dempster Hwy

17
Top
of the
World
Hwy
Eagle ●

Taylor
Hwy

16 7 8
10
12 13

9
11

6
● Keno City

Dawson City

Klondike Hwy

Alaska Hwy

5   Whitehorse
4 ● 3   Alaska Hwy 2
18 Haines Hwy

1
Klondike Hwy

1. Atlin
2. Sign Post Forest
3. MacBride Museum
4. *S.S. Klondike*
5. Takhini Hot Springs
6. Mining Museum
7. Midnight Dome
8. Palace Grand Theatre
9. Diamond Tooth Gertie's

10. Jack London's cabin
11. Bear Creek
12. Steamer *Keno*
13. *Yukon Queen* River Cruise
14. Inuvik
15. Catholic Church
16. Top of the World Highway
17. Wickersham Courthouse
18. Kluane National Park

CANADA'S YUKON

So, you may be asking, what is a chapter about part of Canada doing in an Alaska guidebook? Actually, there are a couple of reasons.

First of all, if you're driving from Southeast Alaska to Alaska's interior, you have to go through a small sliver of Canada's British Columbia and a big hunk of Canada's Yukon. From Haines or Skagway at the northern end of the Southeast Alaska ferry system, you can drive the 152-mile Haines Highway or 98 miles of the Klondike Highway to junctions with the Alaska Highway. From there your route lies northwesterly through Canada's Yukon Territory to the rest of Alaska.

Second, from the traveler's point of view, visiting Canada's Yukon is really part of the North Country experience. Aside from a few artificial differences, like Canada's metric road signs, or gasoline pumped in liters instead of gallons, you'll notice few distinctions between the Yukon and Alaska's interior region. Both are lands of rolling hills, majestic mountains, fish-filled lakes, and vast, untrammeled wilderness areas teeming with moose, caribou, bears, and wolves.

In both interior Alaska and the Yukon, you'll marvel at a sun that nearly doesn't set during the summertime, and in both you'll find friendly, helpful, outgoing folk who revel in their Native heritage, their gold rush past, and their present-day frontier lifestyle.

The main arterial road of the Yukon Territory is the Alaska Highway, referred to by many tourists—but few Alaskans or Yukoners—as the Alcan. (It's rather like calling San Francisco Frisco. Everyone will know what you're talking about, but knowledgeable visitors will observe the local preference.) The fabled road begins at Dawson Creek in British Columbia, meanders through the Yukon Territory to the Alaska border, and ends at Delta Junction, Alaska—a total journey of 1,422 miles.

The two largest cities of the Yukon are Whitehorse, present-day capital of the territory, and Dawson City (not to be confused with Dawson Creek, B.C.). It was near the present site of Dawson City, in 1896, that the discovery of gold on a tributary of the Klondike River set off one of the world's wildest stampedes.

In both Alaska and the Yukon, you'll see numbers on frequent mileposts or kilometer posts beside the highways. These numbers

54

represent miles or kilometers from a highway's beginning. Home and business addresses and even cities are often referenced in miles or kilometers. Whitehorse, for instance, is shown in a Yukon government guidebook as being located at kilometer 1455.3 on the Alaska Highway. In this Canadian section of this book, we'll identify most sites by their kilometer post markings, although in discussing short drives and distances, we'll frequently refer to miles, since most U.S. residents have a better feel for mileage measurements. When, in the next chapter, we're back in Alaska, U.S.A., highway references will be in miles.

Here's a word of explanation about the layout of this chapter. It assumes you'll be traveling northerly through the Yukon to Interior Alaska either from Skagway (over the southern half of the Klondike Highway), Haines (over the Haines Highway), or Dawson Creek at the start of the Alaska Highway. So, to start with, the chapter discusses sights and options along each of these three northbound approaches to Whitehorse. After a discussion of things to see and do in Whitehorse, the chapter describes the northern portion of the Klondike Highway from near Whitehorse to Dawson City. After suggesting a round trip on the Dempster Highway from Dawson City to Inuvik in Canada's Northwest Territories it deals—still Alaska-bound—with the Top of the World Highway north and west from Dawson City to the point where it crosses the border and meets Alaska's Taylor Highway. The Taylor, in turn, is described from northernmost Eagle to Tetlin Junction on the Alaska Highway, 80 miles northwest of the Alaska border.

Finally, the chapter backtracks to Whitehorse and lists your Alaska Higway options between that city and the point where you cross into Interior Alaska and the United States again. Of course, if you're departing Interior Alaska and heading southerly to southeast Alaska or Dawson Creek, British Columbia, the listings should be considered in reverse.

THE KLONDIKE HIGHWAY:
SKAGWAY TO WHITEHORSE

Don't let the start of the **Klondike Highway** out of Skagway scare you. The first 10 or 11 miles climb at a pretty steep grade, from sea level to 3,000 feet plus, but after that the going's relatively

55

level and certainly no worse than other mountain roads in the Lower Forty-eight and elsewhere. The road is two lanes wide, asphalt paved for its 98-mile (159-kilometer) length, and roughly parallels the historic Trail of '98 from Skagway to the Klondike gold fields. It rises from lush, thickly vegetated low country to high, rocky mountain and lake terrain.

You come to **U.S. Customs** just beyond mile 6, but there's no need to stop unless you're southbound, heading for Skagway from Canada. The actual **U.S.–Canada border** lies just before mile 15. Advance your watch one hour, from Alaska to Pacific time. The Alaskan mileposts beside the road now become Canadian kilometer posts. You come to **Canada Customs** and the White Pass & Yukon Route's Fraser Station near kilometer 36. If you're northbound, you have to stop and check in with the Canadian authorities.

At kilometer 43, take the turnout to the east for a spectacular view of **Tormented Valley**, with its little lakes, stunted trees, and rocky landscape of big and little boulders. The historic remains of an ore-crushing mill for the **Venus Mine** can be seen and photographed at kilometer 84. Twelve kilometers farther there's a spectacular view of **Bove Island** and a portion of the Yukon's southern lakes system.

The community of **Carcross,** on the shores of Lake Bennett, lies at kilometer 106. Formerly called Caribou Crossing, the town has hotel accommodations, a general store, gas station, RV campground, cafe, and a gift store called the **Carcross Barracks Gift Shop** where you can have your picture taken with a caribou. At Carcross's **visitor reception centre** in the Old Train Depot (403–821–4431) you can get tourist information—including, if you're into gutsy adventures, details about local skydiving lessons.

If time permits, turn right at kilometer 107 and head northeast on the paved 34-mile Tagish Road to **Tagish**, Yukon Territory, then head south on the good, but mostly gravel 60-mile Atlin Road to ◆**Atlin,** British Columbia. The drive takes a little more than two hours. Atlin is a favorite getaway for Southeast Alaskans, many of whom have summer cottages there. Atlin Lake is a huge, meandering, spectacular body of water with lots of recreational opportunities. In the community itself you can visit the **Atlin Historical Museum** in the town's original one-room schoolhouse, take pictures of the grounded but picturesque old riverboat **M.V. Tarahne,** drink cold, bubbly water at the mineral springs, or hike the local trails. You can rent motorbikes or houseboats, take flight-seeing excursions around the area, or engage a guide for excellent lake and stream fishing. The community has a hotel plus several B&Bs and inns, including **Noland House,** which can accommodate four guests in luxurious, historic rooms. The rate is $85 for a double; call (604) 651–7585. When you leave, you can avoid duplicating about a third of your route back to Carcross by joining the Alaska Highway at Jake's Corner (about 60 miles north of Atlin).

Back on the Klondike Highway, a few minutes' drive beyond Carcross lies **Frontierland Heritage Park,** a six-acre theme park with gold mining, live Dall sheep, an old-time trapper's cabin, the only mounted sabre-toothed tiger in existence, the world's largest mounted polar bear, plus a cafe and gift shop. Adult admission is $3.00. On the same property, but in a separate building, is the **Museum of Yukon Natural History,** a privately owned collection of mounted Yukon wildlife in authentic dioramas. Admission is $3.00. If you visit both Frontierland and the museum, the cost for both is $5.00. Call (403) 667–1055. Hours for both are 8:30 A.M. to 6:00 P.M. daily.

Here's a Yukon superlative for you—a "smallest," not a "biggest." At kilometer 111 you pass the **Carcross Desert,** at 260 hectares (640 acres), the smallest desert in the world. Glaciers and a large glacial lake originally covered the area, and when the glaciers retreated they left sand deposits on the former lake bottoms. The well-named **Emerald Lake,** nestled in the hills farther along at kilometer 120, is incredibly green and colorful, the subject of thousands of photo exposures each year.

At kilometer 157, 98 miles beyond its starting point at Skagway, this portion of the Klondike Highway junctions with the **Alaska Highway.** You're just a few minutes' drive south of Whitehorse. The northern portion of the Klondike Highway, which extends all the way to Dawson City, recommences just north of Whitehorse.

THE HAINES HIGHWAY:
HAINES TO HAINES JUNCTION

The Haines Highway (which several Canadian publications call the Haines Road) runs 152 miles (246 kilometers) from the water's edge in Haines, Alaska, to Haines Junction on the Alaska Highway, west of Whitehorse. They're spectacular miles, sometimes paralleling the path of the old Dalton Trail to the Klondike. In the process they traverse thick green forests in the Chilkat Valley at lower elevations and high, barren, mystical plains once you've climbed over Chilkat Pass. Your travel log will record frequent views of piercing sawtooth mountains plus lakes that contain monster-sized trout. The road is two-lane, asphalt, and open year-around.

About 9 miles from Haines, you enter the **Alaska Chilkat Bald Eagle Preserve** where, in winter, thousands of American bald eagles gather to feast on the still-abundant salmon of the Chilkat River. If you want to stop, use pullouts and viewing areas about 10 miles farther down the road.

At mile 40 you'll arrive at **U.S. Customs,** but if you're Canada-bound you don't have to stop until you cross the **U.S.–Canada border** and come to **Canada Customs and Immigration** a couple of minutes farther on. (Remember, kilometer posts now replace mileposts in metric-minded Canada.)

You'll cross **Chilkat Pass** (elevation 1,065 meters; 3,493 feet) at kilometer 102 and come to **Million Dollar Falls Campground** at kilometer 159. There's pleasant camping (for $8.00) and fishing here, and it's an excellent picnicking choice, even if you don't want to spend the night.

Approaching kilometer 188, you come to the **St. Elias Lake Trail,** a novice- and intermediate-friendly hiking trail through subalpine meadows. It's a 6.4-kilometer (4-mile-plus) trek that offers a good chance to spot mountain goats beyond the lake.

You have another camping and fishing opportunity at big, long **Dezadeash Lake** (pronounced DEZ-dee-ash), home to lake trout, northern pike, and grayling at kilometer 195.

At kilometer 202 you can hike **Rock Glacier Trail,** in **Kluane National Park,** a half-hour walk to the rocky residue of a former glacier and a panoramic view. Rock glaciers are a unique landform created when glacial ice and frost-shattered rock mix and flow downhill.

Haines Junction, Yukon Territory, lies at Haines Highway kilometer 246, nearly 153 miles from the road's start in Haines, Alaska. Whitehorse lies about 100 Alaska Highway miles east.

THE ALASKA HIGHWAY:
WATSON LAKE TO WHITEHORSE

Amazingly, the 2,233-kilometer (1,388-mile) **Alaska Highway** was constructed and connected in eight months and twelve days as a military road during World War II. Construction started March 8, 1942, and ended October 24; it was one of the most amazing road building feats in modern history. The road, then and now, commences in **Dawson Creek, British Columbia,** originating at the huge, picture-worthy **Milepost 0 Monument,** on Tenth Street in downtown Dawson Creek. It ends at Delta Junction, Alaska. It's an asphalt road all the way, though the quality of the pavement varies, and you'll likely encounter gravel detours from time to time as road crews strive to improve the highway and your vacation experience.

The first major Yukon Territory (Y.T.) community you'll come to (and, therefore, our starting point in this book) is **Watson Lake,** at kilometer 1,021. The **visitor reception centre,** at the junction of the Alaska and Campbell Highways, is a good place to pick up the latest data on road conditions as well as visitor attractions in the area—including the mind-blowing ◆**Sign Post Forest,** which started in this way: Back in 1942, the American soldier Carl K. Lindley of Danville, Illinois, one of thousands of U.S. servicemen constructing the highway, got homesick and erected a sign indicating the mileage back to his hometown. Others did the same, and a tradition took hold. Later, after the war, civilian motorists started driving along the road from the Lower Forty-eight states to Alaska, and they erected signs too. In 1995, the count stood at more than 26,000 signs.

Just beyond kilometer 1,162 you cross the Continental Divide, separating lands that drain into the Pacific Ocean from those that drain into the Arctic Ocean. Just off the highway at kilometer 1,294, you arrive in the mostly Native community of Teslin, originally a summer home for Tlingit Indians from Southeast Alaska and British Columbia. The **George Johnston Museum,** open from 9:00 A.M. to 7:00 P.M., houses the largest Tlingit Indian artifact collection in the Yukon. You'll see dioramas, rare historical photographs, George Johnston's 1,928 Chevrolet, and many post-European and early Yukon exhibits. The museum honors Johnston, a Tlingit Indian

59

who was born in 1884 and died in 1972. An expert photographer, Johntson brought the car, a first in these parts, to Teslin. Admission is $2.50 for adults. Phone (403) 390–2550.

Nine miles north of Teslin, at kilometer 1,306, **Mukluk Annie's Salmon Bake** (403–667–1200) serves up salmon and barbecued ribs, steaks, and pork from 11:00 A.M. until 9:00 P.M.. There are also houseboat rides on Teslin Lake every evening at 8:00 P.M., free to salmon bake customers and guests at Mukluk Annie's motel there. **Jake's Corner** and access to the Atlin Road lies beyond kilometer 1,392; you come to Whitehorse city limits at kilometer 1,455, about 40 miles later.

Whitehorse is the Yukon Territory's "big city," a modern community of 23,000. It's home to about two thirds of all the Y.T.'s residents and serves as its hub and transportation center. The town's origins lie in the construction of the White Pass & Yukon Route Railway from the ocean port of Skagway early in the century. Its economy today relies on government, trade, and tourism plus minerals and mining activity.

If you're driving, make the **Yukon Visitor Reception Centre,** at kilometer 1,473.1 on the Alaska Highway, your first stop in the Whitehorse area. It's operated by Tourism Yukon and contains lots of good information and laser disk visuals, especially about Yukon national parks and historic sites. It's also one of your best sources for up-to-date highway data. Call (403) 667–2915. Located beside the centre is the **Yukon Transportation Museum** (403–668–4792), which features North Country transport, from dogsleds and stagecoaches to a WP&YR railcar replica and vintage aircraft. Admission is $3.00. Another source of visitor information, particularly for sites in and around Whitehorse, is the **Whitehorse Chamber of Commerce Information Centre** in town, at 302 Steele Street (403–667–7545).

Not to be missed is the ◆**MacBride Museum** (First Avenue and Wood Street; 403–667–2709), 5,000 rambling but fascinating square feet of artifacts, historic photographs, maps, and exhibits that cover the Yukon from ancient prehistory to the present. The real Sam McGee's cabin (of Robert Service fame) can be seen here, as well as horse wagons and steam engines. Admission is $3.25. The museum is open daily from 10 A.M. until 6:00 P.M.

Everybody does a tour of the ◆**S.S. Klondike,** the largest stern-wheeler to ply the Yukon River, and you should, too. It's

Stern-wheeler *S.S. Klondike*, Whitehorse

located literally on the shores of the Yukon River, near the Robert
Campbell bridge. The 210-foot ship was built in 1929, sank seven
years later, but was refloated and rebuilt in 1937. It continued in
service until the fifties. Now designated a National Historic Landmark, it's been restored to reflect one of the North Country's
prime methods of travel during the late 1930s. Admission is
$3.00. Call (604) 667–4511.

61

And here's a special thing for nostalgia buffs or WW II veterans and their families to do. Nightly in the summer, visitors can attend a one-and-a-half-hour USO-type **Canteen Show** in the Town Hall meeting room of the Gold Rush Inn, 411 Main Street. Music, humor, and entertainment from the wartime forties fill the bill of the evening. Admission is $15; call (403) 668–4500 for more information.

You'll probably never have a better chance to see Yukon wildlife than during a drive-through tour of the **Yukon Wildlife Preserve.** (Contact Gray Line at 403–668–3225.) In hundreds of acres of forests, meadows, and marshlands you can view caribou, elk, bison, moose, mountain goats, sheep, musk ox, mule deer, snowy owls, and rare peregrine falcons. Admission: $18.50. The **Yukon Conservation Society** sponsors free guided hikes around the Whitehorse area during the summer, providing an opportunity to learn about the unique northern flora and fauna as well as the natural history and geology of the land. Call (403) 668–5678 for schedules.

Butchart Gardens it isn't, but **Yukon Gardens** is a worthwhile stop if you're interested in wild and domestic flowers, trees, and shrubs of the Yukon. The strolling is easy, and the color photo opportunities are numerous. Admission is $4.95. Call (403) 668–7972.

For the traveler in search of art, the **Yukon Arts Centre,** at Yukon Place off Range Road (403–667–8575), offers a spectacular view plus the territory's largest art gallery, a theatre, and an outdoor amphitheatre. There is no charge, but donations are accepted. The centre is open weekdays 11:00 A.M. to 5:00 P.M., and Sundays 1:00 to 4:00 P.M. A **Yukon Permanent Art Collection**—showing northern landscapes and lifestyles as portrayed by prominent Canadian artists—is displayed in the foyer of the Yukon Government Administration Building, on Second Street. Open weekdays only, 8:30 A.M. to 5:00 P.M.

In June through August, escorted **Whitehorse Heritage Buildings Walking Tours** originate every hour on the hour 9:00 A.M. to 4:00 P.M. Monday through Saturday at the Donnenworth House, at 3126 Third Avenue. Phone (403) 667–4704. There is a $2.00 fee. If you can't join an escorted tour, pick up the self-guided "Walking Tour of Yukon's Capital" from local merchants.

You don't have to be Anglican (Episcopal) to visit the **Old Log Church** located a block off Main Street on Elliott Street and Third Avenue. The sanctuary building, constructed in 1900 for the Church of England, and the log rectory next door are rich in Yukon's history. Exhibits, artifacts, and relics tell the story of the Yukon's history from precontact life among aboriginal peoples to early exploration and beyond. Admission is $2.50. Services are conducted there Sunday afternoons at 4:30 P.M.

◆**Takhini Hot Springs** lies twenty to thirty minutes from downtown Whitehorse; don't miss it. You get there by driving roughly 9 miles north of the Yukon Visitors Reception Centre on the Alaska Highway, then nearly 4 miles north on the Klondike Highway to the Takhini Hot Springs Road. You then travel about 6 miles west to the well-marked springs area. This place offers some of the pleasantest soaking and swimming waters you'll find in the North Country as well as the opportunity to chat in really relaxing surroundings with Yukoners, Alaskans, and fellow travelers. Facilities here are fully modern, with changing rooms, showers, and a coffee shop on-site. If you're RV camping or tenting, plan to stay in the campground there. Activities, beside bathing and swimming, include hiking and horseback riding. The charge for the hot springs is $3.50, for camping, $8.00 to $10.00. For information, call (403) 633–2706.

If you'd like to pet, feed, photograph, or pose with a herd of reindeer, your opportunity awaits at the **Northern Splendor Reindeer Farm**, about 10.5 miles beyond the Alaska Highway junction on the Klondike Highway. Admission is $3.50; coffee is complimentary. Call (403) 633–2996.

Takhini-Wud Bed and Breakfast is located about 10 miles from the Alaska Highway on the Klondike Highway, just ten minutes from Takhini Hot Springs and five minutes from the reindeer farm and Lake Labarge. You can ride horses, arrange fishing expeditions, or simply relax in a peaceful country setting. Rates start at $65 for a double. Phone (403) 667–4169.

Longtime Yukoners Carla Pitzel and Garry Limbrich operate **Hawkins House Bed and Breakfast** at 303 Hawkins Street, overlooking a city park and swimming pool. They describe their B&B as Victorian luxury, offering such amenities as a 1905 loveseat and bubble baths in a claw-foot tub when you stay in the Victorian Tea Rose Room, and stained-glass windows of old Montreal in the French Room. There's a balcony view of Canyon Mountain and the paddle wheeler *S.S. Klondike*. Rates begin at $100 for a double. Call (403) 668–7638.

From Whitehorse, if you're driving, you have two choices for travel north and west to the main body of Alaska. (The Millers recommend that you choose one option going into Alaska, the other when you drive out.) You can continue on up the Alaska Highway, driving west and then northwest to Haines Junction, Kluane National Park, Beaver Creek, and the U.S. border, or you can drive northerly on the Klondike Highway to Carmacks, Minto, Stewart Crossing, and Dawson City, where you can connect with the Top of the World Highway to the Alaska border.

THE KLONDIKE HIGHWAY; WHITEHORSE TO DAWSON CITY

The northern portion of the Skagway–to–Dawson City Klondike Highway starts at kilometer 1,487 on the Alaska Highway, about 9 miles beyond Whitehorse. The first major stop along the way is Carmacks, at kilometer 357. (Remember, kilometer posts show the distance from Skagway.) The community is historically important as a stern-wheeler steamboat stop on the Yukon River route between Whitehorse and Dawson City. Gold Rush River Tours in the Carmacks Hotel will take you through Five Finger Rapids, a scenic, splashy, fun experience. It's a six-hour round-trip for three persons at $100 each. Call (403) 863–5221 for information about this and overnight tours, canoe rentals, or pike and lake trout fishing. At kilometer 380.5 you can see the rapids from an observation deck built as part of the Five Finger Rapids Day Use Area of trails and picnic sites.

For campers or picnickers, the Yukon government's **Minto Landing Campground,** located at the end of a short road that junctions with the Klondike Highway at kilometer 431.3, is situated right on the grassy banks of the Yukon. An old, abandoned log cabin on the site is particularly picture worthy. Overnight camping costs $8.00.

At kilometer 537 you come to **Stewart Crossing**, where you have the opportunity to take a side excursion (about 150 miles round-trip) over the **Silver Trail** through scenic woods and water country to the mining communities of **Mayo, Elsa,** and **Keno City**. If you plan to overnight in this part of the region, **Mayo Bed and Breakfast** is within walking distance to the scenic Stewart River. The rate is $63 for a double, and there are discounts for payment in cash. Call (403) 996–2221. The Yukon government **Five Mile Lake Campground,** just east of Mayo, is one of the Miller family's favorites, with generous campsites, kitchen shelters, launch sites, a swimming beach, and an obstacle course where kids can work off energy. The charge is $8.00 per night. **Country Charm Bed and Breakfast**, near the same lake, offers a quiet country setting, biking, and hiking. The rate for doubles is $50. Call (403) 996–2918.

The ◆**Mining Museum** at Keno City is a particular delight, with displays that vary from old-time mining equipment to baseball uniforms the local teams wore. There's no admission charge. Hours are 10 A.M. to 6:00 P.M. At **Duncan Creek Gold-dusters,** on the Duncan Creek Road south of Keno City, you can pan for gold for $11 and take a guided tour, usually around 2:00 P.M., of a working mine.

Back on the Klondike Highway at kilometer 715, a few minutes before you arrive in Dawson City you come to a private RV park and gold panning area with the unlikely name of **GuggieVille**. If you're interested in panning for Yukon gold, you can do it here on the massive dredge tailings of the former Guggenheim mining camp. Call (403) 993–5008.

The high point (literally) of a Dawson City visit comes when you drive the Dome Road from its junction at Klondike Highway's kilometer 717 to the top of ◆**Midnight Dome** for a panoramic view of the city, the Yukon and Klondike Rivers, the Bonanza gold fields, and the Ogilvie Mountains. Awesome.

Dawson City, of course, is where it all began—the frenzied, frantic, fabled stampede for North Country gold. It started in 1896 when George Carmack, Skookum Jim, and Tagish Charlie found "color"—lots of it—in a Klondike River tributary called Rabbit Creek, later renamed Bonanza Creek. The rush catapulted into international prominence when the vessel *Portland* steamed into Seattle on July 17, 1897, and the *Seattle Post-Intelligencer* screamed "Gold! Gold! Gold!" in its banner headline. A "ton of gold" was proclaimed in the story that followed. The rush was on.

65

Tens of thousands of gold seekers (most of them ill prepared and without the slightest concept of the rigors they would face) crowded aboard almost any boat that would float out of West Coast ports and headed for Skagway and the White Pass, Dyea and the Chilkoot Pass, St. Michael on the Yukon River, or any of a number of other gateways to the Klondike. Their common goal was Dawson City and the rich gold country around it. It's said that 100,000 gold seekers set out for the Klondike. Some 30,000 made it.

Today the rush to the Klondike continues, but it's a vastly more comfortable odyssey. Travelers come not to extract riches but to see the place where all the excitement happened. Thanks to eleventh-hour rescue restorations by the national and territorial governments, Dawson City looks remarkably as it did a near-century ago, when it sprang up on the Yukon River shores. Old buildings and landmarks were saved from certain rot and destruction. The "Bard of the Yukon" **Robert Service's Cabin** is still there. So is the magnificently refurbished 1899 ✦**Palace Grand Theatre** and ✦**Diamond Tooth Gertie's**, where you can legally gamble away your "poke" at real gaming tables as many a prospector did in '98. At the historic old **1901 post office**, at Third Avenue and King Street (open noon to 6:00 P.M.), your first class letters and postcards will be canceled the old fashioned way— by hand. Collectors can purchase special commemorative stamps.

Before beginning a foray to any of these sites, it's probably wise to stop by Tourism Yukon's **Dawson Visitor Reception Centre**, at Front and King Streets (403–993–5566), to get oriented. While you're there, take time to view some Yukon attractions on laser video disk players and maybe even take part in one of the free **Dawson City walking tours** that originate at the site several times daily. If you plan to extend your trip to Inuvik and Canada's Northwest Territories via the Dempster Highway, cross the street from the Dawson reception centre and get highway and other information from the **Northwest Territories Information Centre** (403–993–6167).

At ✦**Jack London's cabin** near Grant Street and Eighth Avenue you can meet North Country historian and author Dick North daily at 1 P.M. and hear how he discovered London's authentic cabin in the Yukon wilderness. The structure was carefully disassembled, and half the logs were used to re-create the writer's cabin at its present site in Dawson City. The other half went into the construction of an identical cabin at Jack London Square in Oakland, California. Admission is free. At Eighth Avenue and Hanson you'll find the **Robert Service cabin** where poetry, written by "the Bard of the Yukon" is recited at 10:00 A.M. and 3:00 P.M. daily. The cabin is open 9:00 A.M. to noon and 1:00 P.M. to 5:00 P.M. Admission is $2.25.

For a really in-depth look at Dawson's history, visit the old **1901 Territorial Administration Building,** where the Dawson City Museum and Historical Society houses its collection of gold-rush era artifacts, paleontological remains, cultural exhibits of the Han Native people, even a collection of narrow-gauge steam locomotives. There are also vintage film showings and lectures. Admission is $3.50. Call (403) 993–5291.

◆**Bear Creek**, a gold mining industrial complex of some sixty-five buildings that operated from 1905 to 1966, is now open for visitors. Parks Canada interpreters, under the auspices of Klondike National Historic Sites, conduct guided tours daily. The complex, open 9:30 A.M. to 5:00 P.M. daily, is located about 6.2 miles east of Dawson City. Visitors are greeted in the former general manager's residence, and during the course of a tour they see an intact blacksmith shop and the Gold Room, where the precious metal was cleaned, melted down, and cast into bullion. Mining artifacts include a Keystone prospecting drill, a large turn-of-the-century steam-operated water pump, and a hydraulic monitor. There is a $2.25 admission.

It's not far off the beaten path (in fact, it sits on Front Street and First Avenue, on the banks of the Yukon between King and Queen Streets) but it's a must-see if you value restored historical artifacts. We're referring to the ◆**Steamer *Keno,*** built in 1922 in Whitehorse for service between Stewart City and Mayo Landing. It's typical of the breed of shallow-draft riverboats that served the North Country from early gold-rush times until well into the twentieth century.

The largest wooden-hull, bucket-line gold dredge in North America—old **Gold Dredge #4**, two-thirds the size of a football field long and eight whopping stories high—can be seen south of town near the spot where it ceased operations in 1960. The site is beside Bonanza Creek off Bonanza Creek Road, about 7.8 miles south of the Klondike Highway. About 2.5 miles farther south you'll find **Discovery Claim** (and a monument to mark the spot) on Bonanza Creek, where George Carmack, Skookum Jim, and Tagish Charlie made their history-making discovery.

At the **Dawson City Bed and Breakfast**, at 451 Craig Street, you're situated in a quiet, beautiful setting overlooking both the Klondike and Yukon Rivers. Breakfasts are full service. The owners will pick you up at the airport, bus, or waterfront if you don't have your own wheels. Rates are $79 for a double. Call (403) 993–5649.

White Ram Manor Bed and Breakfast is within walking distance of most Dawson City attractions. Look for the pink house at Seventh Avenue and Harper Street. Accommodations include full breakfasts, use of kitchen facilities for other meals, a hot tub, barbecue, and picnic area. Call (403) 993–5772.

From Dawson City you have a splendid overnight riverboat opportunity: Gray Line's ❖ *Yukon Queen* **River Cruise** heads downriver to Eagle, Alaska, utilizing a forty-nine-passenger luxury vessel with meals and full cabin service. Round-trip, one-way, and stand-by rates are available, starting as low as $108. Call (403) 993–5599.

A shorter (one-and-a-half-hour) **Yukon River Cruise and Pleasure Island narrated tour** includes the Dawson waterfront, Han' Native village at Moosehide, a sled dog exhibit, and complimentary coffee. The cost (cruise only) is $15. For $35 you can book a two-and-a-half-hour all-you-can-eat king salmon barbecue and cruise to the island. Call (403) 993–5482.

When you're ready to leave Dawson City, you have three driving choices. You can retrace the Klondike Highway south to the place just outside of Whitehorse where it junctions with the Alaska Highway, then continue north on the Alaska Highway to the main body of Alaska. Or you can take the Top of the World Highway to the place at the Alaska border where it meets the Taylor Highway, which in turn also connects with the Alaska Highway in Alaska. Or, you can keep going north and west via the Dempster Highway to Inuvik, in the Mackenzie Delta, not many miles from the shores of the Arctic Ocean. (Of course, when you've made it to Inuvik, you have to turn around and drive back the way you came. The Dempster doesn't meet or loop with any other highway.)

THE DEMPSTER HIGHWAY: DAWSON CITY TO INUVIK

The **Dempster,** the third choice, definitely deserves considera-
tion. It stretches 741 kilometers (460 miles) from its starting place
about 41 kilometers (25 miles) south of Dawson City on the
Klondike Highway. It ends in **Inuvik,** Northwest Territories,
surely one of the most literally colorful communities in North
America, with almost every hue of the rainbow represented on
homes and buildings.

Along the highway you pass sometimes through valleys
bounded by great granite mountains, at other times over high
flat plains, with rolling hills in the distance. Sometimes your
route is the legendary trail of the valiant North West Mounted
Police who patrolled the region by dogsled in the days before the
highway was built.

Accommodations and service stations are rare along most of
the route, so top off your tank every chance you get. Halfway to
Inuvik, you come at kilometer 364 to Eagle Plains and the **Eagle
Plains Hotel and Restaurant**, which offers thirty-two comfortable rooms, groceries, vehicle services, gas, and a restaurant
that serves the tastiest, most satisfying sourdough pancakes our
family has *ever* devoured. Take the time to examine the display of
historic photos on the walls of the restaurant. They tell the tragic
story of the Mounties' "Lost Patrol" in 1910 and of Inspector
W.J.D. Dempster's finding and retrieval of their frozen bodies.
Other pictures relate the murderous exploits of the "Mad Trapper
of Rat River" and the manhunt organized against him in 1932.
The Mounties, as always, got their man. Rooms cost $90 to $110.
Call (403) 979–4187.

At kilometer 403 you cross the **Arctic Circle** (take pictures of
the monument), and at kilometer 471 you leave the Yukon Territory, enter the Northwest Territories. From now on, kilometer
posts show the distance from this point. At kilometer 86 turn off
the highway to visit the nearby community of **Fort McPherson**. You can fill up on gasoline as well as visit the church graveyard where the hapless Lost Patrol members lie buried. Also, if
you're in the market for a backpack, duffel bag, or an attaché
case, visit the **Fort McPherson Tent and Canvas** factory. The
workmanship is first rate and almost certainly no one in your

69

hiking club back home will have one with the company's distinctive emblem. Call (800) 661–0888 for information.

At kilometer 269 and the community of ✪ **Inuvik**, don't fail to visit the igloo-shaped ✪ **Catholic Church**. Igloo-shaped? It sounds hokey, but the effect when you see it is breathtaking, and the paintings inside, created by *Inuvialuit* painter Mona Thrasher, are more than inspirational. Take time to see, as well, **Ingamo Hall**, a log friendship center with a great hall that has the feel of a baronial mansion.

If you'd enjoy an Arctic country setting for your overnight accommodations, consider the **Arctic Chalet**, a B&B lakeside home and cabins. Olav and Judi Falsnes offer simple but nutritious breakfasts and complimentary canoes. (Caution: Saturday check-ins must be prearranged.) Rates begin at $75 for a double. Call (403) 979–3535. Our favorite government campground in the area (there are two) is the **Chuk Campground**, about 2 miles from town on the Airport Road. Its hilltop location presents a worthwhile view of the Mackenzie Delta, and its breezes tend to discourage mosquitoes. A $10 fee is charged.

For the really ultimate in far north travel, fly to **Herschel Island**, off the Arctic Coast about 150 miles to the northwest (a Yukon territorial park, but accessible from Inuvik) for wildlife viewing as well as a look at the native *Inuvialuit* culture from prehistory through the nineteenth century whaling era. Several air carriers offer the trip. You can also arrange it through lifelong resident Fred Carmichael's **Western Arctic Nature Tours.** The firm can also book plane or boat visits to the village of **Tuktoyaktuk,** on the Arctic Coast, as well as fishing and cruising trips on the Mackenzie River. Call (403) 979–3300.

THE TOP OF THE WORLD HIGHWAY: DAWSON CITY TO THE ALASKA BORDER

Back to Dawson City and the second choice mentioned earlier, driving on the ✪ **Top of the World Highway** to the Taylor Highway. Yes, that's the official name of the road. It begins with a free car ferry ride over the Yukon River and heads west toward the Alaska border and Alaska's Taylor Highway for 127 kilometers (79 miles). The road, you'll find, really lives up to its name. Much

Igloo-shaped Catholic Church, Inuvik

of the time you're on ridge tops looking down on deep valleys. Lots of good scenic photo ops here. It's a good gravel road, but slippery in heavy rains. About 105 kilometers (66 miles) beyond Dawson City, you'll cross the U.S.–Canada border. Stop at the United States border station if you're heading westerly for Alaska and at Canada Customs and Immigration if you're eastbound for Dawson City.

THE TAYLOR HIGHWAY: JACK WADE JUNCTION TO EAGLE AND TELTIN JUNCTION

We're now going to talk about part of Alaska again, even though this chapter deals largely with the Canadian Yukon. Travel on the Taylor Highway is so logically connected with the Top of the World Highway from Dawson City, it just doesn't make sense to have you jump pages into other sections of the book.

At **Jack Wade Junction,** where the Taylor and the Top of the World Highways meet, turn north on the Taylor Highway and drive 65 miles to visit **Eagle,** a small but historically important community in the Alaska scheme of things. Still standing is the ◆ **Wickersham Courthouse** where Judge James Wickersham dispensed frontier justice during Eagle's gold rush days early in the century. Still intact as well are the old Waterfront Customs House, a military mule barn, water wagon shed, NCO (noncommissioned officers) quarters, and other structures that were part of old Fort Egbert. The federal Bureau of Land Management (BLM) has renovated and restored portions of the old fort where, incidentally, Captain Billy Mitchell once served a tour of duty. The Eagle Historical Society conducts daily tours of the community, starting at 9:00 A.M., at the courthouse. The cost is $3.00. You can visit the National Park Service headquarters for the **Yukon–Charley National Preserve** (907-547-2233) on the banks of the Yukon near Fort Egbert. Staffers will show you a video about the national preserve and answer any questions. If you'd like to overnight in Eagle, there's the **Yukon Adventure Bed and Breakfast**, a peaceful home with a large yard and picnic area on the banks of the Yukon. Rates range from $50 for the single Cheechako Room to $60 for the double Sourdough Room. Call (907) 547-2221.

Gray Line of Alaska's luxury river vessel *Yukon Queen* operates between Eagle and Dawson City, Yukon. The company transports passengers between Eagle and Anchorage or Fairbanks by motor coach. Call (800) 544-2206 for details. The *Kathleen,* operated by Upper Yukon Enterprises, offers Yukon and Porcupine River luxury sight-seeing expeditions. Call (907) 547-2254.

After your Eagle visit, backtrack south on the Taylor Highway to Jack Wade Junction. The distance from Jack Wade Junction to Tetlin Junction, and the Alaska Highway, is about 96 miles. When you've gone about 30 of those miles, around mile 66, slow

down and look for **Chicken**. No, this isn't a joke; it's a town...
sort of. It's said the community got its name because the miners
back in the gold rush days couldn't spell *ptarmigan,* which some
called an Alaska chicken anyway. The original mining camp is
now abandoned private property and is closed to general traffic.
If you turn off the Taylor Highway at the Airport Road, you'll
come to the **Chicken Creek Cafe**, known for its pies and baked
goods and the gathering place from which tours depart daily at
1:00 P.M. for old Chicken. Nearby you'll find the **Chicken Saloon**
and **Chicken Mercantile Emporium**, where you can buy a
Chicken hat, a Chicken pin, and, naturally, a Chicken T-shirt.
Chicken Discount Gas and Propane gives you yet another
opportunity to keep your gas tank full.

The Taylor Highway ends (or begins, depending on which way
you're traveling) at Tetlin Junction, mile 1,302 on the Alaska
Highway, where there's lodging, food, and gas if you've per-
ilously coasted in without buying fuel on the Taylor Highway.

THE ALASKA HIGHWAY:
WHITEHORSE TO THE ALASKA BORDER

Back in Canada's Yukon and beyond Whitehorse about 90 miles
lies Haines Junction, at the junction of the Haines Highway from
Haines, Alaska, and the Alaska Highway at kilometer 809. The
community calls itself the Gateway to Kluane. Kluane (pronounced clue-AW-nee) is the Yukon's biggest lake. Its namesake,
◆ **Kluane National Park,** is one of the preeminent wilderness national parks of North America.

Especially for the hiker, mountain climber, canoe enthusiast,
kayaker, and river runner, Kluane National Park is a place to
spend days, not hours. To get oriented, visit the park's **visitor
reception centre**, about .2 mile east of the junction with the
Haines Highway and just off the Alaska Highway. There you'll see
an international award-winning audiovisual presentation about
the park, and you'll be able to pick up information about long
and short hiking trails and canoe-kayak routes. The hours are
8:00 A.M. to 8:00 P.M. daily; call (403) 634–2345.

At privately operated **Kluane Park Adventure Center**, at
the Mountain View Inn, you can book lodges and B&Bs as well as
half-day to weeklong expeditions that run the gamut from rafting

and hiking to heli-hiking, flight-seeing, mountain biking, and fishing. Call (403) 634–2313.

About 35 miles beyond Haines Junction, at kilometer 1693, the Sias family (six generations of Yukoners) operate **Kluane Bed and Breakfast**. Accommodations are heated A-frame cabins with mountain views, showers, cooking facilities, and a beach. Expect full family-style breakfasts here with pancakes and the Sias's own farm fresh eggs. To call, contact the Whitehorse Mobile Operator 2M3924 on Destruction Bay channel.

At the **Sheep Mountain Visitor Centre**, kilometer 1706.8, you can frequently spot a herd of Dall sheep on the nearby slopes. An interpretive trail leads to Soldier's Summit, which was the site of the opening ceremony for the Alaska Highway on November 20, 1942.

The Bayshore Lodge and **Oasis Restaurant,** at about kilometer 1712, offers an unexcelled pristine setting (and a giant lakeside hot tub) on the shores of Kluane Lake. Country-style rooms for two start at $49. The Bumbleberry pie in the restaurant is legendary. Call the owners Jim Stocco and Shirley Steele at (403) 841–4551.

At the village of Burwash Landing, kilometer 1061.5, the **Kluane Museum of Natural History** (403–841–5561) contains major new natural history exhibits featuring wildlife of the region as well as Indian artifacts, costumes, and dioramas. The admission is $3.00.

Here's another North Country travel superlative: **Beaver Creek**, at kilometer 1,934, is Canada's westernmost community. Tourism Yukon's **visitor reception centre** features a special display of wildflowers and dispenses tons of visitor information especially for visitors entering Canada from Alaska. The **Beaver Creek Canada Customs and Immigration** Office at kilometer 1,937.5 is a required stop for visitors entering Canada. At kilometer 1,967.5 you arrive at the **Canada–U.S. border**. Set your clocks back an hour (from Pacific to Alaska time) and start thinking again in miles and gallons.

SOUTHCENTRAL ALASKA

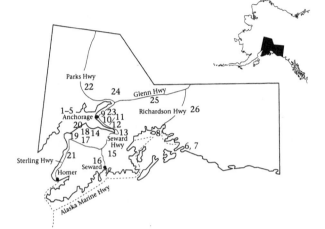

1. Reeve Aviation Picture Museum
2. Tony Knowles Coastal Trail
3. Fort Richardson Alaskan Fish and Wildlife Center
4. Marx Brothers
5. Gwennie's Old Alaska Restaurant
6. Childs Glacier
7. Discovery Voyage
8. Growler Island
9. Potter Marsh
10. Beluga Point
11. Turnagain Tidal Bore
12. Crow Creek Mine
13. Begich-Boggs Visitor Center
14. Resurrection Pass Trail
15. Alaska Railroad
16. Exit Glacier
17. Swanson River Canoe Trail
18. Swan Lake Canoe Trail
19. Holy Assumption of the Virgin Mary Russian Orthodox Church
20. Captain Cook State Recreation Area
21. Clam Gulch State Recreation Area
22. Mary Carey's Fiddlehead Farm
23. Eklutna Village Historical Park
24. Independence Mine State Historical Park
25. Matanuska Glacier
26. Kennicott Glacier Lodge

Southcentral Alaska

More than half the population of Alaska lives, works, and plays in Southcentral Alaska, a region of magnificent glaciers, big lakes (one of them even named Big Lake), forests, fertile river valleys, and many of the tallest mountains in North America. Brown (grizzly) bears, moose, Dall mountain sheep, mountain goats, and wolves thrive hereabouts, and, happily, you'll find no small number of hiking trails and vehicular back roads that offer access for viewing these creatures in their native terrain.

Fact is, there are more miles of asphalt highways, marine highways, byways, airways, and railways in Southcentral than in any other portion of the state. In square miles the region occupies perhaps a fifth of the mainland mass of Alaska. In shape Southcentral Alaska is a roughly 250-mile-deep arc of land and waters bordered on the south by the Gulf of Alaska, on the north and west by the curving arc of the Alaska mountain range, and on the east by the Canadian border—except at the very bottom, where the Southeast Alaska panhandle comes up to join the main body of Alaska.

Before the arrival of Europeans in the eighteenth century, this region and Alaska's interior was the domain of mostly Athabascan Indians, a tough, resourceful people who lived by hunting moose, caribou, and bear as well as lesser game and birds. They harvested fish from saltwater shores and freshwater streams. Among their many skills was working in leather, sometimes richly adorned with beads fashioned from hollow porcupine quills and other natural materials. Those skills survive today, especially in the form of colorful decorative beadwork—greatly prized by visitors and residents alike—sewn onto moccasins, vests, and other leather goods.

Southcentral's modern history began in 1741 with the arrival of Russians sailing for the Czars (Vitus Bering and Alexei Chirikov), followed by the English (Captains James Cook and George Vancouver) and other Europeans in the 1800s. After the Alaska Purchase of 1867, Americans came sporadically to the region seeking gold and other resources. But it was not until 1915 and the beginning of construction of the Alaska Railroad from Seward to Fairbanks that the area began to come into its own. Anchorage—a city created as construction and managing headquarters for the line—came into being. It later boomed, especially during and after World War II, when military installations swelled the population. In recent years the development of Alaskan petroleum resources has created additional growth in Anchorage and other communities.

Visitors find the weather surprisingly mild in this region of Alaska. Around Anchorage, for instance, summertime temperatures range in the comfortable midsixties and seventies. Thanks to the sheltering heights of the Alaska Range, wintertime temperatures usually hover between ten and twenty-five degrees—above zero—although they occasionally plunge to twenty or more degrees below. Whenever you come, be prepared for an extraordinary vacation in this part of Alaska. It teems with opportunities both on and off its major roadways.

ANCHORAGE

Since Anchorage is the transportation hub of Southcentral Alaska, this chapter treats it as the hub, as well, for planning trips in the region. After first describing the city and its immediate environs the chapter describes the water world and marine highway routes of Prince William Sound to the southeast, the more southerly highways (including the Seward and the Sterling) of the Kenai Peninsula, then the highways (George Parks, Glenn, and Richardson), which head northerly toward Denali National Park and other points in interior Alaska.

Anchorage is Alaska's "Big Apple," a large (for Alaska) metropolitan, cosmopolitan community of oil executives, college professors and students, business and transportation managers, tradespersons, artists, and no small number of working stiffs who keep the wheels of all this commerce turning. Curiously, Anchorage is Alaska's largest Native village as well; thousands of Indian, Eskimo, and Aleut Natives have chosen to live and work in Alaska's largest city.

Anchorage is also the transportation hub of Alaska. Jet flights go and come at Anchorage International Airport from every region of Alaska, from the other states of the United States and from Asia and Europe. The state-owned Alaska Railroad headquarters here and extends southerly to Seward, on Resurrection Bay, and Whittier, in Prince William Sound, and north to Denali National Park and Fairbanks. Three major state highways begin in

77

or near Anchorage: the Seward Highway to the Kenai Peninsula, the Glenn Highway to Tok and the Canadian border, and the George Parks Highway to Denali National Park and Fairbanks. Off these arterials you'll find scads of lesser roads that lead to remote villages, near–ghost towns, backwoods lodges, and lots of wilderness terrain for exploring, fishing, photography, and fun.

First, within Anchorage itself: Number one stop on any off-beat traveler's itinerary should be the **Alaska Public Lands Information Center,** at Fourth Avenue and F Street downtown (907–271–2737). Housed in the old Anchorage Federal Building, circa 1939, the center contains scores of really helpful state and federal exhibits, videos, wildlife mounts, transportation displays, and even a trip-planning computer to assist in organizing your travels. Once you have finished there, head diagonally across the street to the Anchorage Convention and Visitors Bureau's **log cabin visitor information center** (907) 274–3531. Within the cabin's main room you'll find friendly local volunteers and tons of printed material to assist you in planning your stay in the city.

By all means, ask for the visitors bureau's excellent free visitor's guide, which contains more than one hundred pages of tourist information, including a better-than-average walking tour of the downtown vicinity. Among more than two dozen sites noted: the **Alaska Railroad Depot** and old locomotive **Engine Number 1,** built in the early 1900s and used in constructing the Panama Canal as well as the Alaska Railroad; **Elderberry Park** and the **Oscar Anderson House,** the city's first (1915) wood frame home, open for viewing; and **Oomingmak Musk Ox Producer's Coop,** where you can see and purchase garments made from Arctic musk ox qiviut (pronounced KEE-vee-ute), the softest yet warmest wool-like material on earth.

At 343 West Sixth Street, tucked away in the south wall of the otherwise bustling Fifth Avenue Shopping Mall, is the ◆**Reeve Aviation Picture Museum,** which displays more than 1,000 vintage photos of Alaska's most famous bush pilots and military aviators. Bob Reeve was the legendary bush pilot–founder of Reeve Aleutian Airways. The museum is open Monday to Friday 9:00 A.M. to 5:00 P.M. There is no charge.

The ◆**Tony Knowles Coastal Trail** (named after the former Anchorage mayor and now Alaska governor Tony Knowles) merits special mention. This wide, asphalt trail starts at the west end of Second Avenue and follows the meandering shore of Cook Inlet for 10 scenic miles around woods, inlets, and lakes to **Kincaid Park**. Best of all, the Knowles Trail junctions along the way with other segments of Anchorage's outstanding network of bike and pedestrian paths. Ask for a trail system map at the visitor center.

Although the selection is not always large, some of the best buys in Alaska Native art can be found in the gift shop at the **Alaska Native Medical Center**, at Third Avenue and Gambell Street. Call (907) 257–1150 for information. The hours vary, but the shop is usually open from 10:00 A.M. until 2:00 P.M. Another good source of authentic Native art is the **Alaska Native Arts and Crafts Association,** at 333 West Fourth Avenue (907–274–2932). The **Anchorage Museum of History and Art**, at Seventh Avenue and A Street also has a small shop with tasteful, authentic art objects for sale. The gift shop number is (907) 343–6195. For recorded information about the museum, call 9907) 343–6173.

Another very Alaskan shopping opportunity exists in the open-air **Saturday Market,** staged each week in summer at the Lower Bowl parking lot, at the corner of Third Avenue and E Street. You can pick up made-in-Alaska arts and crafts, antiques, fresh produce, fish, and garage sale items. Hours run from approximately 10:00 A.M. until 6:00 P.M. No charge for admission.

The ◆**Fort Richardson Alaskan Fish and Wildlife Center**, located in Building 600 on the Fort Richardson Military Reservation accessible off the Glenn Highway about 7.5 miles northeast of town, isn't just for soldiers and their families. You, too, can view some 250 mounts of Alaska wildlife, including bears, moose, caribou, sportfish, birds, and other critters. The center is open year-round, with free admission. Call (907) 384–0431 for hours. The **Elmendorf Wildlife Museum,** which has 200 game and bird species, is at the Air Force base north of the city and similarly opens its doors to the public in Building 4-803. To reach the base turn north on Reeve Boulevard from the Glenn Highway, about .7 mile from the highway's start at Medfra Street. Turn right on Post Road and proceed to the base entrance. The hours are noon to 5:00 P.M. Tuesday through Thursday. For information call (907) 552–2282.

One of the best things the Alaska legislature ever did was set aside **Chugach State Park**, nearly half a million acres of wild and wondrous mountain valleys and alpine country, right smack dab next to Anchorage. From numerous gateways along city roads and state highways, you'll find access to gentle and tough trails to hike, lakes to fish, rivers to kayak or canoe, and wildlife to see and photograph. Among the latter are moose, Dall mountain sheep, mountain goats, plus brown (grizzly) and black bears. For maps and more information, call (907) 345–5014.

You'll find Anchorage one of the pleasantest communities in Alaska to be hungry in. For dinner it's almost impossible to beat ✦**Marx Brothers,** located downtown in one of Anchorage's oldest houses, at 627 West Third Avenue. It can be pricey (entrees range from $15 to $35), but where else will you find the likes of Alaska halibut in macadamia nut crust with coconut curry and mango chutney? Phone (907) 278–2133. If your taste buds run to Greek or Italian cuisine, try **Villa Nova Restaurant,** at 5121 Arctic Boulevard (907–561–1660).

You can devour great hamburgers at the **Arctic Roadrunner** from two locations, 2477 Arctic Boulevard (907–279–7311) and 5300 Old Seward Highway (907–561–1245). For chicken done fast and right, the **Lucky Wishbone,** at 1033 East Fifth Avenue, (907–272–3454), is a favorite among Anchorage folk.

✦ **Gwennie's Old Alaska Restaurant** is sort of outrageous, but it, too, is a favorite among locals for breakfast, lunch, and dinner. The big, rambling structure features lots of historical photos and relics on the walls and a menu that features Alaskan reindeer omelettes, smoked salmon, and king crab. Prices are moderate. It's located at 4333 Spenard Road. Phone (907) 243–2090.

Visitors often feel intimidated by the place and pass it by, but if you want to rub elbows (literally) with Alaskans in a frontier saloon setting, drop by **Chilkoot Charlie's**, Anchorage's best known watering hole. Called Koot's by the locals, it's located at 2435 Spenard Road. Forget reservations. Just come out, and they'll shoehorn you in somehow.

Alaska state and federal employees stretch their per diem dollars in Anchorage by staying at the small (thirty-eight rooms) **Voyager Hotel** downtown, at 501 K Street. The ample rooms each have a queen-size bed and a couch that makes up into a twin, full kitchen facilities, and TV. They serve fresh complimentary coffee in the lobby each morning. To stay at the Voyager, you'll need reservations almost any time of year. Call (800) 247–9070 or (907) 277–9501.

If you stay at the **Six Bar E Ranch Bed and Breakfast**, your quarters may be a converted horse barn stable or a spacious room with sauna in a large log home. You can browse among lots of antiques plus international and Alaska memorabilia. Breakfasts are full and fabulous, and the talk around the table is frequently in several languages. It's located at 11401 Totem Road, off O'Malley Road just past the Alaska Zoo. Netherlands-born hostess Margriet Ekvall also owns and operates **Earth Tours**, an agency with an emphasis on hiking, canoeing, and camping. B&B rates start at $55 for two. For information call (907) 346–2655.

Angie and Tom Hamill operate **Birch Trails Bed & Breakfast,** at 22719 Robinson Road, from their home in the Anchorage bedroom community of Chugiak. Their entire downstairs is dedicated to guests. There is a private entrance, two bedrooms, shared bath, stocked kitchenette, game and exercise area, Alaska library, outdoor deck with hot tub, and views of the Chugach Mountains. They serve heaping gourmet breakfasts. The Hamills also offer hiking, river rafting, and fishing packages. In winter (and summer, on wheels) they operate **Birch Trails Sled Dog Tours.** Call (907) 688–5713.

Anchorage International Hostel, at Seventh Avenue and H Street (practically downtown), is quite large for Alaska, but since Anchorage is the travel hub for most of the state, its ninety-five beds fill up early. Reservations are a must; request them by mail from 700 H Street, Anchorage, AK 99501. Bring your own sleeping bag if you have one; otherwise you can rent one. There are showers, a kitchen, sitting rooms, storage, and phones. The hostel is wheelchair accessible. The rate is $12.00 for adults. For information, call (907) 276–3635. This same number serves hostels in Girdwood and Seward.

Anchorage-based **Alaska Two Wheel Tours** (907–522–1430) isn't your usual bike touring outfit. What these folk offer are long-distance tours, some rigorous and some more leisurely. Their All Around Alaska Tour, for instance, is a twenty-day affair that takes in hot springs, frigid glaciers, and scads of sites and attractions in between, all around the Southcentral region. Their Kodiak King Crab Festival offering includes a seven-stage road

81

race; you can be a racer or a spectator. Their Hope-to-Seward mountain bike excursion travels 85 miles of Resurrection Pass mountain trails. Or, they'll outfit you in Anchorage to explore the community's 150 miles of superlative bike and pedestrian paths.

Here's another quality bike tour, this one offered by **Saga Alaskan Bicycle Adventures.** They call it Bicycle Alaska, and it includes travel by train from Anchorage to Denali National Park, a van ride to Fairbanks, in Alaska's interior, pedal power down the Richardson Highway to Valdez, on Prince William Sound, and a ferry/train/bike combination back to Anchorage. For more information on this and other options, call (800) 770–SAGA.

If you're a winter fan, Anchorage can be particularly fun. Organized sled dog races take place virtually every January and February weekend at the Tozier Sled Dog Track in south Anchorage. And nobody, but nobody, fails to feel the excitement when the biggest winter sled dog racing events of the year roll around in February and March.

First is the **Anchorage Fur Rendezvous**, staged in mid-February. This "Mardi Gras of the North" runs through two weekends and includes the World Championship Sled Dog Race, which begins and ends right downtown on Fourth Avenue. Literally thousands of cheering Alaskans line the way. The "Rondy" also features some rather outrageous activities among its hundreds of scheduled events, including an outhouse race, featuring privies being pushed and pulled on skids. Another riotous event is a canoe race—down the icy slopes of a hill since all the water in the area is long since frozen over. There are also snowshoe obstacle races put on by senior citizens, snow machine races, ice sculpting competitions, Eskimo blanket tosses, a grand parade, dances, Native crafts fairs, and outdoor fur auctions.

Several tour companies have created tours built around the Fur Rendezvous as well as Alaska's premier sled dog race, the 1,000-mile **Iditarod** Classic, running from Anchorage to Nome on the Bering Sea. **Alaska Sightseeing/Cruise West** offers a five-day Anchorage Fur Rendezvous Festival Tour as well as a five-day package that culminates with the start of the Iditarod. Other features include visits to the Iditarod Trail Museum, excursions around Anchorage and Turnagain Arm (including Portage Glacier), the Matanuska Valley, and the Iditarod Trail Mushers banquet. Prices start at $649, double occupancy. For details, call (800) 666–7375.

Far North Tours offers several ways to experience the Iditarod, including a $60 Iditarod Restart tour that takes clients out to the official race restart at Wasilla, in the Matanuska Valley. (The downtown Anchorage start is largely ceremonial.) The company also offers a $195 Fly the Iditarod Trail tour. It includes an Alaska bush plane trip to Skwentna, one of the official checkpoints along the trail. Most ambitious is a seven-day affair that includes the Mushers banquet, the start in Anchorage and restart in Wasilla, the bush plane trip to Skwentna, plus a personal dogsled tour. It costs $1,100, double occupancy. Call (800) 478–7480.

PRINCE WILLIAM SOUND

Curious thing about Prince William Sound. It took the nation's all-time awfullest oil spill—the *Exxon Valdez* disaster of 1989—for most people to learn about one of the continent's most gorgeously pristine regions. The vessel, you'll recall, went aground on Bligh Reef, ruptured its hull, and spilled more than 11.3 million gallons of North Slope crude oil onto more than 1,500 miles of coastline. The deadly pollution, killing uncounted thousands of birds and sea mammals in its path, extended as far as the Alaska Peninsula, 600 miles away. Yet there's some good news. Although the sound will continue to suffer from subsurface oil contamination for decades to come, from a visual perspective it has largely recovered. Myriad glaciers, islands, and mountains await visitors aboard huge cruise ships, tiny kayaks, day boats, and state ferries. Whales of several species spout, roll, and sound in the waterways. Hundreds of thousands of birds again inhabit the trees and cliffside rookeries throughout the region. Bears wander along otherwise deserted beaches. Mountain goats frolic high (but visibly) on the peaks overhead.

As in Southeast Alaska, Prince William Sound's communities are not connected by road, but many who live there consider that a virtue. Actually, you can drive *to* the sound by first taking the Seward Highway from Anchorage to Portage, then piggybacking your car aboard the Alaska Railroad's short shuttle through mountain tunnels to Whittier. (For particulars, see the Seward Highway, in the Kenai Peninsula section.) Or you can drive on portions of the Glenn and Richardson Highways to Valdez. Cordova, the third of Prince William Sound's three principal communities, can't be reached by regular highway, but the state ferry *Bartlett* regularly calls there as well as at Whittier and Valdez. Call (800) 642–0066 for more information.

Here's a rundown on these towns: **Whittier** is principally a jumping-off (rather, a sailing-off) place. The community is, in reality, comprised of an excellent dock and wharf area, a few waterfront buildings and—dominating the scene—two very tall and prominent buildings (that are skyscrapers by Alaska standards) called Begich Towers and the Buckner Building. The U.S. Army built the structures during World War II to house servicemen and their families stationed at the site. Today the fourteen-story Begich Towers has been converted into condos and about half the population of Whittier lives there. The Buckner Building is now vacant. Another building, Whittier Manor, houses a good share of the rest of Whittier's residents.

The **Alaska Marine Highway System** (800–642–0066) operates the state ferry *Bartlett* between Whittier and Valdez during the summer (one way, $72 for an auto and $58 each for adult passengers), as do commercial tour operators, including Stan Stephens Cruises. Stephens offers the opportunity for an overnight on Growler Island in a permanent tent camp. (See Valdez, in this section, for more details.)

If you don't plan to drive your car aboard the ferry for Valdez, don't bring it to Whittier on the rail shuttle. There's really no place for you to drive it there. On the other hand, if you'd enjoy a really different circle trip from Anchorage, drive your car aboard the shuttle train, bring it aboard the ferry to Valdez, then disembark for a drive up the Richardson and Glenn Highways back to Anchorage, or stay on the Richardson all the way to Fairbanks. If time permits, take the *Bartlett* ferry all the way to Cordova before disembarking at Valdez. The highway ferry trip, of course, works either direction.

From the Port of Whittier, several cruise and charter operators offer round-trip day cruises of the sound or one-day excursions from Whittier to Valdez. Captain Brad Phillips operates his deluxe catamaran *Klondike Express* daily in these waters, into numerous coves and bays and past dozens of glaciers. Captain Phillips calls this tour Twenty-six Glaciers in One Day, but you'll actually see many more. The chances of spotting whales, mountain goats, and other wildlife are excellent. For information about

this tour, priced at $119 from Whittier, call (800) 544–0529.
Major Marine Tours packages an all-you-can-eat salmon dinner cruise from Whittier to Blackstone Glacier and back. The price is $135, including van and rail transportation from downtown Anchorage to Whittier. Call (800) 764–7300 for information.

Sound Adventure Charters operates Dude Fishing trips, which feature a hands-on commercial seine fishing experience aboard the 50-foot *FV Pagan*. Guests actually help with several salmon sets as well as check crab and shrimp pots. When the trip is over they take generous shares home. The cost is $500, plus $90 for an Alaska state commercial fishing license. The company's $150 Blackstone Glacier Day Cruise includes hot tubbing among icebergs as well as sight-seeing and sportfishing. For details about these and other trips, call (907) 783–3153.

Now about **Cordova.** For travelers who enjoy "untouristy" destinations, it is a great little place for poking around, mixing with the locals, exploring on one's own. Now mostly a fishing and fish-processing town, Cordova had its start as the saltwater port for shipping copper ore brought down on the Copper River & Northwestern Railway from the Kennecott mines.

You can drive about 50 miles to the face of one of Alaska's most accessible drive-up glaciers, ✦**Childs Glacier,** on the Copper River Highway, east of town. You can also cross the historic **Million Dollar Bridge** (if you're game; it's been only "temporarily" fixed and sort of slanty ever since the 1964 Alaska earthquake) for a view of **Miles Glacier** as well. The Childs Glacier, separated by a stream from the elevated, excellent U.S. Forest Service interpretive center there, is extremely active. If you wander down to the stream level and the glacier calves off a big hunk of ice, run for higher ground. The surge wave can be sizable and dangerous. On the drive out from town, keep your eyes alert for bears; this author saw two on his last trip. Other sights along the way: beaver dams, picturesque marshlands, lakes and mountain vistas, silver salmon spawning streams, and trumpeter swans.

The **Reluctant Fisherman Inn** at 407⁄501 Railroad Avenue (complete with a photogenic mermaid sculpture) is located downtown, overlooking Cordova's busy harbor. The restaurant features locally caught seafood, and if you didn't bring wheels, you can rent a car there. Rates for doubles start at $115. Call (907) 424–3272.

85

A major national news magazine recently noted: "A cruise on the *Discovery* would be the prize of anyone's trip to Alaska." No question about it, any of the options offered on a ✦ *Discovery Voyage,* including three-day getaways and a six- or eight-day cruises, rates only the highest marks among off-the-beaten-path trips in this part of Alaska. The twelve-passenger, 65-foot *Discovery,* a classic yacht owned by Dean and Rose Rand, carries kayaks and skiffs for landing parties and features close-up viewing of fjords, glaciers, bird rookeries, sea life, and wildlife on shore. Hot showers, sumptuous food (including fresh seafood harvested on the trip), and knowledgeable staff make this a top-rated experience. For reservations and information, call (800) 324–7602.

The city of **Valdez** (Alaskans say "Val-DEEZ") calls itself the Switzerland of Alaska. Actually that's not too far off the mark. The range of Chugach Mountains that arch behind and around the city are certainly in a class with the Alps. But Valdez has at least one attribute the Swiss can only dream of—an ocean view of fish-filled waters and forested islands.

The town boasts at least one additional distinction. The 800-mile **Trans-Alaska Pipeline** from Prudhoe Bay, in the Arctic, terminates here in a major, 1,000-acre terminal operated by **Alyeska Pipeline Service Company.** Alyeska loads more than a million gallons of crude oil daily onto huge oceangoing tankers docked at the site. For a two-hour bus tour of the facility, call Valdez Tours at (907) 835–2686. The cost is $15.

A good starting point for any visit to Valdez is the **visitor information center,** at Chenega Street and Fairbanks Drive downtown. You can view films about the 1964 Good Friday Earthquake, which all but destroyed much of the old town near the water, and you can pick up a map showing the present location of historic homes from Old Valdez. Many were relocated when it was determined the old sites were no longer safe for occupancy. Nearby, at Chenega Street and Egan Drive, is the **Valdez Museum,** where exhibits range from slot machines to gold rush gear and a restored 1907 fire engine.

Operating vessels both from Valdez and from Whittier, **Stan Stephens Cruises** offers several cruising options, including some with a bountiful midcruise salmon, halibut, and chicken feast in the big dining hall on ✦ **Growler Island,** facing Columbia Glacier. Other trips offer overnights at Stephens's comfortable camp of large heated tents on the island. Depending on the cruise you take, excursions also sail past a shoreline gold mine, Bligh Reef, intriguing little bays and inlets, long silvery waterfalls cascading from high mountain cliffs, bears onshore, and whales, sea lions, and sea otters in the water. The last trip we took, on Stevens's *Nautilus II,* we saw three of the latter swimming peacefully at dockside before our trip even got under way. The company's cruise to and from Valdez, with one night on Growler Island, costs $188.50. For information, call (800) 992–1297.

If you're into people-powered water sight-seeing, **Anadyr Adventures** of Valdez (907–835–2814) provides deluxe charter boat–supported kayaking trips to remote and awesome parts of Prince William Sound. Trips range from one to ten days and can accommodate novices as well as expert paddlers. Three-hour local trips start at $52 a person, overnight excursions at around $260 per day including transportation to the kayaking site and meals.

If you've traveled this far into Alaska and still haven't taken a river rafting trip, this may be the place to do it. Valdez-based **Keystone Raft and Kayak Adventures** (800–328–8460) provides five trips daily down the nearby Lowe River through high-walled Keystone Canyon. The company also offers one day floats through Class III and Class IV whitewater on the Tonsina River, four days on the Talkeetna River, five or ten days on the Chitina and Copper Rivers in the Wrangell Mountains, and kayak trips on waters around the state. Rates vary from $30 on the Lowe River to $1,275 for ten days in the Wrangell Mountains.

THE KENAI PENINSULA

Deep in the bowels of the Alaska Historical Library, in Juneau, resides a rare and treasured second edition of Jonathan Swift's *Gulliver's Travels,* an account written in 1726 about fictional Lemuel Gulliver's adventures in Lilliput, a nation of little people, and in Brobdingnag, the land of giants. What is especially intriguing about the book for Alaskans is Swift's map of Brobdingnag—a huge land mass extending westward from northern North America.

Remember that Vitus Bering and Alexei Shelikof, the men who discovered Alaska while sailing for the Russian Czars, did so in 1741. The second edition of Swift's book is dated MDCCXXVII— 1727, 14 years before the Russian voyages of discovery. Yet

Swift's map bears a resemblance (some say a close resemblance; others say, not really) to Alaska, complete with a little stretch of land that could be the Kenai Peninsula, extending from Southcentral Brobdingnag.

The comparison becomes more intriguing still when you realize that in modern Brobdingnag/Alaska roam many of North America's "most giant-sized" creatures, including record-sized brown (grizzly) bears, even bigger polar bears, and large concentrations of mammoth whales and walrus in adjacent seas. In addition, on the peninsula noted both in Swift's book and in modern guides you can see and photograph huge moose.

The Kenai, probably more than any other locale, is where Alaskans themselves play and recreate. Lake, river, and saltwater fishing is superlative. Hiking trails are widespread and wide ranging. Moderate-sized and tiny communities offer traditional homespun Alaska hospitality. Access is easy by highway, rail, and air from Anchorage.

Because the Kenai is much used by Alaskans, particularly from Anchorage, it's wise to avoid weekend and holiday visits, when traffic on the only road access from Anchorage, the Seward Highway, can be horrendous. Most of the time, however, the 127-mile asphalt road is more than pleasurable as it skirts saltwater inlets, circles around big and little lakes, and penetrates thick, vast forest expanses. It richly deserves its prestigious designation by the U.S. Forest Service as a National Forest Scenic Byway.

THE SEWARD HIGHWAY: ANCHORAGE TO TERN LAKE JUNCTION

Following are some of the sight-seeing opportunities along the several highways that serve the peninsula, starting with the 127-mile **Seward Highway,** south of Anchorage. The Seward Highway mileposts you see along the side of the road, incidentally, measure the distance from Seward. So the parking area at Potters Marsh at mile 117.4, for instance, is 117.4 miles from Seward and 9.6 miles from Anchorage.

All along the highway be on the lookout for wildlife, especially moose. The Kenai is home to a national wildlife refuge, and the abundant moose population is the reason for it. At mile 117.4

and at mile 116 you'll see turnoffs for ◆**Potter Marsh,** a state wildlife refuge where you can view extensive waterfowl, shorebirds, arctic terns, and American bald eagles plus king, pink, and silver salmon. A boardwalk crosses the marsh. Between mileposts 106 and 110 on the Seward Highway, look frequently to the craggy tops of the rocky cliffs that rise from the road. If you look carefully, more often than not you'll spot mama **Dall mountain sheep** and their youngsters staring curiously down at you. Do not, of course, stop your car on the highway; there are several turnoffs where you can safely stop then walk back for easy viewing.

If you collect unusual critters to log in your life book of wild animals, stop at ◆**Beluga Point,** at mile 110.3. Here, if you're just a little bit lucky, you may see the small white beluga whales that congregate in these waters. The best viewing is probably around high tide. At low tide the point is also a good place to witness a tidal bore. (See below.)

Bird Creek State Campground, just past mile 101, is not only a pleasant place to camp or picnic, it provides one of the better vistas for watching one of Alaska's more spectacular natural phenomena—the ◆**Turnagain Tidal Bore** that comes rushing through Turnagain Arm at low tide daily. Get a tide book (free at many service stations, sporting goods stores, and banks), and check the times for low tide at Anchorage. Then to get the correct time for the Bird Creek overlook, add about two hours and fifteen minutes to whatever time is listed. What you'll see is a frothing, foaming wall of sea water—sometimes as high as 6 feet—come surging into the constricted inlet. Don't, by the way, even think of wading out onto the mudflats that are exposed in these and other Cook Inlet areas. The mud is like quicksand. Foolish waders have drowned during incoming tides after becoming mired in the muck and mud.

At mile 90 the Seward Highway junctions with the 3-mile Alyeska access road to **Girdwood, Alyeska Resort,** and ◆**Crow Creek Mine.** Girdwood is less a city and more a still-woodsy gathering place of some 300 Alaskans, most of whom love to ski (usually at adjacent Alyeska Resort) and many of whom work at shops, stores, or eateries either at the resort, in Girdwood, or nearby. Many Anchoragites have condominiums here. The community isn't exactly planned or laid out, but it's small enough to be easy

89

to wander around in. The residents are more than friendly and accommodating. At the resort (a world-class ski area in the winter months), you can take a tram ride ($15) 2,300 feet up the mountain for hiking, for casual but gourmet dining in the $16 to $20 range at **Seven Glaciers Restaurant** (907–754–2237), or for just taking in the sweeping view of Turnagain Arm.

At the Crow Creek Mine, you can pan for gold along creek beds still rich with the precious metal. The managers will even teach you how and point out likely areas for prospecting. Sure, it's sort of touristy, but there really is plenty of gold along these creek banks. Many Alaskans come here on weekends for recreational panning. Of course, you get to keep all the "color" you find. When you're through, you can refuel the body with sourdough pancakes or sandwiches in the **Bake Shop** (907–783–2831) at Alyeska Resort, or partake of moderately priced pizza, pasta, or seafood at **Chair 5 Restaurant** (907–783–2500) in downtown Girdwood. The **Double Musky** (907–783–2822), with its huge (14 to 20 ounces) French pepper steak, at $24, is another favorite among locals and visiting Alaskans.

If you're overnighting in Girdwood, consider **Alyeska Bed and Breakfast.** Mark and Laura Lyle will even arrange custom breakfasts, in bed if you like, in their one- and two-bedroom suites. And by all means, partake of the hot tub. Prices range from $100 to $110; details from (907) 783-1222. Another good choice is John and Anne Herschleb's **Fireweed Inn Bed and Breakfast** on Tahoe Road. The B&B is a two-room suite over the Herschleb's garage and detached from their home. Rate is $70, single or double. Call (907) 783–3153. **Alyeska Booking Company** will be glad to book you into these or the two dozen other B&Bs and condominiums they represent in the area. They can also arrange local flight-seeing, river rafting, and bike rentals. Call (907) 783-4386 for more information.

Hostel enthusiasts can check out the **Alyeska Home Hostel** about ½ mile from the Alyeska Resort. This is a small, unpretentious, ten-guest cabin with a couple of rooms upstairs, another on ground level, a kitchen, woodstove, and small sitting room. There's no shower, but it does boast a sauna out back. The charge is $10 per person. To get there drive the Alyeska Road past Glacier Creek, make a right turn on Timberline Drive, then another right on Alpina for about .25 mile. The hostel is on the right; you'll see the sign. For reservations, call (907) 276–3635, the same number as the Anchorage International Hostel.

Back on the Seward Highway. If you're heading for the **port of Whittier,** on fabled Prince William Sound, watch for the pull-offs where you exit the highway to board the **Alaska Railroad "piggyback train"** at mile 80.3. What you do is drive your vehicle up a ramp and onto a railroad flatcar. (Railroad personnel will direct you.) Your car or RV will be secured, and you'll ride inside your own vehicle with a fabulous view during the forty-minute, 12-mile ride across valley floors and through two tunnels to Whittier. Call (907) 265–2607 for recorded schedules and information. For more information about things to see and do in the waters there, see the section on Prince William Sound. At mile 80 you'll come to a second ramp plus a parking area for your vehicle if you want to park and ride in a passenger railcar. By all means, leave your car at the lot if you're not taking the ferry from Whittier to Valdez. As was noted earlier, there's really nowhere to drive in tiny Whittier. The cost for the piggyback option is $56 for the car and driver. The railcar option costs $16. For reservations and information, call (800) 544–0552.

At mile 79 you can take a driving tour of **Big Game Alaska** (907–783–2025), the state's only drive-through wildlife park, to view moose, elk, buffalo, musk ox, caribou, and other North Country creatures from your own vehicle. Admission charge is $5.00 for adults.

Farther south on the Seward Highway, beyond mile 79, the highway junctions with the Portage Glacier Road. This 5.5 mile road leads to Alaska's most visited travel attraction, **Portage Glacier,** and perhaps Alaska's least known wildlife species, the glacier iceworm.

At the glacier the U.S. Forest Service operates ◆ **Begich-Boggs Visitor Center,** a comprehensive observation structure where, in good weather or foul, you can view the glacier, the frequently iceberg-clogged lake that the ice river flows into, and all kinds of interesting glacial exhibits. Each day a huge chunk of glacier ice is hauled into the center, where you can touch, rub, and pose with ice that fell as snow on the glacier perhaps a century ago. Incredibly, there are tiny but visible organisms, popularly called iceworms, that live in glacial ice. In the summer you can head out with U.S. Forest Service naturalists daily for an iceworm safari (no charge) to track down some of Alaska's littlest creatures. The center is open daily in summer 9:00 A.M. to 6:00 P.M. Call (907) 783–2326.

The Gray Line of Alaska sight-seeing vessel *Ptarmigan* makes frequent one-hour excursions from lakeshore to within .25 mile of Portage Glacier's glistening face. This is Alaska's most economical ($21) glacier cruise. Forest Service naturalists accompany each trip. For information and reservations, call (800) 544–2206.

At Seward Highway's mile 56.7 you have two somewhat confusing choices. If you're coming from Anchorage, turn right to access the **Hope Highway;** turn left to stay on the road to Seward. The Hope alternative is well worth exploring. The road leads to the community of **Hope** and one of Alaska's most celebrated backpacking experiences.

First, about the road and the community: At the turnout just beyond mile 2, you have at least a chance of seeing moose in the Sixmile Creek Valley below. Just past mile 11 there's a big, paved turnoff with a view of Turnagain Arm. At mile 16.5, turn on Hope Road for "downtown" Hope, a picturesque, tiny community of year-round homes for a handful of residents and getaway cabins used by urban Alaskans. The road leads past the post office, then to the waterfront, a popular site for anglers. The town had its start as a mining center in 1896. Today it offers a secluded base for hiking, fishing, and just getting away from it all.

Just past mile 16 and before you get to Hope, turn south on Resurrection Creek Road for the trailhead of the ◆ **Resurrection Pass Trail,** one of Alaska's finest backcountry hiking routes. It ends 38 miles later at about mile 53 on the Sterling Highway. In between, trekkers experience alpine ridges and lakes, scenic valleys, and vast panoramas plus the opportunity to observe moose, Dall mountain sheep, mountain goats, and bears. Spaced about a half-day's hiking distance apart are eight U.S. Forest Service rental cabins. (For information call 907–271–2599.)

Back on the Seward Highway, between miles 47.5 and 44.5 you'll find numerous turnoffs that offer excellent photo ops for pictures of Upper and Lower Summit Lakes and the spectacular mountains that rise behind them. If you're driving from Anchorage to Seward in one day, the log cabin **Summit Lake Lodge,** at mile 45.8, offers a good refreshment stop with moderately priced old-fashioned eggs-meat-and-potatoes breakfasts plus full lunch and dinner menus.

You come, just before mile 38, to Tern Junction where the Seward Highway junctions with the Sterling Highway. If you're Seward-bound, continue straight ahead on Alaska Highway Route 9. If you're headed for Soldotna, Homer, and other Sterling Highway points, turn right on Route 1.

THE SEWARD HIGHWAY: TERN LAKE JUNCTION TO SEWARD

Moose Pass, at mile 29.4, would be easy to miss if you blinked but it's an interesting little town (population about 150) and has a motel, general store, and restaurant. At Estes Brothers Grocery there's a big waterwheel that turns a working grindstone. If you collect pictures of unique signs, the one here reads MOOSE PASS IS A PEACEFUL TOWN. IF YOU HAVE AN 'AXE TO GRIND' DO IT HERE. If you're looking for an interesting spot to stretch your legs, there's a 1.3-mile paved biking and walking trail that skirts the edge of Trail Lake. Trail Lake Lodge (907–288–3101) offers a lakeside salmon bake plus a menu of steaks and seafood.

At Nash Road junction (mile 3.2 on the Seward Highway), turn left off the highway, then left again on Salmon Creek Road to find **The Farm Bed and Breakfast.** Host Jack Hoogland calls the rooms here elegantly casual. They come with private baths, decks, and entrances. The setting is one of trees and greenery. Rates are $75 for two with private bath; call (907) 224–5691.

The highway ends at mile 0 and the **city of Seward.** The community is relatively old by Alaska standards, having had its start in 1903, when railroad surveyors selected this site at the head of Resurrection Bay as an ocean terminal and supply center. Actually, there was a small Russian settlement there prior to 1903. Since 1923 the town has served as the farthest-south point on the 470-mile route of the Alaska Railroad and prides itself today on being the "Gateway to Kenai Fjords National Park."

The four-hour ◆**Alaska Railroad** trip from Anchorage to Seward, incidentally, is one of the North Country's most rewarding excursions. The journey departs Anchorage at 6:45 A.M. each morning in summer and leaves Seward at 6:00 P.M. for the return trip. Sights along the way include the dramatic coast of Cook Inlet, major lakes and streams, forest country, deep gulches and gullies, and (at least every time I've made the trip) abundant

93

wildlife, including moose and bears. During my last journey (northbound), the engineer had to stop the train just outside of Seward because a big fat black bear sat resolutely on his haunches right in the middle of the track—and showed no inclination to move. Finally he meandered to the side, much to the delight of photographers who were hoping for a better picture angle. For information about rail-only travel or rail/yacht combination tours that include cruising Resurrection Bay and Kenai Fjords National Park, call (800) 544-0552.

To get a quick glimpse of both old downtown Seward, the small boat harbor, and all the history in between, hop aboard the **Seward Trolley.** This sight-seeing bus departs from the railroad station and other points every half hour daily in summer. The fare is only $1.50 for adults or $3.00 for an all-day pass. It may be the cheapest tour in Alaska.

Two hiking destinations, among many others, are especially notable. From a trailhead at about mile 2 on the Lowell Point Road, you can walk, at low tide, along a 4.5-mile forest and beach trail to **Caines Head State Recreation Area,** where World War II bunkers and gun emplacements serve as reminders of Alaska's strategic location during a time when a Japanese invasion of North America seemed plausible.

Mt. Marathon, which rises from the community's edge from just above sea level to 3,022 feet, offers another satisfying trek. But if you don't like crowds, avoid the peak on Independence Day. On July 4 each year the town continues a tradition begun in 1909 with a wager between two "sourdoughs." The bet: whether or not a person could run from midtown to the top of the mountain and back in less than an hour. The outcome: Yes, it can be done—so far in a record time of forty-three minutes, twenty-three seconds. These days, competitors come from other towns, states, and even nations to scramble to the summit, then run, leap, slide, and fall during the helter-skelter descent witnessed by cheering crowds of spectators along the route.

For those who like their hikes escorted, with knowledgeable guides to explain colorful flora, fauna, and local history, Mary Thompson's **Kenai Peninsula Guided Hikes** offers guided easy 3-mile family trail walks ($45 per person), moderate hikes about 6.5 miles long ($60), and 14-mile challenging treks ($75). Call (907) 288-3141.

A small but informative **National Park Service Visitor Center** with information on nearby **Kenai Fjords National Park** is located at 1212 Fourth Avenue, on the Seward waterfront. It sits among structures that house sight-seeing, charter, fishing, and souvenir shops. The center operates 8:00 A.M. until 7:00 P.M. daily in the summer, offering short slide shows, interpretive programs, other exhibits, and short walks.

You really won't find any hideaway eating places in Seward, but for lunch and dinner locals and visiting Alaskans often choose **Ray's Waterfront,** at 1316 Fourth Avenue at the small boat harbor (907–224–5606), especially for fish and seafood. Prices are in the $8.00 to $12.00 range for lunch, $15.00 to $25.00 for dinner. Another frequent choice among locals, especially for seafood, is the Harbor Dinner Club of 224 Fifth Avenue, downtown. Call (907) 224–3012. Prices range from $5.00 and $10.00 for lunch, $15.00 to $23.00 for dinner.

◆**Exit Glacier** is one of the few glaciers in the North Country whose face you can actually approach on foot. It's located at the end of Exit Glacier Road, which junctions at mile 3.7 on the Seward Highway. En route to the glacier, you initially pass by small clusters of homes, then drive through thick forests and a steep-walled valley for about 8 miles to a National Park Service visitor parking area. A series of paths and trails lead to the snout of the 3-mile-long ice river. *Caution:* You'll see whole groups walking right up to the ice to pose for photos; that's a dumb thing to do. Huge pieces of ice can fall at any time. Stay safely back; you can still get some great pictures. If you're a hiker, you'll find options from short nature trails to an all-day trek to the Harding Icefield. There are bears and moose in the area, and, as at Portage Glacier, you can find iceworms in the ice. Look for them in the early evening; they avoid the sun. If you don't have a vehicle, **Kenai Fjords Tours** schedules a $19 daily bus tour to the glacier at 2:00 P.M. Call (907) 224–8068 for times. **Northern Nomad Adventures** offers a similar excursion. Call (907) 224–7026 for information about this tour and others in a restored classic 1952 suburban Nomad.

Of course, to really appreciate Kenai Fjords National Park, you need to see the fjords from the water. Several excellent day cruise operators offer half day or longer narrated excursions through Resurrection Bay to see whales, sea otters, a sea lion rookery, puffins, eagles, glaciers, mountains, and other features of the magnificent Kenai Fjords landscape. Times and rates vary. There are two-and-a-half-hour tours offered by **Alaska Renown Charters** for $40 (907–224–3806) and four-and-a-half-hour trips (complete with an all-you-can-eat crab and shrimp buffet) for $64 and $74 offered by **Major Marine Tours** (800–764–7300). **Kenai Fjords Tours**, which originated the first waterborne excursions in the bay in 1974, offers a variety of choices, from four hours at $59 to full-day trips at $99. For details and reservations, call (800) 478–8068. Other credible operators include **Mariah Charters and Tours** (907–224–8623) which offers a four-hour excursion for $55, nine hours for $90.

To get really close to nature in the bay, book an escorted day kayaking trip with **Adventures and Delights Eco Tours** for $95. Extended five- and ten-day tours go farther into the Kenai Fjords National Park and into Prince William Sound. Call (800) 288–3134.

If you'd enjoy sleeping in a National Historical Site, book yourself into the **Van Gilder Hotel,** a small but comfortable hotel in the older business district in downtown Seward. It was built in 1916 as an office building but became a hotel in 1921. The rates begin at $50 for a room with shared bath. Call (907) 224–3079.

North of town at mile 16 on the Seward Highway, you'll find the **Snow River Hostel**, a log-constructed, fourteen-bed hostel with a family room, showers, kitchen, and laundry. Bring your own sleeping bag. The managers, Denise and Woody Walker, have their own home next door. The rate is $10 per person. For information, call (907) 276–3635, which is the same number as the Anchorage International Hostel.

The Sterling Highway: Tern Lake to Homer

Seward, of course, is as far as you can go by road on the Seward Highway, which covers the eastern side of the Kenai Peninsula. At its Tern Lake junction with the Seward Highway at mile 37, however, the paved Sterling Highway heads west, then south along the western side of the Kenai. Strangely, the mileposts along the Sterling Highway measure distances from Seward, even though the road doesn't go there. The road ends at its southernmost point, at the tip of the Homer Spit at mile 179.5.

For the traveler who enjoys luxuries while traveling, the rustic but regal **Kenai Princess Lodge** (800–426–0500) is accessible from the road at mile 47.7. Activities include horseback riding, river rafting, flight-seeing, hiking, fishing, and touring from the lodge throughout the rest of the peninsula. Or just relax in a hot tub. Note the chandelier in the lobby made from deer antlers. Rates begin at $79 off season, $169 during peak season. The adjacent **Kenai Princess RV Park** (also 800–426–0500) provides one of the nicest private campgrounds in the state.

The small town of **Cooper's Landing**, spread out along the road before and after mile 48, offers various visitor facilities, including fish guiding services, cabins, and shops.

Alaska Wildland Adventures offers a number of quality river trips from their launch site at mile 50.1. If you're looking for a bit of adventure, ask about their seven-hour Kenai Canyon Raft Trip through a remote, nonmotorized section of the Kenai River. It includes some spirited Class III rapids and a lunch on the shores of pristine Skilak Lake. The cost is $95. In case you prefer a more peaceful trip, the company offers a Kenai River Scenic Float through a portion of the Kenai National Wildlife Refuge, where there are frequent sightings of moose, eagles, Dall sheep, waterfowl, signs of beaver, and sockeye salmon. The cost is $42. Alaska Wildland also packages half- or full-day Kenai River Sportfishing trips, on which you can angle for salmon, rainbow trout, and Dolly Varden. Costs vary from $97.50 to $175. For details, call (800) 478–4100.

Just down the road, at mile 50, Gary and Carol Galbraith's family-operated **Alaska Rivers Company** offers a half-day scenic float excursion for $39 or a full-day scenic, sometimes splashy, canyon experience for $80. Both trips include homemade picnic lunches, professional guides, and excellent wildlife viewing prospects. The Galbraiths also do guided hikes and have traditional Alaska log cabins—rustic but very comfortable—for rent on the shore of the Kenai River. The cost for two is $65. Call (907) 595–1226.

With pickups in both Cooper's Landing and Anchorage, **Jon James Adventures, Ltd.** has Kenai River float and fishing trips plus historic tours of Hope and Cooper Center. The prices are $39 for four-hour floats, $135 for full-day fishing, $139 for the two-hour historical tours. The firm also packages tours in Southwestern and Arctic Alaska. In Anchorage, call (907) 276–2272; in Cooper's Landing (907) 595–1598.

97

At mile 58 you have a choice to make, and a **U.S. Fish and Wildlife Service information station** to help you make it. You can continue on the paved Sterling Highway westerly to mile 75.2, or you can take the southerly 19-mile gravel Skilak Lake Loop Road to its junction with the Sterling at mile 75.2. We recommend the latter. The gravel road isn't bad, and opportunities for photography, fishing, hiking, and wildlife spotting are excellent.

Hidden Lake, along the gravel road, is a particular delight, with a first class U.S. Fish and Wildlife Service campground that features paved roads, campfire programs at an amphitheater, and a deck for spotting wildlife. *A warning note:* Beautiful **Skilak Lake**, like many of the large lakes on the Kenai, can be extremely dangerous. Horrific winds can arise suddenly on the water. If you plan to take out a small boat, stay close to shore and wear a life jacket.

After Skilak Loop Road junctions with the Sterling Highway at mile 75.2, the Sterling Highway continues westerly to mile 83.4, where you have another off-highway choice. If you're transporting a canoe, the choice is an easy yes. The Swanson River and Swan Lake Roads head north, then east, for nearly 30 miles, accessing two of the most highly acclaimed canoeing routes in the North Country. The ◆**Swanson River Canoe Trail** is 80 miles long and connects more than forty lakes with 46 miles of the Swanson River. Portages between lakes are short, less than a mile over relatively easy terrain. The ◆**Swan Lake Canoe Trail**, separate from the Swanson River route, covers 60 miles and connects thirty lakes with forks of the Moose River. Both trails lie within the Kenai National Wildlife Refuge.

The opportunities for viewing wildlife—especially moose, eagles, trumpeter swans, and tundra swans—are enormous. For maps and additional information, call the refuge manager at the Kenai National Wildlife Refuge (907–262–7021), and ask for the free U.S. Fish and Wildlife Service pamphlet "Canoeing the Kenai National Wildlife Refuge." Information is also available at the USFWS cabin at mile 58, the Kenai National Wildlife Refuge Information Center in Soldotna, and at local information centers in Kenai and Soldotna.

At mile 94.2 you face still another vexing little decision. This time your options are three. You can continue westerly on the Sterling Highway to Soldotna (the city center is only a mile down the road), then keep driving southerly on the Sterling toward the end of the road in Homer. Or you can turn northerly at what is called the Soldotna Y on the Kenai Spur Highway to the city of Kenai, then drive on to Captain Cook State Recreation Area. The third choice is to drive on to Soldotna, visit that city, then backtrack the short distance to the Kenai Spur Highway. After you've finished exploring the spur road and the city of Kenai, you can then bypass Soldotna and drive southerly on the Kalifornsky Beach Road to rejoin the Sterling at mile 108.8. I recommend the latter choice.

First, about **Soldotna**. If you want to fish the Kenai River for king salmon and other species, this community of about 3,700 offers a large number of charter boat fishing services. You can also fish on your own from the shores of the river; many do. Among the sights to see: the **Soldotna Historical Society Museum**, which includes a small "village" of historic log buildings, among them the 1958 territorial school, the last one built in Alaska before statehood. Damon Hall, at the village site, contains an excellent display of Alaska wildlife mounts. Still other mounted wildlife displays can be seen at the **Kenai National Wildlife Refuge Visitor Center**, at the top of Ski Hill Road. This is a prime location to get information about canoeing, hiking, camping, or just sightseeing in the refuge, which was established by President Franklin D. Roosevelt in 1941 as the Kenai National Moose Range.

Catherine Cassidy operates her home-based **Tours on the Kenai** from locations in both Soldotna and Kenai. She provides two different three-hour van tours. One is called Romancing the Salmon and covers commercial fishing thereabouts from 1882 to the present. Tales from the Land takes in homestead sites, Old Town, a Russian Orthodox Church, and homesteading history as well as contemporary points of interest. Tours depart from the parking lot at the Riverside House Hotel, in Soldotna, and from the parking lot of the Kenai Visitor Center, in Kenai. Call (907) 260–3369 for a schedule of departures and tours. The cost is $30 for adults.

Another home-based tour operation is Soldotna-born Terri Cater's **Legacy Tours** (by reservation only), which put you in touch with the legacy of the area's indigenous peoples, Russian fur traders, miners, and homesteaders. This company picks up at hotels and B&Bs in Soldotna and Kenai. The cost is $35 for a half-day tour, $75 for a full-day excursion to Seward, and $75 for a trip to Homer. Call (907) 262–5724 for schedules and details.

Now retrace your steps back to the Y at mile 94.2 on the Sterling Highway, where the Kenai Spur Highway heads northerly. The city of Kenai lies about 11 miles up this road.

It's probably best to start a **Kenai** visit at the **Kenai Bicentennial Visitors and Cultural Center** (907–283–1991) near Main Street and the Kenai Spur Highway. There you'll find a cultural museum and wildlife displays as well as friendly staff to give directions around the far-flung community.

Kenai, you'll find, is one of those curious cities that don't really seem to have a downtown, yet this is a site where Native peoples and Russian fur traders have settled for centuries. The Russian heritage is dramatically expressed in the ❖**Holy Assumption of the Virgin Mary Russian Orthodox Church**, not far from the visitor center. The original church was founded in 1846 by a Russian monk, Egumen Nicolai. The present three-domed structure was built a half century later and is one of the oldest Russian Orthodox houses of worship in Alaska. Tours can be arranged (donations accepted) at the parish house. The nearby **St. Nicholas Chapel** was constructed in 1906 and covers the grave of the founding monk. In the same vicinity is **Fort Kenay**, a log structure built during the 1967 Alaska Purchase Centennial to commemorate the original 1869 U.S. Army installation. It housed some one hundred men and officers. The admission charge is $2.00.

Walk to **Beluga Lookout**, at the end of Main Street, for possible sightings of the white beluga whales that visit these waters. Fishing for lunker king salmon, monster-sized halibut, and other species is, for many visitors, what Kenai is all about. Like Soldotna, a large number of guides and charter boats call Kenai home.

From their floatplane base on Island Lake, in North Kenai, **Air Adventures** (907–776–5444) offers a wide variety of wildlife viewing tours that range from 45-minute flight-seeing excursions starting at $50 per person for a party of six, to two days of guided bear watching in a wilderness tent camp, priced at $575 per person for a party of three. They also package airborne fishing adventures.

The ❖**Captain Cook State Recreation Area**, at the very end of the Kenai Spur Highway, is one of Alaska's unsung and relatively undiscovered state parklands—probably because it's at the end of a single road. But especially if you're a camper, it's well worth the drive. **Discovery Campground,** near the end of the road, merits special mention. Here you'll find a locale of rolling hills, wooded spruce plateaus, and beautiful vistas of the Alaska Range across Cook Inlet. The volcanic peaks Mt. Spurr, Mt. Redoubt, and especially Mt. Iliamna stand out across the water (as do thirteen oil platforms).

Three warnings: On the tidelands, observe the warnings and don't let an incoming tide catch you off guard. Delicious berries are thick in the area, and they are there for the picking, but avoid the bright red or white poisonous baneberry. And third, if you get into a standoff with a bear, leave the site and the berries to him (or her). Don't even think of trying to shoo the bruin away.

After you've "done" the Kenai Spur Highway, you can retrace your travel to Kenai and the Soldotna Y at mile 94 on the Sterling Highway, then continue south down the Sterling. The more scenic choice, though, is to head west, then southerly on the Kalifornsky Beach Road down the coast to Kasilof, at mile 108.8 on the Sterling Highway.

If you're neither a hunter nor an angler, but you'd still like to do something very Alaskan, stop at mile 117.4 and head for ◆ **Clam Gulch State Recreation Area** (where there are 116 campsites) to join hundreds of locals on the shore for the grand old Alaska sport of razor clam digging. *Be aware of three concerns:* Don't drive down the extremely steep beach road to sea level unless you have a four-wheel-drive vehicle. Don't go digging without a valid Alaska sportfishing license, available at various sporting and retail establishments. And, again, don't get stuck offshore on an incoming tide. The best clamming occurs on minus tides and varies from month to month. Locals are more than happy to share their knowledge and technique. You'll find similar clamming opportunities at the Ninilchik Beach Campground, which is part of **Ninilchik State Recreation Area**, at mile 134.5.

At about mile 135 you'll come to a side road that leads to the old original **Ninilchik Village** and the beach. Take the time to explore this site, which includes a few old log buildings. A white Russian Orthodox church, still in use, overlooks the village from a photogenic hilltop setting. Modern **Ninilchik** stretches down the road from roughly mile 135.5. If you don't like crowds, avoid the area on Memorial Day and other holidays, when thousands converge for the fishing thereabouts.

At mile 157 on the Sterling Highway, the collector of superlatives will want to turn off the main highway and drive on the Old

Sterling Highway past the Anchor River to another turnoff, this one on the Anchor River Beach Road. At the end of this road lies the **Anchor Point State Recreation Site**. There, on an overlook platform facing Cook Inlet, stands a big sign marking "North America's most westerly highway point." You can't drive your car anyplace west of this point on the connected highways of the United States and Canada. Incidentally, more than a million razor clams are taken each year on the beaches between Anchor Point and Kasilof up the highway.

You come to **Homer,** one of the author's favorite Alaska places, at mile 172 and beyond, crossing onto the Homer Spit at mile 175. The Sterling Highway ends here just short of 142 miles from its beginning at Tern Lake Junction and nearly 233 miles from Anchorage.

The community, you'll find, enjoys mild and usually pleasant weather throughout the year. It's small enough to be cozy but large enough to have everything you need. The hiking, fishing, photography, and nature-watching opportunities are enormous. There's lots of Alaska history (and pre-history) here, and the people—though individualistic to the core—are as open and friendly as you'll find anywhere. No wonder author and radio personality Tom Bodett (of Motel 66 "We'll leave the light on for you . . ." fame) chooses to live here.

First, a little orientation: Most residences, city services (hospital, fire department, library, city hall), and government offices are located in what you might call Homer proper. The **Pratt Museum,** which emphasizes natural and cultural diversity on the Kenai Peninsula, has a marine "touch tank" aquarium, a botanical garden, and a museum store. It's located at 3779 Bartlett Street in downtown Homer. Admission is $3.00 and children under eighteen are free. The hours are 10:00 A.M. to 6:00 P.M. daily.

Also located downtown is the world-renowned **Alaska Wild Berry Products** plant, where you can sample some of Alaska's tastiest berry products as well as other goodies. You can watch the processing and packing action through glassed observation windows and browse in the gift shop. Open daily in summer at no charge.

Most visitor attractions and services are located on the 5-mile-long narrow gravel bar called the **Homer Spit.** The spit, which never sat very high above sea level, dropped 4 to 6 feet during the 1964 Alaska earthquake, but nonetheless continues to be the site of countless visitor shops, eateries, commercial wharfs, docks for waterborne sight-seeing and fishing cruises, parking places, campsites, and a prime port for the Alaska Marine Highway System's oceangoing ferry *Tustumena*.

The **Salty Dawg Saloon**, one of Alaska's best known frontier bars, is located on the spit, as is **Alaska Maritime Tours** (two doors beyond the Salty Dawg), which offers daily half-day birdwatching/wildlife tours to Gull Island and the picturesque, waterlocked, incredibly photogenic community of **Seldovia**. Seldovia originated as a Russian sea otter hunting station. Today the water-oriented community of 400-plus residents relies on fishing, fish processing, some timber operations, and summer tourism. The city's picturesque boardwalk dates back to the 1930s. Birders can collect lots of views of bald eagles here, as well as sea and shore birds and sightings of sea otter from excursion boats are common. Alaska Maritime also offers full-day birding excursions to the **Barren Islands**. Cost is $100 for each tour. Call (907) 235–2490.

Another first-rate water trip takes you aboard the private **Kachemak Bay Ferry *Danny J.*** around Gull Island to the artists' colony of **Halibut Cove**. In Halibut Cove you can explore a dozen blocks of wooden boardwalks that connect homes and galleries. Among the more well-known artists in residence is Diana Tillion, whose painting in octopus ink has earned her a national reputation. The cost for a half-day ferry trip is $35. Call (907) 296–2223. If you enjoy nautical travel under your own steam, **True North Kayak Adventures** takes small groups of experienced and inexperienced kayakers into the wild beauty of Kachemak Bay for full-day close encounters of the sea otter kind (plus porpoises, sea lions, and shorebirds). Call Central Charters at (907) 235–7847 or Jakolof Ferry Service at (907) 235–2376 for reservations and to arrange your water taxi ride from Ramp Number One behind the Salty Dawg Saloon to the kayak company's base across from Homer. The price is $140, including all equipment, instruction, a hearty lunch, and the water taxi.

Rainbow Tours, on Cannery Row Boardwalk on the Homer Spit (907–235–7272), will book you for a guided **Kachemak Bay Natural History Tour** by boat and by foot, during which you'll observe 15,000 nesting seabirds on Gull Island, view sea mammals (including an occasional whale), explore beaches and intertidal areas, and learn about the marine life, local flora and fauna, and the Alaska Native prehistory of the locale. This is an all-day tour, 9:00 A.M. until 6:00 P.M. daily, priced at $55 for adults. Bring your own lunch, rubber boots, and rain gear.

Homer, you'll find, abounds in charter boats, especially for halibut fishing. The town, in fact, calls itself the Halibut Fishing Capital of the World. You'll see incoming anglers hang their halibut on scales at the dock and record catches in the 50, 100, even 200 to 300 pound class.

Cranes' Crest Bed and Breakfast (at 59830 Sanford Drive; 907–235–2969) enjoys a 1,200-foot elevated view of Kachemak Bay, Homer Spit, mountains, glaciers, and coves—not to mention sandhill cranes, wild flowers, berry bushes, and moose. For adventurous youngsters in your party proprietor Kate Gill can even provide a metal "igloo" where the young ones can "camp out" in their own sleeping bags. Queen-sized bedroom with private bath runs $70, including full breakfast.

Seaside Farm Hostel is many things: It's a large working homestead in the best Alaska tradition, a B&B, a campsite for tenters, a place to rent cabins—and a hostel with overnight accommodations in the main ranch house and a large cabin. There's an open-sided kitchen on-site for hostelers and campers. Hostel prices range from $12.00 to $15.00, campsites cost $6.00, cabins are $55. For reservations, call (907) 783–2099.

George Parks Highway—Southern Section: Anchorage to Denali National Park

Now, back to Anchorage. Truth to tell, it's a little difficult sometimes to know exactly which highway you're traveling on in Alaska. The **George Parks Highway** between Anchorage and Fairbanks is a good example because for the first 35 miles of the trip you're really on the Glenn Highway, which eventually takes you to Tok. The George Parks Highway starts at its junction with the Glenn at about mile 35 on the latter road, but the mileposts on both show distance from Anchorage. To read about places to see and things to do on the first 35 miles out of Anchorage, see the discussion of the Glenn Highway–Tok Cutoff in the Glenn Highway section of this chapter.

The George Parks Highway, it should be noted, is among Alaska's best. You encounter some rough spots and frost heaves along a few portions (so keep road speeds within safe limits), but generally it is among the wider and most modern in the state. It cuts through some of Alaska's most urbanized country as well as some of the state's wildest and most scenic. You can see Denali (Mt. McKinley), North America's highest mountain, from a number of places, and the highway provides access to two of the state's most popular state and national parks.

At about mile 35.5 you can access the **Mat-Su** (for Matanuska-Susitna) **Visitors Center**. Especially if you plan a side trip to Palmer, a few miles east on the Glenn Highway, stop for information.

About mile 39.5 you come to the Wasilla city limits and shortly thereafter Wasilla's Main Street. There your choices are several: Head north a block to 323 Main Street and visit the community's **Dorothy G. Page Museum** (907–373–9071), a visitor center, and historical park. Go north as well to access the Wasilla Fishhook Road to **Independence Mine**, or turn south across the railroad tracks to drive along the **Knik Road.** Especially if you're interested in learning more about sled dog racing, head left on this road and drive for a couple of miles to the **Iditarod Trail Committee Headquarters and Visitor Center.** (Look for the large, colorful sign.) You can view historical mushing exhibits and films, see sled dogs, meet a musher, and shop for mushing souvenirs. The center is open daily in summer and does not charge admission. Phone (907) 376–5155. At mile 13 visitors are welcome (by appointment) at **Knik Kennels**, since 1948 the world's largest sled dog kennel and the home of numerous famous canine athletes. Admission is free. Call (907) 376–5562. Nearly 14 miles down the road from the Parks Highway junction and about ½ mile after you come to the village of Knik, you'll find the **Knik Museum and Sled Dog Mushers' Hall of Fame.** In addition to mushers' portraits, mushing equipment, and Iditarod Trail historical exhibits, you can see artifacts from Knik village's gold rush (1898–1916) beginnings. The museum building itself dates back to that period. Admission is $2.00. Call (907) 376–7755. It's open from noon to 6:00 P.M., Wednesday through Sunday.

If your transportation preferences don't include pooch power, how about an airboat ride to Knik Glacier for a walk on the ice?

The price is $60 for a four-hour tour. Or a llama trek into the back country? This option starts at $50. **Knik Glacier Adventures** offers these and other tours, plus log cabin rentals for $55 a night, at mile 7 on Knik Road. Call (907) 746–5133 for reservations or details.

If you want to overnight near Wasilla and still feel out of the mainstream, **Yukon Don's Bed and Breakfast Inn** features a fabulous 360-degree view of rural Mat Valley at mile 37.5 on Parks Highway. Rates begin at $75. Call (907) 376–7472.

At mile 47, turn left on Neuser Drive for .75 mile to the road's end at the **Museum of Alaska Transportation and Industry.** It features, in the words of the Mat-Su Visitors Bureau "ten acres of neat ol' stuff," including airplanes, locomotives, farm and construction rigs, plus "trucks and vehicles that built Alaska." Admission is $3.00 for adults, $7.00 for families. Call (907) 376–1211. Hours are 10:00 A.M. to 6:00 P.M.

Just past mile 52 on the George Parks Highway, the Big Lake Road leads to (you guessed it) **Big Lake** and any number of lodges, B&Bs, eateries, service stations, shops, fishing supply stores, public and private RV facilities, and several smaller lakes joined to the big one. If you're interested in a different kind of overnight experience, consider **Big Lake Houseboat Rental**, located at the Klondike Inn on Northshore Drive, which will lease you a six-guest houseboat on which you can cruise more than 50 miles of shoreline. The rate is $225 to $250 depending on boat size. Call (800) 770–9187. Suggestion: Big Lake is one of Anchorage folks' favorite weekend getaway locales. Plan your own Big Lake visit Monday through Thursday to miss the madding crowd.

Lucky Husky Racing Kennel (an Iditarod race viewing point) at mile 80 on Parks Highway, offers year-round sled rides, kennel tours, and a movie plus major mushing adventures in the winter. You can even purchase a puppy. Kennel tour admission is $5.00; dogsled ride (on wheels) is $10.00. Phone (907) 495–6470.

Nearing mile 99 from Anchorage, you come to a 14.5-mile spur road to **Talkeetna,** one of several Alaska communities often compared to *Northern Exposure*'s mythical city of Cicely on TV. There's a visitor center right at the Parks Highway junction, and 1 mile down the road lies ◆**Mary Carey's Fiddlehead Farm**, reputedly the only one in the world. You can meet longtime Alaskan book author (and character) Mary Carey as well as purchase her gourmet pickled and frozen ferns, buy autographed copies of her books, and shop for ivory carvings, soapstone sculpture, and other Native arts. Phone (907) 733–2428.

Near the end of the spur road, stop in at the **Talkeetna Historical Society Museum**, located on the village airstrip, which is almost in the middle of town. Formerly a schoolhouse built in the middle thirties, the museum contains displays and information from its gold mining past as well as items commemorating the life of famed bush pilot Don Sheldon. Talkeetna is definitely a walk-around town, so pick up a walking tour map at the museum, then wander about, taking pictures of the community's WELCOME TO BEAUTIFUL DOWNTOWN TALKEETNA sign, the historic old **Talkeetna Roadhouse**, the old **Fairview Inn**, and various other log and clapboard houses and structures spread along Talkeetna's streets and paths.

Steve Mahay's **Mahay's Riverboat Service** offers three very different Susitna River experiences for visitors: a two-hour McKinley View River Cruise for $34.50, a one-hour Sunset Cruise priced at $19.50, and a "wild and wet" jet boat ride that features nonstop spray-in-your-face frantic action and 360-degree full power spins. "This ride," says Mahay, "is not for the fainthearted." The twenty-minute ride costs $19.50. Call (907) 733–2223.

When they're not busy airlifting climbers to base camps on Denali (Mt. McKinley) in the spring and early summer, Talkeetna's several excellent bush flight services take visitors on airborne flight-seeing forays around North America's tallest mountain, sometimes even landing on a glacier's icy surface. Among the companies offering such services is Jim Okonek's Talkeetna-based **K2 Aviation** (907–733–2291), whose services also include statewide air tours and a variety of Denali Park air tour options. Prices for flight-seeing out of Talkeetna start as low as $70. K2 also flies into several remote backcountry lakes with cabins, such as Goat Lake, where the cost is $35 a night for a cabin plus $600 airfare. The firm's **Climber Bunkhouse**, just off Main Street near the river, is used by mountaineers during the climbing season but is available for other visitors the rest of the summer. The cost is only $12 per night. Bring your own sleeping bag.

K2's **Explore Air Statewide Tours** (sort of a funny name, eh?) are especially intriguing. A party can charter an appropriate size and type of aircraft (wheels or floats), then receive unrestricted flight services at a fixed daily rate—sort of like a Hertz or

Avis unlimited miles car package, except the client also gets the services of a pilot guide. Typically, people charter the plane for two or three days. One of the most popular itineraries includes a visit to remote North Coast and western Eskimo villages. Prices range from $1,600 to $2,000 per day per party, so for a party of six the cost would be less than $335 per person per day. There's no limit to where the trip goes.

Talkeetna's longest operating (since 1948) air taxi service is Cliff Hudson's **Hudson Air Service** (800–478–2321). Two generations of bush pilots can take you on scenic flights, land you on Denali's glaciers, and provide wildlife viewing excursions. Talkeetna, incidentally, is also accessible by daily summer Alaska Railroad train service from Anchorage or Fairbanks. Call (800) 544–0552 for information.

Denali National Park and Preserve, of course, gets lots of attention, and properly so. But there's another Denali Park, **Denali State Park**, which deserves more mention than it gets. You enter this park at mile 132 on the Parks Highway, and you're within its boundaries until mile 169. In between, you can enjoy fine dining or lodging with indescribable views of Denali at **Mary's McKinley View Lodge** at mile 134.5 (907–733–1555). This is the same Mary whose fiddlehead farm you passed a few miles back. Or you can pitch a camp in the stellar lake, stream, and forest country at **Beyer Lake Campground** at mile 147. The overnight fee is $10. *Caution:* Especially if you go hiking in the woods there make noise. Grizzlies roamed the area last time we camped at this site.

At roughly mile 210 on the Parks Highway you arrive at **Cantwell** and the junction of the Parks and Denali Highways. Before hurrying on to Denali National Park, spend a little time around this small community, which many pass by. (For details, see the section on the Denali Highway in the chapter on Interior Alaska.)

The entrance to **Denali National Park and Preserve** lies just past mile 237. For information about exploring and enjoying this grand national parkland, see the following chapter on Interior Alaska.

GLENN HIGHWAY: ANCHORAGE TO GLENNALLEN

The Glenn Highway is one of the most traveled routes in Alaska. It's also one of the most scenic. The sky-piercing Mentasta and

Wrangell Mountains abut this route. It dissects long, wide valleys of spruce, alder, and birch forests, and in the Matanuska and Susitna Valleys it courses through Alaska's principal agricultural districts. The Glenn provides the principal access between Anchorage and Tok on the Alaska Highway.

Alaskans often talk about the Anchorage–Tok link as if it were one road. (And, indeed, the state Department of Highways designates it, plus part of the Seward Highway and all of the Sterling, as Alaska Route 1.) To be accurate, however, we should note that the 328-mile route actually consists of two separate highways and part of a third—the Glenn itself, which extends 189 miles from Anchorage to Glennallen; a 14-mile portion of the Richardson Highway, from Glennallen to Gakona; and the 125-mile Tok Cutoff, extending from Gakona to Tok, where it junctions with the Alaska Highway.

We'll explore the Glenn and Richardson sections of the highway in this Southcentral Alaska section of the book; you'll find the Tok Cutoff portion in the following chapter on Interior Alaska.

Leaving Anchorage on the Glenn, you pass access roads to Elmendorf Air Force Base and Fort Richardson and about 13 miles out, you come to a community called **Eagle River**, most of whose residents work in Anchorage. From downtown Eagle River, drive 12.5 miles easterly on the Eagle River Road to the **Chugach State Park** and the park **visitor center**. There's lots of good information to be picked up here, including hiking maps and updates on recreation sites in one of Alaska's and America's largest state parks. Enjoy lunch and a panoramic mountain view on the veranda outside the center, take a short hike on nearby trails, and check out nature walks and lectures by state park rangers. For information during summer months, call (907) 694–2108.

Eklutna Village and ◆**Eklutna Village Historical Park,** 26 miles from Anchorage, is another of those priceless little places that many pass by in their rush to get from Anchorage to some other, more publicized travel attraction. Through historical records, oral history, and archaeology, the Athabascan village can trace its occupancy of this area back an astonishing 350 years. To get to the park, exit left off the Glenn Highway at Eklutna. The road leads to the nearby park. A half-hour tour starts with an orientation in the Heritage House, which has art displays and lifestyle exhibits. The tour then leads, on a guided gentle walk, to a tiny little Russian Orthodox church built in the 1830s. Visitors then move on to a

109

Spirit Houses at Eklunta Village Historical Park

more modern church, and finally to the village cemetery, where the dead lie buried beneath small, colorfully painted "spirit houses." Admission is $3.50. Phone (907) 696–2828.

Just before mile 30 on the Glenn, you have the opportunity to turn right onto the Old Glenn Highway. Both the Glenn and the Old Glenn end up in Palmer, but the older route offers options such as a view of **Bodenburg Butte**, access to a nice view of **Knik Glacier**, and the opportunity to see original Matanuska Valley colony farms. At the **Williams Reindeer Farm** on Bodenburg Loop Road (which begins at mile 11.5 on the Old Glenn) you can see, pet, and even feed reindeer. Admission charge is $3.00. Call (907) 745–4000.

At the end of the Old Glenn Highway, and at mile 42 on the Glenn, lies **Palmer**, borough seat for the Matanuska Susitna Borough and a major hub for trade and agriculture in the Mat Valley. It's also the site during the eleven days preceding Labor Day each year of the **Alaska State Fair**. (Actually, other celebrations in the state share that designation, but none is so large and well attended.) It's here, incidentally, you can see and photograph the valley's huge and famous vegetables, including cabbages that sometimes reach one hundred pounds. There are lots of other food and animal exhibits as well as carnival-type rides and—perhaps most fun of all—political booths filled with Alaskan activists gathering petition signatures and giving out information about whatever is politically hot at the moment.

Just beyond Palmer, the partly paved, partly gravel **Fishhook Road** at mile 49.5 on the Glenn Highway offers a delightful side trip to wide-open spaces and vistas. If you're an equestrian, turn right on Gordy Drive at mile 5.2 for **Rafter T Ranch Trail Rides** (907–745–2884). The ranch offers guided and unguided horseback excursions starting at $25 per hour. The main attraction along the road, however, is fascinating ◆**Independence Mine State Historical Park**, about 17 miles from the Glenn Highway junction. Here during the summer months you can take escorted tours through old mining structures that date back to the thirties. The cost is $3.00. Call (907) 745–2827. There's no charge for gold panning in the park, and rangers at the visitor center (the old mine manager's house) will direct you to the best prospects. Located on a private inholding within the 761-acre park is the A-framed **Hatcher Pass Lodge**, perched at a 3,000-foot elevation and offering cabins, rooms, and meals. The rate is $110 for a double. Call (907) 745–8797. Eventually the 49-mile road junctions with the George Parks Highway.

Just off the Glenn Highway at about mile 50, a former farm from the old colony days now houses the **Palmer musk ox farm**, the only one of its kind in the country. About seventy of the animals (sort of a scaled-down water buffalo with long hair) live there. Their highly prized qiviut wool is knitted (only by Alaska Natives) into hats, scarves, and other items. An ounce of qiviut is eight times warmer than an equal amount of sheep's wool. The farm is open to the public from 9:00 A.M. to 7:00 P.M., May through September. Admission is $7.00. For information, call (907) 745–4151.

If you'd like to walk on a glacier—minus the expense of a high-priced helicopter tour—the ◆**Matanuska Glacier** offers a rare opportunity to do so. Turn off the Glenn Highway at mile 102 and take the gravel road to **Glacier Park Resort** (907-745-2534), which is perhaps a rather grand description for a pretty basic camping and tenting area plus gift shop, laundry, showers, liquor store, and snack foods. It nonetheless merits its $6.50 admission fee for adults ($3.50 for children) because from the parking lot, you can stroll right up onto the glacier. If you use common sense, it's safe, but be cautious on the ice. It can be slick. And be on the lookout for crevasses that can run deep and cold. Other ways and places to view the glacier include the **Matanuska Glacier State Recreation Site** and camping area at mile 101, the state highway pullout just past mile 101.5, and **Long Rifle Lodge**, beyond mile 102, where you can dine with a view of the ice river. The interior view at the lodge, incidentally, includes 25 wildlife mounts. Overnight rates start at $40 for a double. For dining or lodging reservations, call (800) 770-5151.

B&B usually means "bed and breakfast," but at mile 111.5 you'll find **Bunk 'n' Breakfast,** operated by Dee Larson. Rustic cabins sleep six guests (bring your own sleeping bag) at $15 a night. Farther along the highway, at mile 113.5, lies **Sheep Mountain Lodge** (907-745-5121), established nearly a half century ago. If you can tear yourself away from the lodge's hot tub and sauna, there's great sheep viewing by telescope as well as excellent hiking in the area. Rates start at $85.00.

Another worthwhile side trip, just short of 20 miles each way, takes you to **Lake Louise** via the Lake Louise Road, which begins just before mile 160 on the Glenn Highway. Several fine fishing and outdoor lodges as well as a state recreation area and campgrounds are located on this lake in one of the North Country's premier water/mountain/glacier settings. In addition to providing B&B accommodations for $85 per night, the long-established **Evergreen Lodge** (907-822-3250) operates flight-seeing tours, guided fishing, fly-outs to a remote cabin, and an innovative seven-night safari that includes daily fly-outs or driving excursions for sight-seeing, wildlife photography, visits to the Kennecott Mine, hiking, glacier viewing, and sauna time. Your experience is wrapped up in an edited video souvenir complete with music, voice, and titles. The cost is $1,425.

If you're tenting or driving an RV, **Tolsona Wilderness Campground** lies .75 mile north of the noise and traffic of the highway at mile 173 and is set in the forest beside Tolsona Creek. One of its newer attractions is a primitive 1-mile hiking trail to an active mud spring, where gases bubbling up from lower Cretaceous and upper Jurassic formations carry fine particles of silt to the surface to form a 2,075-foot hill from which the springs emerge. The spring itself flows year-round and is a source of water for wildlife, especially in the cold and frozen months of the year. The fee for tenters is $10, for RV hook-up campsites $15. Call (907) 822-3865.

The Glenn and Richardson Highways meet and blend at Glennallen. Beyond this community, for 14 miles you're really traveling on the Richardson Highway and therefore the mileposts indicate miles from its start at Valdez. Then, at Gakona Junction, the Richardson continues north to Delta Junction and Fairbanks while the **Tok Cutoff**, on the Anchorage–Tok route we're discussing here, courses northeasterly. You're right, it can be a little confusing, so be alert.

And . . . not to confuse you further, beyond Glennallen you're really traveling in Interior Alaska, so for information about the more northerly portions of this route, refer to the chapter on Interior Alaska.

THE RICHARDSON HIGHWAY—
SOUTHERN SECTION: VALDEZ TO GAKONA JUNCTION

When you drive on the 368-mile Richardson Highway, you're traveling along a historic gold rush route first pioneered in 1898 as the Valdez–Eagle Trail. The trail at that time, however, began with a treacherous start literally over the ice of Valdez Glacier, a fact that devastated or turned back many a would-be prospector before he ever started his trek to the gold fields. The following year Captain W.R. Abercrombie created an alternate route through Keystone Canyon and across Thompson Pass, bypassing the glacier. The route—first a sled dog and horse trail, now paved and fully modern—has been a major Alaskan land link between Prince William Sound and the Interior ever since. Today the Richardson connects Valdez with Delta Junction and Fairbanks. As the road approaches its second century, a few of its pioneer

113

(but now renovated) roadhouses remain along the way, reminders of the era when warm, welcome accommodations were spaced a day's horse or dog team travel apart.

The canyon drive into or out of Valdez is one of Alaska's most spectacular, with high, steep walls and no small number of breathtaking waterfalls. The surrounding mountains are likewise high, rugged, and spectacular. It's in this area and on these death-defying near-vertical mountain slopes each winter that the community hosts the **World Extreme Skiing Championships.** The event attracts practitioners of the daredevil sport from all over the world, and it's fast becoming a favorite spectator sport (with surprisingly good binocular views from the highway) among Southcentral Alaskans. For more information, call (800) 770–5954.

It sounds pleasurable and it is: **Blueberry Lake State Recreation Site**, with loop entrances at both mile 23 and 24 along the Richardson, is a visual delight and a favorite campground for Alaskans. An alpine area situated above timberline, the site offers a sweeping sight of Keystone Canyon as well as close-up views of dwarf plants and other flora usually associated with northern tundra. It's also the natural habitat for Alaska's state bird, the willow ptarmigan. Flocks of dozens are not uncommon. The state camping fee is $10 per night.

At mile 26 you come to 2,678-foot **Thompson Pass**, where winter snowfall totaling nearly 1,000 inches has been recorded. The long, tall poles alongside the road guide snowplows and snowblowers in the snowy season. About 2.5 miles beyond the pass is **Worthington Glacier State Recreation Site**, where you'll find displays and exhibits explaining the huge river of ice. You can, if you'd like, drive up practically to the glacier.

At about mile 83 you come to the paved, 35-mile **Edgerton Highway** to **Chitina** (pronounced CHIT-na; the second "i" is silent), which connects at the highway's end with the 60-mile gravel **McCarthy Road**. This road, in turn, leads over a former railroad bed to the near-ghost towns of **McCarthy** and **Kennicott**, within Wrangell–St. Elias National Park. Take the time to drive at least to Chitina, stopping en route perhaps at **Kenny Lake Mercantile and RV Park** (at mile 7.5) to top off your gas tank or, if you're pulling a rig, to drop off your RV and proceed unencumbered. In fact, you can even leave your car and RV here if you wish. This is a pickup point for scheduled van service to McCarthy and Kennicott. Call (907) 822–9863 for details. If you enjoy collecting nature scenics, stop at mile 23.5 at bubbling, forested Liberty Creek and thunderous Liberty Falls in **Liberty Falls State Recreation Site**, another of the author's all-time favorites. The highway itself bisects rolling hills and takes in views of wide, forested valleys, grand lakes, and the imposing peaks of the Wrangells. If you're really lucky, you may even see bison herds across the Copper River.

The **National Park Service** has a ranger office in Chitina, and the staff there can tell you about park and local attractions as well as conditions on the McCarthy Road, which begins where the Edgerton ends. Picturesque Chitina is almost a ghost town—just ask the locals, who have painted humorous, ghostly pictures on a few of the town's abandoned turn-of-the-century structures. Hand-hewn log cabins, western-style stores, and rusting old cars, trucks, and wagons give testimony to the town's gold rush past.

If you're game, by all means continue beyond Chitina on the **McCarthy Road**, but be advised it can be a slow, bumpy, and narrow. It can also be pretty muddy in the rain. Still, the rewards are many when you make it to the road's end at the Kennicott River. **McCarthy**, the town for which the road is named, lies across the river and hopefully you can access it easily by a footbridge across the water. We say "hopefully" because the bridge is scheduled to be finished by the time this book comes off the press. If it isn't, you can do what many hundreds of visitors have done for decades—pull yourself across the river on a hand-powered tram! It's not all that difficult, but do wear gloves to protect your hands.

About two dozen hardy souls call McCarthy home, including lifelong Alaskans Gary and Betty Hickling, who operate **McCarthy Lodge restaurant and saloon** as well as the **Ma Johnson Hotel** (circa 1916). Visitor rooms, all of which are located in the hotel, are in the early twentieth century tradition, long and slender and furnished in Victorian decor. The hotel does, however, offer modern shared baths. The $180 rate for two includes three meals daily for each person. The Hicklings also operate a hostel called the **Bunkhouse.** The nightly cost is $25; bring your own sleeping bag. Call (907) 554–4402 for more information.

The **McCarthy Museum**, housed in the old railway depot, displays items and photographs from the community's mining glory days. Five miles down the road (van pickup is available)

115

Abandoned Kennicott Copper Mine

lies the abandoned town and copper mine of **Kennicott** and ❖**Kennicott Glacier Lodge**. a thoroughly modern, thoroughly elegant 26-room lodge built in the style and decor of the surrounding old structures. Rates for the Kennicott Glacier Lodge, including transport from McCarthy, a guided tour of the ghost town, and three meals a day begin at $115 per person per night, double occupancy. Call (800) 582–5128 for details. There's lots of exploring and poking around to be done in this National Historic Landmark community.

Two bush flight services based in McCarthy offer a wide variety of flight-seeing, hiker drop-off, and transportation services, including flights to Kennicott and Kennicott Glacier Lodge.

116

Wrangell Mountain Air (800–478–1160) and **McCarthy Air** (800–245–6909) can serve you from McCarthy or from Chitina as well as from Glennallen or even Anchorage. Sample rates: Wrangell Mountain Air will ferry you from Chitina to McCarthy (thus relieving you of a long bumpy ride) for $60; McCarthy Air prices thirty minutes of flight-seeing from McCarthy over valleys, glaciers, and historic mining sites at $40.

St. Elias Alpine Guides (907–277–6867) offers a wide selection of options, including a Root Glacier Hike (half day, $55), a Kennicott Glacier Fly-In (full day, $165), fly-in rafting on the Kennicott River ($195), and a full day of mountain biking through the forested high banks of the Nizina River ($80). Howard Mozen's **Copper Oar** runs a number of rafting adventures from McCarthy, ranging from two hours on the Kennicott River to nine days on the Chitina and Copper Rivers, travelling all the way to Cordova. Prices vary from $45 for the short ride to $2,100 for the longest. Call (907) 554–4453, May through September, or call (907) 566–0771 anytime.

Back on the Richardson Highway, you come to the turnoff for **Copper Center** just beyond mile 100. The highway officially bypasses this community which grew out of a nineteenth-century trading post, but you shouldn't. Turn right onto the *Old* Richardson just past mile 100. The historic old **Copper Center Lodge**, still serving travelers as it has since 1897, is today fully modern, but well preserved. Rates start at $70 for rooms with shared bath, $75 for rooms with private facilities. Call (907) 822–3245. The lodge's restaurant serves sourdough pancakes made with a starter that can be traced back more than a century. Next door, in a small log cabin, you'll find one of two small but worthwhile stops for history buffs. **The George Ashby Memorial Museum** houses mining, trapping, Indian, and pioneer relics and displays. Half the cabin is an authentic old log bunkhouse. And within the museum you can walk through the actual iron doors of the old Copper Center Jailhouse. There is no charge, but donations are accepted. The other (relatively recent) historical stop is the log **Chapel on the Hill**, at mile 101 on the *Old* Richardson Highway, constructed in the early forties by U.S. Army servicemen. Daily free slide shows give visitors a visual look at Copper Valley and its features.

The park headquarters and visitor center for the **Wrangell–St. Elias National Park and Preserve** (the

117

nation's largest, at 13.2 million acres) is located at mile 105.5 on the *Old* Richardson Highway, just north of Copper Center. The park, which is the size of six Yellowstones, contains nine of the 16 highest peaks in the nation—not to mention countless glaciers, forested valleys, and many species of wildlife. The headquarters is your source of information about park hiking, camping, road access (extremely limited), and attractions. Call (907) 822-5235.

Driving north from Copper Center, the old segment of the Richardson Highway junctions with the north end of the bypass at mile 106, and you're officially back on the Richardson. At mile 115 the highway junctions at **Glennallen** with the Glenn Highway from Anchorage. For the next 14 miles, the Richardson Highway and the Glenn Highway–Tok Cutoff route are the same. Near mile 129 and Gakona Junction, the Tok Cutoff heads northeast, while the Richardson continues north to Delta Junction and Fairbanks.

And now, although there's no official boundary between Southcentral Alaska and the Interior, this is probably a good place to separate the two regions. For information about the northern portion of the Richardson Highway, see the next chapter on Interior Alaska.

INTERIOR ALASKA

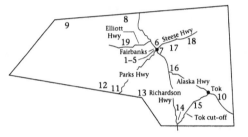

1. stern-wheeler *Discovery III*
2. Creamer's Field Migratory
   Waterfowl Refuge
3. University of Alaska Museum
4. Alaskaland
5. Native Village
6. El Dorado Gold Camp
7. Gold Dredge Number 8
8. Anaktuvuk Pass
9. Athabasca Cultural Journeys
10. Alaska's Mainstreet
    Visitor Center

11. Denali National Park
12. Camp Denali
13. Denali Wilderness Lodge
14. visitor center
15. Huck Hobbit's Homestead
    Campground and Retreat
16. Rika's Roadhouse/Big Delta
    State Historical Park
17. The Resort at Chena Hot
    Springs
18. Arctic Circle Hot Springs
19. Manley Hot Springs

INTERIOR ALASKA

From one point in Alaska's Interior region—the summit of Denali (Mt. McKinley)—climbers can literally look down on every other mountaintop, hill, ridge, valley, and plain in North America. (Although McKinley is the name the federal government officially recognizes for the continent's highest peak, Alaskans, noting that President William McKinley, of Ohio, never once laid eyes on even a little mountain in Alaska, greatly prefer to use the beautiful Athabascan Indian name for the peak, *Denali*, which means the high one. Entreaties from the Alaska Legislature and Alaska's delegation in Congress to officially change the name, however, have fallen on deaf ears. The Ohio Congressional delegation seems always to succeed in blocking the change.) The view from Denali may explain why Interior Alaskans speak in such expansive terms about their region of sky-piercing mountains, rolling hills, long and mighty rivers, sub-Arctic tundra lands, and vast taiga forests. This is gold mining country and has been since Felix Pedro's 1902 strike near present-day Fairbanks. It's oil country as well, at least in the sense that a large share of the 800-mile Trans-Alaska Pipeline passes through the Interior on its way from Prudhoe Bay to the coast at Valdez.

And the Interior is grand traveling country. It's a land of long roads and riverways and remote fly-in lodges and cabins. It is also a place with a rich Athabascan Native culture, and a place of grizzlies, moose, caribou, wolves, and scores of smaller species. It's a warm and balmy region in the summer (though temperatures can plummet to sixty *below* in the winter).

Fairbanks, about 300 miles from the border and the second-largest community in Alaska, serves as transportation and travel hub for the region, and for that reason we describe the many facets of Fairbanks at the beginning of this chapter. We then deal with pleasurable things to see and do along Interior Alaska's roads and highways, most of which (but not all) lead to or from Fairbanks. We will examine the Interior portions of the state's four multiregion highways in the same order in which they appeared in earlier chapters. Specifically we'll describe the Alaska Highway from the border (where we left off in the Yukon chapter) to the highway's end at Delta Junction. We'll examine the northern portions of the George Parks Highway connecting

Anchorage and Fairbanks and the Glenn Highway–Tok Cutoff route, which runs from Anchorage to Tok. And of course we will cover the northern portion of the Richardson Highway that begins at Valdez and ends in Fairbanks. We'll look, too, at the Steese Highway from Fairbanks to Circle City on the Yukon River. Not to be overlooked in these pages are the smaller and often-overlooked Denali Highway and the Elliott Highway; they're noted, too.

FAIRBANKS

A bustling, busy, dynamic city is **Fairbanks**, on the banks of the Chena River. Fairbanksans call it the Golden Heart of Alaska, and it was indeed gold in the early years of the century that brought about the founding of the town.

When, in 1901, Captain E.T. Barnette set out from St. Michael, at the mouth of the Yukon River, aboard the stern-wheeler *Lavelle Young,* he intended to establish a trading post in the gold prospecting area at Tanana Crossing, about halfway between Valdez and Eagle. He didn't get that far, however. The ship couldn't navigate the shallow Chena River beyond present-day Fairbanks, so he established his post there. And a fortunate choice it turned out to be. Felix Pedro, an Italian prospector, discovered gold in the area a year later, and a "rush" to Fairbanks soon followed.

The **Fairbanks Convention and Visitor Bureau Information Center**, right downtown on the banks of the Chena River at 550 First Avenue, provides lots of up-to-date information on things to see and do, places to go, restaurants, and overnight options. For the traveler seeking off-the-beaten-path options, an even more important resource is, once again, the **Alaska Public Lands Information Center**, which you'll find on the lower level of Courthouse Square, at Cushman Street and Third Avenue. Here you'll see displays, wildlife mounts, cultural artifacts, and basic information about the Interior's outdoor touring, camping, and recreational opportunities. There is no admission charge. Call (907) 456–0527.

Captain Jim Binkley's ◆ **stern-wheeler *Discovery III* cruise** is Fairbanks' most popular tour; it's also very much an off-the-beaten-path and educational experience. Twice daily, at 8:45 A.M. and 2:00 P.M., the vessel departs from its docks at 1975 Discovery Drive (southwest of downtown) for a cruise down the Chena and

Tanana Rivers. En route, as the hustle and hurry of Fairbanks fades further and further behind, passengers learn about the Native Athabascan peoples of this area—some of whom are onboard as guides—as well as the history of gold rushes and oil booms and homesteading hereabouts. They watch as huge fish wheels, powered by stream currents, scoop fish into large holding baskets from the rivers they're cruising. If they're lucky, they even see moose in the woods along the shore. Finally, the vessel stops at a river island for a visit at **Old Chena Indian Village.** There, musher David Munson (whose wife Susan Butcher has won the grueling 1,000-mile Iditarod sled dog classic four times) demonstrates sled dog mushing. There, too, as visitors wander from site to site on the island, they see how Athabascan Indians and Eskimos from farther north smoke fish, tan wildlife hides, sew leather, bead garments, and live in a harsh, but bountiful environment. The cost is $33.95. Call (907) 479–6673.

If you're interested at all in birds, ◆**Creamer's Field Migratory Waterfowl Refuge**, only 1 mile from downtown, provides great viewing of huge flocks of ducks and geese in the spring and fall, and sandhill cranes during the summer months. You can walk along a 2-mile self-guided nature trail and visit the restored farmhouse that now serves as visitor center. The start of the trail is located at 1300 College Road. College Road is one of Fairbanks's principal east-west thoroughfares. It is located about 1 mile north of downtown. Donations are accepted. Call (907) 452–1531.

Close by Creamer's Field, on College Road at the **Tanana Valley Fairgrounds**, you can shop at the **Tanana Valley Farmer's Market** for fresh veggies, meats, bakery items, flowers, and craft goods on Wednesday from noon to 5:00 P.M., Saturday from 9:00 A.M. until 4:00 P.M. It's the only market of its kind in Interior Alaska.

At the ◆**University of Alaska Museum**, on the UA Fairbanks campus, northwest of downtown, you can view natural and historical exhibits, such as an incredible 36,000-year-old Steppe bison that was almost perfectly preserved in Alaska's permafrost until its discovery in this century. Also on display are contemporary wildlife mounts (including a really humungous brown bear), the state's largest exhibit of gold, Native art, plus an exhibit on the *aurora borealis* (northern lights). Admission is $5.00 for adults; the museum is open daily. Call (907) 474–7505 for details.

For your photo collection of strange beasties of the Arctic, tour the university's considerably less visited **Large Animal Research Station**, off Yankovich Road north of the main campus. There, among other animals, you'll find the shaggy, horned musk ox, once hunted to extinction within Alaska. With the help of imported animals of the same species from Canada, the animals are making a comeback. UAF also offers tours of the **Geophysical Institute**, where scholars ferret out knowledge of the earth's deepest regions and the heaven's northern lights. And for the botanically inclined, the university will give you a guided visit to the Agricultural and Forestry Experiment Station's **Georgeson Botanical Garden**. For information about these tours or a look at the whole campus, call (907) 474–7581.

In 1967, wanting to commemorate the one hundredth anniversary of Alaska's purchase from Russia in a lasting way, the people of Fairbanks and the State of Alaska created a forty-four-acre pioneer theme park called Alaska 67. Renamed ◆**Alaskaland** after the official year of celebration ended, the park continues in business on Airport Way, with a wide variety of things to see and do. There's no admission charge to enter Alaskaland, but there are fees to visit some portions of the park. Among various things to see and do, you'll find a genuine stern-wheeler riverboat (the **S.S. Nenana,** a national historic landmark), a **Gold Rush Town** of relocated and restored homes and stores from Fairbanks's early days, the frontier **Palace Theatre and Saloon,** a miniature mining valley, a newly created pioneer air museum of early aircraft, plus one of the two best salmon bakes/barbecues in Alaska. (The other is in Juneau.) Circling it all is the **Crooked Creek & Whiskey Island Railroad,** not terribly authentic, perhaps, but it is fun and a good way to get the lay of the land before you start wandering around the acreage.

For the culturally curious, one of Alaskaland's most interesting locales is the ◆**Native Village,** where Athabascan Indian young people proudly entertain and educate visitors with stories and ancient dances. In the village museum, where you'll note a pleasant faint scent of cottonwood-smoked animal skins, you'll see a wide variety of artifacts, tools, weapons (such as a bear-killing spear), and art, including masterful beadwork. The young people share legends, history, and their techniques of survival in one of the harshest environments on earth. There's also an Athabascan *kashim,* a log house with sod roof, as well as a traditional underground sod home of the type once used by Alaska's Eskimo peoples. There is a modest admission fee to the village. For general information about Alaskaland, call (907) 459–1087.

Here's a chance to collect another Alaska superlative. If you're a golfer and want to play some really far out golf, be aware that two courses in Fairbanks lay claim to being the farthest north golf course in the world. Friends in the city tell me the **North Star Golf Club** is actually a tad more northerly (though on the opposite side of the city) than the **Fairbanks Golf and Country Club**—but who's measuring? The thing to do is play them both. You'll find North Star northeast of town off Old Steese Highway on Golf Club Drive. Call (907) 457–4653 for tee times. The Fairbanks Golf and Country Club is located northwest, near the intersection of Farmers Loop Road and Ballaine Road. Phone (907) 479–6555.

You can relive some of Fairbanks's gold heritage at a working gold mine and visitor operation called ◆ **El Dorado Gold Camp,** about 9 miles northwest of Fairbanks on the Elliott Highway. You'll be treated to a short train ride on a tour of old and new "diggin's" at the mine, then a demonstration of how sluicing and panning for gold works. Once you're ready, they turn you loose with a pan of your own and some ore that's guaranteed to contain "color." You can keep all you find. The experience runs $24.95. Call (907) 479–7613.

Historic old ◆ **Gold Dredge Number 8,** at mile 9 on the Old Steese Highway, is a restored relic from an important mining era in Alaska's gold country. Between 1928 and 1959 this huge, floating hulk, five decks high and 250 feet long, scooped $3 billion worth of gold from creeks near Fairbanks. You can take a guided tour of the now-inoperative dredge for $10.00, which includes panning for gold yourself or searching for ancient mammoth tusks, teeth, and other Ice Age bones like the ones in a collection on display. Time your visit Monday through Saturday for lunch at the Dredge Bar & Restaurant, right at the dredge site, or on Sunday for a sourdough pancake feed. Call (907) 457–6058.

Lots of people arrive in Alaska and regret they left their camping equipment, bicycles, or canoe at home. Independent Rental, Inc. at 2020 S. Cushman in the heart of Fairbanks, will rent not only these items but also inflatable rafts and boats, fishing gear, tools, even video cameras. Call (907) 456–6595.

Among the smaller, Alaska-based tour companies operating out of Fairbanks is Terry and Patty McGhee's **Trans-Arctic Circle Treks Ltd.** They offer van tours as short as a single day along the Elliott and Dalton Highways with a 6-mile cruise on the Yukon River ($105 per person) or as long as three days and two nights on the Dalton Highway to Prudhoe Bay and the Arctic Ocean ($148 per day). Other options include Mt. McKinley and the Kantishna Mining District ($119) and exploring the Denali Highway, which the McGhees call "Alaska's best kept secret" ($95).

Alaska is one of those places where, even if you don't imbibe, you really ought to visit a few of the more colorful frontier saloons. In Fairbanks, at least three watering holes match that description: the **Palace Theatre and Saloon** at Alaskaland; the **Dog Sled Saloon** in the Captain Bartlett Inn, itself rather a colorful log motel, at 1411 Airport Way; and the **Malemute Saloon,** at the Ester Gold Camp just off mile 351.7 on the George Parks Highway. The latter is one of those atmospheric places frequented by locals as well as visitors where patrons throw peanut shells on the sawdust floor and gawk at the artifacts and the art junk on the walls. In the glow of a single lantern each evening an Alaska sourdough recites Robert Service's epic poems of the Yukon.

It's not cheap, but you can book one of Alaska's highest rated backcountry flight tours from Fairbanks via **Frontier Flying Service** (907–474–0014). It's the company's full-day excursion to ⬧**Anaktuvuk Pass** north of the Arctic Circle on the northern edge of the Brooks Range. The pass is both a geographic location and a Nunamiut ("People of the Land") Eskimo village. Your surroundings are the majestic peaks encompassed in Gates of the Arctic National Park. During the course of your flight-seeing and four-hour ground tour in the village, you'll meet the hardy, friendly people who still live largely a subsistence caribou-hunting and fishing lifestyle. You'll walk through the village with a local resident, tour the Simon Paneak Museum, and visit Gates of the Arctic U.S. Park Service headquarters. The cost is $250 round-trip.

Larry's Flying Service (907–474–9169) also operates a number of worthwhile flight-seeing tours from Fairbanks, including one to Anaktuvuk Pass. The flying portion of this trip takes in portions of the Trans-Alaska Pipeline and the Dalton Highway as

Malemute Saloon, Fairbanks

well as Gates of the Arctic National Park. The cost is $250. Another flight-seeing service, the **Fairbanks Flight Train** (907–474–0757), takes you on a sixty-to-ninety-minute excursion with an onboard narrator-naturalist, flying over the pipeline, the small community of Fox, gold mines, and Gold Dredge Number 8, plus Tanana and Minto flats, where you may see moose, geese, and bears. Fares vary from $79 to $89. The company will pick you up at your hotel.

◆**Athabasca Cultural Journeys** is the name of a bush adventure that begins with a small plane flight from Fairbanks to the Native village of Huslia and continues by boat up the Koyukuk River to an authentic Athabascan fish camp in the **Koyukuk National Wildlife Refuge.** An Indian family will serve as your hosts during a four-day visit, during which you may well see moose, caribou, bear, otter, and beaver plus eagles, hawks, owls, and other birds. Accommodations are clean, roomy canvas tents with extra wide cots. Generous meals may include moose-meat stew. There's time for recreational fishing and visits to archaeological sites as well. For details, call (800) 423–0094.

If you're looking for a classic, woodsy Alaska wilderness-type lodge located within a fifteen to twenty minutes' drive from downtown, Tom Ridner's **North Woods Lodge,** on Chena Hills Drive, is the answer to your quest. The main lodge is constructed from massive logs and can handle a group of any size, from a couple to several families traveling together. Guests can relax on a large deck running the full length of the building or soak up some "midnight sun" at the end of a day in a twelve person Jacuzzi hot tub. Bedrooms average about $60, but accommodations in the hostel sleeping loft can run as low as $15. A separate 10-by-12-foot cabin with two twin bunks rents for $40 for two. Call (907) 479–5300.

Also set on Chena Ridge among towering spruce with panoramic views of the Tanana Valley, the Alaska Range, and Fairbanks is **Forget Me Not Bed and Breakfast** and Mike and Susan Wilson's newest addition for nostalgic railroad aficionados, the **Aurora Express.** The latter consists of three former Pullman cars and a caboose, the Golden Nelly, all elegantly restored and refurbished as comfortable sleeping accommodations. For those who prefer an equally elegant but traditional setting, their 5,000-square-foot lodge home offers a variety of choices, including the 650-square-foot Lilac and Lace Suite with cathedral ceilings, a king-size bed, and a private bath with a tiled 6-foot Jacuzzi. A typical breakfast at this B&B would be sausage, an onion-mushroom-cheese omelet, cranberry muffins, hash browns, fresh fruit, juice, and coffee. Call (907) 474–0949.

Speaking of B&Bs, **G.O. Shuttle Service,** in Fairbanks, offers shuttles from the airport or rail or bus depot to any of the B&Bs in town. Fares run about $7.00 per person. It also provides tours and transfers to other points of interest in Fairbanks. Phone (907) 474–3847.

Fairbanksans, when they dine out, often choose the downtown **Plate and Palette Gallery Cafe,** at 310 First Avenue (907–451–9294), for its wholesome food served with a touch of flair in an art gallery setting. **Pikes Landing,** on the Chena riverbanks, at 4438 Airport Way, is another favorite. We usually choose the casual outdoor setting, on the large deck (907–479–6500). Or

127

try the **Two Rivers Lodge** (907–488–6815), at mile 16 on the Chena Hot Springs Road, where your choices range from seafood to steaks and Cajun cuisine.

THE ALASKA HIGHWAY: U.S. BORDER TO DELTA JUNCTION

Now, back to the Alaska Highway where, in the Yukon chapter, we left off at the U.S. and Canada border. Your first stop in Interior Alaska, mandatory if you're coming in from Canada on the Alaska Highway, is the **U.S. Customs and Immigration Station** at mile 1221.8, right at the international boundary. The station sits sort of out in the middle of nowhere, with no large community nearby.

At mile 1229, similarly situated, the **U.S. Fish and Wildlife Service** maintains a log cabin visitor center with an observation deck and outdoor exhibits about Alaska's wildlife. There's more of the same indoors, along with animal mounts and lots of good information about Alaska's fish, birds, and other wild critters.

The **Naabia Niign Athabascan Indian Crafts** store (907–778–2297) is located at the junction of the Alaska Highway and the Northway Road, at mile 1,264. If you'd like to examine intricately and colorfully beaded moccasins, mukluks (boots), mitts, vests, and other apparel, this is an excellent place to do so. There's also a campground with full services at the site.

At mile 1302 you come to the Tetlin Junction, a meeting of the Alaska Highway and the **Taylor Highway,** which extends north to Eagle. The Taylor, in turn, provides access to the Canadian Yukon Territory's **Top of the World Highway** to Dawson City, Yukon. For information about these roads, see the sections after Dawson City in the chapter Canada's Yukon.

You'll come to the next major highway junction at mile 1,314, right in the middle of **Tok** (rhymes with poke), where the Alaska Highway, heading sort of west, meets the Tok Cutoff–Glenn Highway from southwesterly Anchorage. Just before the junction, you'll see the **Alaska Public Lands Information Center** (907–833–5667), where you can get tons of information about state and federal lands, waters, and outdoor recreation. Audiovisual aids, wildlife mounts, and helpful staff will provide you with the latest about places and things to do both on and off the beaten path. Also worth a visit is ◆ **Alaska's Mainstreet Visitor Center** (907–883–5775), operated by Tok's chamber of commerce. The center, also at the above-mentioned junction, is located in the largest log structure in the state. It features a number of mounted wildlife and birdlife dioramas. If you'd like to meet an Alaska character right out of *Northern Exposure*—except she's for real—check with the Mainstreet Information Center to see when Tok's best-known author, "Tent Lady" Donna Blasor-Bernhardt, will be on hand. She'll tell you about the year she and her family spent living in a tent, sometimes shivering through temperatures as low as 69 degrees *below* zero. You can visit the site at her **Winter Cabin Bed & Breakfast**, 3 blocks off the Alaska Highway at mile 1,316.5. Cabins are newly built log units, nonsmoking, fully furnished, with a shared bathhouse, and include continental breakfasts. The nightly charge is $60 to $80. Call (907) 883–5655.

Here in Tok the locals take sled dog racing, Alaska's official state sport, very seriously. You can see mushing demonstrations at the **Burnt Paw** gift shop, beyond mile 1,314 on the Alaska Highway, nightly except Sunday at 7:30 P.M. and at the **Westmark Hotel**, near the Alaska Highway–Tok Cutoff junction. (Check at the desk for times.) You can also take a sled ride at **Mukluk Land** theme park, at mile 1,317. Sleds, of course, are on wheels in the summer, since the snow is long gone. Incidentally, Donna Bernhardt's original tent is on display at the park.

Speaking of sled dog racing, winter visitors can see mushers and their dogs almost any weekend working out or racing on the Tok Dog Mushers Association trail, which starts at their log headquarters building at mile 1,312.8 on the Alaska Highway. Spectators can view the 20-mile course from many points along the highway.

If you'd like to start your day and your visit in a thoroughly Alaskan way, try the **sourdough pancake breakfast with Alaska reindeer sausage** at the Sourdough Campground, 1.5 miles south of the junction on the Tok Cutoff. The cost is $6.25. Phone (907) 883–5543.

The **Tok International Hostel** operates mid-May through mid-September in a big tent with ten beds in dorm "rooms" at each end and a kitchen/sitting area in between. Water is carried in, and restroom facilities are of the outhouse genre. Still, it's clean, comfortable, and the price, at $7.50 per person, is reasonable.

129

Bring your own sleeping bag. To get there, turn south onto Pringle Drive at mile 1,322.5 on the Alaska Highway, then follow the signs less than a mile. For reservations, call (907) 883–3745.

Offering a variety of accommodations, John and Jill Rusyniak's **Cleft of the Rock Bed and Breakfast**, 1.5 miles down Sundog Road, 3 miles northwest of Tok, has guest rooms and suites plus log and frame cabins. It's situated in a black spruce forest with bike trails nearby. The rates range from $55 to $85. Call (800) 478–5646. **Cheryl's Old Fashioned Bed and Breakfast** is located in **Rita's Campground and RV Park** (907–883–4342), at mile 1,315.7 on the Alaska Highway. Rita and Doug Euer's campground has been one of the Millers' favorite private camp sites since their first stay there in the 1960s. The B&B is a private log cabin in wooded surroundings, adjacent to an elevated Athabascan Indian food cache. (A cache is rather like a tiny one-room log cabin built on stilts eight feet or so off the ground and accessible only by ladder. Rural residents use them to store food out of the reach of bears and other wild creatures.) Breakfasts are continental; you can use campground grills and picnic tables anytime. The rates are $15 and up for the RV park, $155 for a double at the B&B.

When you get to **Delta Junction**, at mile 1,422, you've come to the end of the Alaska Highway. From that point on north, the road to Fairbanks is the **Richardson Highway**, and the mileposts beside the road indicate distance from Valdez. Delta Junction's Richardson Highway milepost is 266. For information about the Richardson from Delta Junction north, see the section in this chapter on the Richardson Highway.

THE GEORGE PARKS HIGHWAY—
NORTHERN SECTION: DENALI TO FAIRBANKS

The George Parks Highway, you'll recall, runs for nearly 360 miles from near Anchorage on the shores of Cook Inlet, to Fairbanks. In our Southcentral chapter, we followed the course of this excellent highway to Denali National Park and Preserve, where this section picks up this road once more.

For many, ◆**Denali National Park** is the high point of an Alaska vacation. (No pun was intended, but as a matter of fact, the top of Denali mountain, at 20,320 feet, *is* the highest point in

North America.) And in the surrounding parklands, visitors may well see more game—moose, grizzly bear, caribou, Dall mountain sheep, perhaps even wolves plus any number of smaller creatures and birds—than anywhere else they travel in the state.

It should be noted, however, that much of the park and its environs are by no means off the beaten path. In particular, the strip along the George Parks Highway near the mile 237 park entrance overwhelms with hotels, lodges, motels, cabins, RV parks, and varied visitor services. Most of the overnight accommodations there are roomy, nice, and comfortable, like **Sourdough Cabins,** at mile 238.8 (907–683–2773) and some of them, such as the **Denali Princess** (800–426–0500) and **Denali Parks Resorts** (800–276–7234) properties, are quite superior. But the sheer numbers of such places provide ample evidence that many thousands of visitors beat down this path every summer. So where, if you're a dedicated offbeat traveler, can you stay? And what can you do away from the crowds?

Actually you have options, not the least of which is to pitch a tent or park your RV at one of seven National Park Service campgrounds within the park itself, then hike in the backcountry hills, valleys, mountain slopes, and open spaces in splendid isolation. Be aware, however, that overnight backcountry hikes require a permit, and the number of backcountry users permitted in a given area is limited. *Another caution:* Campsites within the park are often hard to come by, so it's wise to reserve months ahead if you can by calling the reservations line, (800) 622–7275. If all advance-reservation camping slots have been assigned for the days you plan to visit, you may be able to reserve space up to two days in advance on a first-come first-served basis at the **Park Service visitor center** on the main park road .5 mile inside the park boundary.

If you enjoy day hikes, check the bulletin boards and with the ranger on duty at the information center for the times, location, and degree of hiking skills required for various ranger-escorted treks not only in the park entrance area but at bus-accessible points along the single road that bisects the park and at the **Eielson Visitor Center** and **Wonder Lake**, near the road's end.

If you're not a camper, consider spending a few days at award-winning ◆**Camp Denali** at the western end of the park road, just outside the National Park Service boundary. This is one of

Alaska's best-loved backcountry eco-tourism lodges and has been since its founding nearly a half century ago. Guests enjoy breathtaking views of Denali and other peaks of the Alaska Range from hillside log cabins. Meals are served family style in the main lodge building. Short walks and wildlife-viewing hikes, guided by experienced wilderness interpreters provide fascinating insight into the nature of things. Canoeing, biking, rafting, flight-seeing, gold panning, and evening natural history talks provide further options. Call (907) 683–2290 in the summer, (603) 675–2248 during winter.

Also at the far western end of the road lies **Kantishna Roadhouse** and the former gold mining town of Kantishna, now a wilderness resort. The accommodations are in a new log lodge and cabins. Attractions include the Smokey Joe Saloon, escorted nature walks, wagon tours, and horseback rides plus mountain biking, gold panning, and fishing. Rates, including round-trip bus transportation from Denali train depot, all meals, and most activities, start at $260 per person per night in a twin room. Call (800) 942–7420.

Another option, this one a remote lodge accessible only by a twenty- to thirty-minute bush flight from Denali Airport, also lies outside the park boundary. ♦**Denali Wilderness Lodge**, in pristine Wood River Valley, contains twenty-eight hand-hewn log buildings set in a tiny enclave among 2,000 square miles of wilderness. Structures include a rustic but luxurious main lodge and wildlife museum (one hundred game mounts from around the world), more than a dozen cabins, each with private bath, and various support cabins. Guests hike and ride horseback on guided and unguided sight-seeing and photography treks. Meals are bountiful and of gourmet quality. Price for a single-day tour runs $210 per guest; overnight tours cost $295 per guest for the first night in a twin room, $200 for additional nights. For more information, call (800) 541–9779.

Within Denali Park itself, you'll spot most wildlife during bus or motor-coach tours that run daily on the single park road. Although the Park Service no longer offers free shuttles on the road as it once did, a new program of low-cost bus rides represents a "best buy" option for frugal travelers. The price now for a trip on the road ranges from $12 to $30 per adult, depending on a visitor's destination in the park. Discounts are available for three- and six-day passes. Note that travelers can now book shuttle reservations and buy tickets through the same toll-free number they can use to reserve campsites, (800) 622–PARK. Narrated tours in roomier coaches cost $28 for a 15-mile tour lasting three to four hours, or $51 for a 50-mile excursion lasting six to eight hours. The latter tour includes a box lunch. Call Denali Park Resorts at (800) 276–7234 for reservations.

My wife and I enjoyed one of our pleasantest-ever water trips during a visit to the park a few years ago. We booked **Denali Raft Adventures'** two-hour, splashy, exciting Canyon Run rubber raft experience through rapids called Cable Car, Coffee Grinder, and Ice Worm. The company has two- and four-hour options, including one in which you can wield a paddle as part of the crew. Two-hour raft trips run $36, four-hour trips, $56; four-hour paddle trips are $61. Denali Raft headquarters is located at mile 238, .5 mile north of the park entrance on the George Parks Highway. Call (907) 683–2234.

The **Denali Hostel** sits about a dozen miles north of the park entrance and provides bunks at $22 per guest. The fee includes coffee and muffins each morning, Visitors come here from all over the world. If you arrive by train, look for the hostel van. With only seventeen beds, reservations are a must. Call (907) 683–1295.

There are, in addition to park ranger–escorted hikes, several quality commercial firms that offer treks and climbs that vary from tender to tough. Whether, for instance, you're gung ho to climb all the way to the summit of North America's highest peak—a rigorous, dangerous climb only strong and experienced mountaineers should attempt—or you'd be satisfied with a less demanding hike across Curry Ridge ("which any fit person can enjoy"), **Alaska-Denali Guiding, Inc.** provides an ample variety of hiking and climbing opportunities. The Talkeetna-based company specializes in guiding small groups in the Denali National Park area. Prices range from $740 for five-day hikes to $2,650 for Denali summit ascents. Call (907) 733–2649.

Among several offerings from Denali-based **Osprey Expeditions** is a six-day combination horseback–rafting adventure in Denali National Park's backyard. For three days, clients ride through high country with excellent prospects of seeing Dall mountain sheep, bear, moose, and caribou. The final three days include rafting on the glacier-fed Yanert Fork of the Nenana River, through class II, III, and IV rapids. This tour costs $1,550.

The company also operates in the Copper River Valley, Talkeetna, and other locales. Call (907) 683–2734. **Mountain Trip, Inc.**, with headquarters in Anchorage, is another professional guiding firm, this one with a record of fifteen years of leading climbers up Denali as well as other mountains. They also package mountain biking excursions on the Denali Highway and other such roads. Their sixteen- to twenty-four-day Mt. McKinley West Buttress and Traverse expedition runs $2,600. Call (907) 345–6499.

For the traveler seeking an easy but unmechanized way to sight-see, **Sugarloaf Wilderness Trail Rides** offers horseback rides along the northern boundary of the national park through Dry Creek Valley as well as other locales and options. Costs start at $60 for one and a half hours. Call (907) 683–2402 for reservations. The company will provide transportation from your hotel.

Back on the George Parks Highway, roughly 300 miles north of Anchorage, you come to **Nenana**, on the Tanana River. (Nenana is pronounced nee-NAN-a; Tanana is TA-naw-naw.) Don't breeze through without stopping at least to see the **Alaska Railroad Museum**, in the old (1923) railroad depot building alongside the tracks on Front Street. The old-fashioned pressed tin ceiling is a particular curiosity, and if you happen to be a pin collector, as I am, you can pick up lapel pins commemorating not only the Alaska Railroad but various other U.S. and Canadian rail systems as well.

Also worth a look-see is the 1905 log **St. Mark's Episcopal Church**, whose altar is adorned with elaborate Athabascan beadwork. It's located at Front and A Streets, east of the depot. At Nenana's sod-roof log **visitor center** on A Street, just off the Parks Highway, volunteers will tell you about Alaska's most popular annual statewide guessing game—a contest in which the winner can earn more than $150,000 by predicting when the ice will break up on the Tanana River. For information, call (907) 832–9953. From Nenana, **Alaska Tolovana Adventures** will rent you a canoe for $25 a day, guide you on two- to seven-day canoe tours, or take you by riverboat to the restored and historic (1923) **Tolovana Lodge** in the Minto Wildlife Range. Call (907) 832–5569 for details. If you want to overnight in Nenana, consider Carl and Gerrie Jauhola's **Finnish Alaskan Bed and Breakfast**, at mile 302 on the Parks Highway. The B&B nestles on a birch-forested hillside, with a view of the Alaska Range.

Guests are free to enjoy the Jauholas' outdoor Finnish sauna. Rates start at $50 for a double. Call (907) 832–5628.

Past mile 325 the Parks Highway enters the Fairbanks North Star Borough (county). The old (1936) **Ester Gold Camp,** (800–676–6925) which has a hotel, saloon, and dining facilities, lies about ½ mile off the highway, beyond mile 351. At mile 358 you arrive at the exit to the city of **Fairbanks**.

Glenn Highway–Tok Cutoff— Northern Section: Glennallen to Tok

A word of review about the Glenn Highway–Tok Cutoff from Anchorage to Tok. The route, you'll recall, is actually three segments: 189 miles of the Glenn from Anchorage to Glennallen, 14 miles on the Richardson, and a final 125 miles on the Tok Cutoff. This section begins where the section in the Southcentral Alaska chapter left off, at **Glennallen**, where the Copper Valley Chamber of Commerce operates a log cabin ◆ **visitor center**. The center itself is worth a stop and a picture, since plants actually grow from the cabin's sod roof. This is authentic Alaskana. Many a sourdough used this same material for insulation on log cabins in the remote bush country.

Fourteen miles farther, at the Richardson Highway's mile 128.6, the Tok Cutoff begins. **Gakona Junction** is mile 0. Tok, our destination, is located at milepost 125. At mile 2, stop at least for an evening meal (no lunches) at the **Carriage House** dining room of the **Gakona Lodge & Trading Post**. The lodge, built in 1905, originally served travelers on the old Richardson Trail and is now on the National Register of Historic Places. The dinner menu ranges from $6.00 cheeseburgers to $13.95 filets.

At mile 53 on the Tok Cutoff, the **Grizzly Lake Ranch** offers B&B accommodations plus **Knight Riders Horse and Buggy Rides** along back roads and forested trails. B&B rates start at $45, and the buggy rides cost $60 for an hour for two. Call (907) 822–5214.

Just past mile 65 you come to the 45-mile **Nabesna Road** and one of your few opportunities to actually drive into **Wrangell–St. Elias National Park**, one of the wildest, most mountainous and least developed in the U.S. park system. Just beyond the junction, at Slana, you'll see the Slana **National Park Service Ranger Station.** Inquire about road conditions, especially the last dozen miles or so, which can be quite rough. Just before mile 4, you enter the park itself. For the dedicated backwoods aficionado ❖**Huck Hobbit's Homestead Campground and Retreat** has two 12-by-12-foot log cabins to rent. To get to the homestead, turn left on the side road at mile 4, drive 3 miles to the signed parking place for your vehicle, then walk an additional mile of trail to Huck Hobbit's place. He'll meet you at the trailhead if you feel nervous about the hike. He will also rent you camping space and a tent if you need one, has canoes available, and will point you in the direction of the best fishing and berry picking. The rates are $25.00 a night for a cabin and an additional $5.00 for breakfast or $10.00 for a tent and camping place. Call first for reservations at (907) 822–3196. There are several other lodges and overnight accommodations toward the end of the road, including **End of the Road Bed and Breakfast** (907–822–3426) at mile 42. The rates are $60 for two. Driving beyond this point is not recommended unless you have four-wheel drive.

The Glenn–Richardson–Tok Cutoff route from Anchorage to Tok ends at mile 125. (For information about Tok, see the section in this chapter on the Alaska Highway.)

THE RICHARDSON HIGHWAY—NORTHERN SECTION: GAKONA JUNCTION TO FAIRBANKS

In this section we take a look at the northern portion of the historic Valdez-to-Fairbanks Richardson Highway, commencing at the Gakona Junction where the Richardson meets the Tok Cutoff at mile 128.5.

The terrain along the Richardson continues to reveal tall, majestic mountains, countless big and little lakes, and thick forests. You stand a good chance of seeing moose alongside the road (pay special attention to small ponds, where a huge animal may rise up and break the surface after having scoured the pond's bottom for succulent plantlife) as well as caribou and perhaps grizzly bear. The Trans-Alaska Pipeline shows itself at various times.

If you missed out on king salmon fishing either in the saltwater of Southeast or Southcentral Alaska, you can, surprisingly, make up for it here on the Gulkana River. **Gulkana Fish Guides** offer jet boat and raft trips June through July from their headquarters at mile 128.5. The rates are $95 for five hours. Call (800) 962–1933.

If you'd like to go hiking and let a lovable llama from South America carry your lunch and gear, the **Paxson Llama Works** offers a range of treks, from $17.50 for 1 or 2 miles to $125 for a full day's outing. Murray and Kristy Howk also offer evening scenic (not whitewater) raft floats to view wildlife and waterfowl. The rate is $48 for two and a half hours. You can overnight at the nearby historic (1903) **Paxson Lodge** at mile 185.5. Llama trek reservations are available through the lodge; call (907) 822-3330.

The Richardson Highway junctions at **Paxson** with the **Denali Highway** at mile 185.5, and if you don't plan to drive all 135 miles to Cantwell and Denali National Park, at least consider round-tripping some of the first 21 paved miles of the road. The panoramic views—of glaciers, lakes, and majestic, snow-covered peaks—from the tops of hills, rises, and turnoff viewing areas are just breathtaking.

At mile 266 the Richardson Highway and the **Alaska Highway** meet at **Delta Junction.** Actually, this is where the Alaska Highway ends. The Richardson continues north to Fairbanks and mileposts beside the road continue to measure distance from Valdez.

The **Delta Junction Information Center** (907-895-9941), at the junction of the two highways, is a good place to stop for visitor information and road condition updates. Especially if you had your picture taken at the Alaska Highway milepost 0 monument in Dawson Creek, B.C., you'll want to do the same at the highway's end monument at the information center.

The name **Delta International Hostel** perhaps conjures up an image of sophisticated, cosmopolitan lodging. It isn't. It's kind of hard to find, bare bones (there's no electricity, and toilets are "down the path"), has just one big sleeping room, and it's constructed, in fact, on stilts about 12 feet above the ground. Hostelers who lodge there give high marks for the friendly management, the tranquility of the setting, and the thoroughly Alaskan experience. Bring your own sleeping bag. You definitely need wheels. Drive just north of Delta Junction to mile 271.7 on the Richardson Highway, then turn on the Tanana Loop Road, driving for about a mile until you come to the Tanana Loop Extension. Drive another mile, turn left when you get to (no joke) Main Street USA, and keep going for approximately a mile to the end of the road. It sounds confusing, but you'll see signs along the way. The hostel is open in summer only. For reservations call (907) 895-5074. The rate is $7.00 a night.

Peggy's Alaskan Cabbage Patch Bed and Breakfast offers accommodations in a modern Alaska home and serves up old-fashioned full breakfasts. To get there, from the visitors center, drive 2 miles toward Fairbanks on the Richardson Highway. Turn right at Jack Warren Road and go about 6.3 miles to a dirt road called Arctic Grayling. Peggy's is the second driveway on the right. Says Peggy Christopherson: "Look for the cabbage patch and the pigs." Rates are $60 for a double. Phone (907) 895–4200.

Among Alaskans, at least, Delta Junction is probably best known for its herd of 500 or so bison (American buffalo). They're the outgrowth of small numbers of the animals established there in the 1920s and roam freely over the 70,000-acre **Delta Bison Range.** Occasionally the bison spill over into adjacent barley farm fields, and farmers are not amused. If you want to see the herd, you stand a pretty good chance at the visitor viewpoint just past mile 241 on the Richardson. If you'd like to tour the workings of a **Trans-Alaska Pipeline pumping station**, you can do so at mile 258. Call (907) 869–3270 for times and details. Soon after, at mile 275, a terrific photo op awaits where the pipeline crosses over the Tanana River.

Not to be missed is ◆ **Rika's Roadhouse** at **Big Delta State Historical Park**, just upstream from the pipeline river crossing. The roadhouse is right out of Alaska's history. Built in 1910 and purchased by Rika Wallen in 1923, it served for decades as a major overnight stop on the Richardson wagon road and highway for travelers between Valdez and Fairbanks. Today the roadhouse has been restored, as have a sod-roofed museum building, an old U.S. Army Signal Corps station, and other historic structures. Staff in 1920s garb will guide you around the park, where you'll find artisans at work as well as live farm animals. The **Packhouse Restauran**t is one of the best you'll find along Alaska's road system and features breads from the Alaska Baking Company on-site and homemade soups. There is no admission charge to visit the roadhouse, but tent or RV sites at the state campground run $6.00 per night. Phone (907) 895–4201.

Harding Lake, 1.5 miles off the Richardson Highway from mile 321.5, is a great place to swim, have a beach picnic, or camp overnight. Avoid it Friday night through Sunday, however. Lots of Fairbanksans drive down for the weekend, and it gets pretty crowded. The camping fee is $6.00 per night.

As you approach Fairbanks, don't let your desire to get there lead you to bypass the **Chena Lakes Recreation Area**, accessible from a 2-mile side road at mile 346.7. Whether you're RV camping or simply looking for a superb picnic spot, this place is definitely worth a look-see. (It's not to be confused, incidentally, with the Chena River State Recreation Site in Fairbanks, nor with the Chena River State Recreation Area on the Chena Hot Springs Road.) The Chena Lakes Rec Area is a sprawling, lake-oriented, 2,178-acre site with scores of campsites, lots of picnic areas, swimming beaches, even a children's playground. There's at least one island with camping and picnic facilities. Again, local Alaskans tend to use it most heavily on weekends and holidays.

Also worth a stop before you arrive in Fairbanks is **Santa Claus House** in (where else?) **North Pole**, Alaska. The large shop, located at mile 349, is packed with Christmas-type gifts, including Santa Claus letters for kids that Santa will mail and postmark from North Pole in December.

The Richardson ends at mile 364. If you started your Alaska Highway-Richardson trip in Dawson Creek, B.C., you've traveled 1,520 miles.

THE STEESE HIGHWAY: FAIRBANKS TO CIRCLE CITY

Although it's paved for only 44 of its 162 miles from Fairbanks, the Steese Highway is one of the most satisfying among the backroads in Alaska. Along the way you see the sites of old mining camps and new ones, hot springs spas, gorgeous rolling hills and mountains, small authentic Alaska communities, some of the most intensely colorful wildflower viewing to be found anywhere, and the Chatanika and Chena River Recreation Areas. We've found midweek travel easier, with less gravel dust in the air than on weekends, when many Alaskans head for hot springs spas and good fishing along the route.

You've barely been traveling northwest along Steese Highway from its beginning at the junction of the Richardson and Parks Highways when, at mile 4.9, you come to the **Chena Hot Springs Road**. The road is paved and generally well maintained but drive carefully; it can be bumpy. For a good portion of its nearly 57 miles, the road travels through the **Chena River Recreation Area**, with lots of scenic spots for camping, picnics, fishing, and wildlife viewing.

About 23 miles down the road, you'll come to Pleasant Valley Road. Turn right, drive .75 mile, then turn right again for .5 mile to arrive at **Northern Light Runners Dog Sled Rides and Kennel Tours**. In winter you can book sled dog expeditions that run from a half day locally to a week in the Brooks Range. Summer or winter you can tour the ninety-six dog kennels and meet some of the champion canines who have raced Iditarod, Yukon Quest, and other major sled dog events. Operator Kathy Swenson was the first woman musher to win Europe's Alpirod International race. The admission charge for tours is $10. For information, call (907) 488–7216.

If you want to stock up on groceries or other supplies along the way, stop at mile 23.5 on the hot springs road at **Tacks' General Store and Greenhouse Cafe**, a genuine, old-fashioned general store and an institution in these parts. The greenhouse is full of flowers and colorful hanging baskets. Generous breakfasts, incidentally, are served until 8:00 P.M. The home-baked pies are arguably the best in Alaska.

At road's end you'll find lodging, a restaurant, bar, and other facilities at ◆ **The Resort at Chena Hot Springs,** with its spring-fed pool, hot tub, and 2,800-square-foot redwood deck with ten-person spa. Accommodations range from luxury hotel rooms (starting at $70 in summer; $105 in winter) to rustic cabins that rent for $35 a night, summer only. Activities, besides soaking, include horseback riding, canoeing, hiking, mountain biking, and hayrides. Phone (907) 452–7867.

Back on the Steese Highway, one of the best places to see the **Trans-Alaska Pipeline** up close is about 10 miles north of downtown Fairbanks, just off the highway. The pipe, in fact, is elevated, so you can stand right under it and have your picture taken while countless gallons of crude oil flow over your head.

Also at the site is an Alyeska Pipeline Service Company information center with interpretive displays, which is open daily, May to September. Phone (907) 456–9391.

The **Old F.E. Gold Camp**, at mile 27.5 at **Chatanika**, is right out of Alaska's glory mining days. The F.E. (for Fairbanks Exploration) Company operated from 1926 to 1957 and is today on the National Register of Historic Places. On-site you'll see lots of vintage mining gear from the forties, thirties, and even earlier. In the buildings you'll come across Alaska artifacts and antiques, including a 200-year-old brass bed. The camp offers overnight accommodations as well as items of Alaskana. Rooms in the bunkhouse or cabins start at $27.50. The restaurant features fresh Alaskan fish dinners and on Saturday and Sunday mornings, sourdough pancake buffets.

If you happen to be traveling on the Steese Highway about the time of the Summer Solstice (June 20 or 21), plan to celebrate the change of seasons the way many Fairbanksans do—by driving to **Eagle Summit** (mile 108) for a midnight picnic and a view of the sun dipping close to the horizon *but not quite setting*, then rising again to start a new day and a new summer season. The summit lies south of the Arctic Circle, but this phenomena is possible because of its 3,624-foot elevation.

◆ **Arctic Circle Hot Springs** (907–520–5113), near Central Alaska on the Steese Highway, is a don't-miss-it experience. This is one of Alaska's oldest (1930) visitor destinations and an Alaskan favorite. Today, though thoroughly modern, rooms at the resort continue to reflect the style and furnishings of the early 1900s. If you prefer something more rustic, you can rent a log cabin.

The warm waters of the Olympic-size swimming pool are, of course, the resort's best known feature, but the spa also offers Jacuzzis, hot tubs, a colorful log saloon, an RV park, and hillside campsites. At mealtimes the home-cooked food includes fresh vegetables from the resort gardens. You can bunk in the fourth-floor hostel dorm for $20 per person or rent bare-bones cabins for as little as $59 per couple (no running water, bathrooms, or kitchens). Deluxe cabins and apartments go for $90 per couple. To get to Circle Hot Springs, take the turnoff at mile 127.8 on the Steese and drive to mile 8.3 on the Circle Hot Springs Road.

The Steese Highway dead ends at mile 162, at the picturesque community of **Circle**, a community of mostly Native Alaskan residents. The town got its name when early prospectors thought it straddled the Arctic Circle. It doesn't—the circle lies 50 miles north—but the town does sit on the banks of the Yukon River, which made it a busy transportation and trading hub during the early and middle years of the century.

A company with the unlikely name of **L&L Fishing & Hunting Plus** provides hourly, half-day or full-day tours on the Yukon River for $40, $62.50, and $125, respectively, aboard a 20-foot, covered and heated riverboat, with a platform for viewing and photography. Sights include wildlife, abundant bird life,

141

Fishweel

a Native burial area, a walking tour through an upriver locale of abandoned homes, and an active trapper's site. You can also view fish wheels, which are large wheels with big-mounted scoops on their outer rims. The current of the river turns the wheel and these scoops, in turn, capture fish swimming by and deposit them in baskets. Call (907) 488-4028.

142

ELLIOTT HIGHWAY: FAIRBANKS TO MANLEY HOT SPRINGS

Most of the travelers you'll meet on the **Elliott Highway**, especially beyond the road's mile 73.1 junction with the Dalton Highway to Deadhorse, will be Alaskans. And chances are they'll be heading to or coming from one of Fairbanks's favorite getaway destinations, **Manley Hot Springs**. It's one of three popular hot springs spas in the region, the others being Chena Hot Springs and Arctic Circle Hot Springs, at the ends of access roads off the Steese Highway.

The Elliott Highway takes off from the Steese about 11 miles north of Fairbanks, and for the first 28 miles or so it's paved. Beyond that it's gravel, but not a bad road at all, although it gets slick in places when it rains. There are, as well, some roller coaster rises and falls, but if you keep your speed at a reasonable rate, it's no problem.

At mile 1.2 on the Elliott, you come to **El Dorado Gold Mine**, a worthwhile stop that's both a commercial operation and a visitor attraction. (For a description, see the Fairbanks section.)

At mile 49.5 you can visit **Wildwood General Store and Fox Farm Tour**, run by the Joe and Nancy Carlson family. Ask one of the family members about how the store had its start as a lemonade stand operated by a few of the Carlsons' sixteen adopted children.

Roughly 21 miles later you come to a junction with a 2-mile access road to **Livengood** (pronounced LYV-en-good). It was a major gold camp at times in the first half of the century, but now only one hundred or so live in the area. Just past mile 73, the Elliott junctions with the Dalton Highway supply road to the North Slope, Deadhorse, and Prudhoe Bay.

At mile 94.5 you come to a generous double pullout on the south side of the road. From here you have a good view of Minto Flats, the Tanana River, and the foothills of the Alaska Range. After mile 97 keep your eyes peeled northerly for great views of Mts. Sawtooth, Wolverine, and Elephant. At mile 110 the highway junctions with an 11-mile access road to the Native village of **Minto** (there's a lodge that provides meals and a general store, if you're looking for a place to eat or buy snacks), and 40 miles farther down the Elliott, you come to ◆**Manley Hot Springs**.

Very Alaskan, this place. **Manley Roadhouse** is one of a vanishing breed of accommodations that once were common along the sled dog and horse trails of the north. This one was built in 1906, when the community served as a trading center for mining districts in the area. The roadhouse accommodated riverboat crews, miners, and commercial travelers. Today owner Robert E. Lee offers visitors the chance to revisit those days in his roadhouse with single and double sleeping accommodations, a rustic, antiques-filled sitting room, and the Roadhouse Bar, with Alaska's largest back bar. Rooms start at $150 for doubles, $65 for cabins. For reservations, call (907) 672–3161.

Manley Hot Springs Resort offers a swimming pool fed by mineral hot springs, restaurant, bar, rooms, and log cabins as well as an RV park, laundromat, and showers. From the resort you can rent boats for grayling, sheefish, and pike fishing or book tours to fish camps and gold mines. Winter visitors can sign up for sled dog tours. Due to the northern latitudes and being away from the lights and haze of the big cities, the *aurora borealis* (northern lights) are at their best in locales such as these. Rooms start at $650. Call (907) 672–3611 for reservations.

Denali Highway: Paxson to Cantwell

They used to call the **Denali Highway** one of the worst roads in Alaska. It's still bumpy in places, a washboard in others, and you do have to watch for potholes. But if you keep your speed down and your eyes open, you can drive its 135 miles from Paxson on the Richardson Highway to Cantwell on the George Parks Highway without fear or foreboding. At its Cantwell end, it's only a few minutes to the entrance of Denali National Park. Because of the road's relatively high elevation, right at timberline or a bit above, you can enjoy lots of high tundra views. Sights of Alaska Range peaks are frequent and fabulous.

Perhaps because the Denali's old and unsavory reputation won't quite die, the road receives surprisingly less traffic than you would expect, considering its location. And because of its sparse traffic, the highway today is much appreciated by stream and lake anglers who don't care for bumper-to-bumper "combat fishing" crowds. There are several state and private RV campgrounds along the way as well as private lodges.

144

Off-road vehicle enthusiasts enjoy its designated routes, and mountain bikers and hikers also regard highly its marked and unmarked trails. *A caution, though:* If you're heading far off the road, be sure to carry a compass. It's distressingly easy to get turned around in the woods, or even in open tundra, if clouds close in. From your first entry onto the road at Paxson (mile 0), keep your eye out for brown (grizzly) bears, moose, and other wild critters. They're often spotted.

The Denali is paved at its start, but the asphalt ends at mile 21. **Tangle Lakes Lodge** is located at mile 22. If you're a bird nut, as the Millers are, stop to talk with the owners, Rich and Linda Holmstrom. Rich can convey some of the most accurate birding information on the highway, including the whereabouts of ptarmigans (Alaska's state bird), Arctic warblers, gyrfalcons, wandering tattlers, and many other oft-sighted species. The Holmstroms offer cabin, canoe, and three meals for two persons for $135. For more information, call (907) 822–7302.

Comes mile 135.5, and you've arrived in **Cantwell,** which began life as a rail line flag stop and continues to be served by the Alaska Railroad on its run between Anchorage and Fairbanks. Newer businesses have located near the intersection of the Denali and George Parks Highways, but if you'd like to peek into Alaska's yesteryear, stop by for a meal, lodging, or beverage at the **Cantwell Lodge** (907–768–2300) in the older section of town, 2 miles west of the junction. Meals (summer only) range from $7.00 for a hamburger and fries to $17.00 for a steak.

145

ALASKA'S FAR NORTH

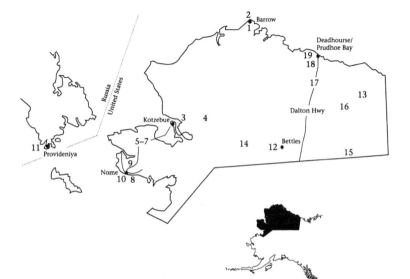

1. Barrow
2. Arctic Safari Tours
3. Kotzebue
4. Village/Wilderness Excursion
5. Kotzebue Cultural Fish Camp Experience
6. Museum of the Arctic
7. Arctic Circle Adventures
8. gold dredges
9. Pilgrim Hot Springs
10. Olson Air Service's Siberian Sight-seer
11. Bering Air
12. Sourdough Outfitters
13. Kongakut and Sheenjek Rivers
14. Peace of Selby
15. Fort Yukon
16. Arctic Village
17. Dalton Highway
18. Deadhorse
19. Pipeline Mile Zero

Alaska's Far North

Alaska's Far North, more than any other region, is a land of extremes. As its name implies, this region lies farther north than any other in the state or nation. It's the only part of the United States lapped by the Arctic Ocean's summer waters and barricaded by its winter pack ice. At its northernmost reaches, the region enjoys the country's longest period of daylight—eighty-four continuous days of constant daylight from May 10 to August 2. In contrast, during the dark days of winter, the sun literally does not rise for sixty-seven days. At least one of the region's wildlife species, the polar bear, can be found nowhere else in the nation. And, of course, Alaska's Far North is home to North America's largest oil field, Prudhoe Bay.

Although some may imagine the Far North as drab and lifeless, the tundra country, especially in summer, can turn virtually ablaze with wildflowers, berries, and other colorful plantlife. Millions of birds migrate to the northern tundra from North and even South America each spring. Especially during flight-seeing tours, but during road trips as well, you stand a good chance of seeing grizzly bears, caribou, and moose.

Among Native peoples of the region, there are two groups of Eskimos: Inupiats on the shores of the Alaska mainland and the Yu'pik Eskimos, who reside in Gambell and Savoonga on St. Lawrence Island, a large island in the Bering Sea only 40 miles from Russian Siberia. A small number of Nunamiut inland Eskimos live at Anaktuvuk Pass, about 260 miles north-northwest of Fairbanks, while Athabascan Indian communities may be found as far north as Arctic Village in the Brooks Range, 290 miles north of Fairbanks and roughly 100 miles north of Fort Yukon.

Major Communities of the Far North

◆ **Barrow** is just about as far off the beaten path as you can get and still have your feet planted on North American soil. Located 330 miles north of the Arctic Circle, the mostly Eskimo town is, in fact, the northernmost community in the Western Hemisphere. That's only one of the superlatives you can collect during a visit here. Barrow is also the seat of government for the North Slope Borough, which at 88,000 square miles, ranks as the largest municipality in the world. (A borough, in Alaska, is rather like a county in the Lower Forty-eight, but not really... It gets kind of complicated.)

In spite of its remoteness, you can get to Barrow easily. Alaska Airlines, provides daily jet service from Anchorage and Fairbanks, and once you've arrived, you'll find several ground tour organizations with one- and two-day excursions designed to maximize your time at the Top of the World. Biggest of these is **Tundra Tours**, which also operates the fully modern **Top of the World Hotel.** On Tundra's tours you'll travel beside the Arctic Ocean, pass through an old U.S. Navy research site, visit a Distant Early Warning System installation, take a short trek on the tundra for a look at an old-time traditional hunting camp, and finally reach the northernmost point your bus can take you. From there you can disembark and go beachcombing, and maybe even stick your toe in the chill Arctic Ocean waters. Contact Tundra Tours or the Top of the World Hotel at (907) 852–3900. A tour of Barrow from Fairbanks, booked by Alaska Airlines Vacations (800–468–2248), costs $363 including airfare; if you stay overnight it costs $405.

Northern Alaska Tour Company offers village tours as well, emphasizing the Inupiat Eskimo culture with a program of traditional dance and song plus demonstrations of skin sewing, Native games, and the Eskimo blanket toss. The tours also explore Arctic shores. One-day tours run $365 from Fairbanks and $525 from Anchorage. Call (907) 474–8600.

And here's still another Far North superlative: Sheila Taranto operates the world's northernmost limo service, **Tundra Taxi and Limo Service.** She also runs ◆ **Arctic Safari Tours,** serving small groups guided personally by Sheila, who's lived in the Arctic for fourteen years. During the tour you may see caribou (or even a polar bear in winter!) plus beach and village sites and lots of bird life. Sheila can also rent you a car ($75 a day for a Lincoln Continental) or truck ($60) if you want to explore on your own.

Another hotel choice in Barrow is the **Barrow Airport Inn**, with rates at $100 per night. Call (907) 852–2525.

One final superlative for Barrow: **Pepe's North of the Border** is indisputably the farthest north Mexican restaurant in North America. By Lower Forty-eight standards it's expensive (everything has to be flown in from "down south"), but the food is good and you can meet the locals there. Phone (907) 852–8200.

149

Alaska's largest Eskimo community, ◆ **Kotzebue**, lies 26 miles north of the Arctic Circle, 550 air miles from Anchorage, and 200 miles from the shores of the Russian Far East. This fascinating Eskimo community, truth to tell, is probably easiest seen as part of a package tour. You can, if you want, put all the elements together yourself, but there's really only one hotel, the principal transportation option is a tour bus, and the sights you probably want to see are covered in regular bus tours. The principal tour operator is **Tour Arctic** (907–442–3305).

The easiest way to book one-day or overnight visits is through **Alaska Airlines' Vacations** (800–468–2248), whose airfare-inclusive tours from Anchorage start at $330 for one day and $445 for two days, including an overnight at the fully modern **Nullagvik Hotel**. The carrier also packages combination tours of Kotzebue and Nome from $445. Tour Arctic offers an add-on ◆ **Village/Wilderness Excursion,** which features a bush flight to the Kobuk Valley. During this trip you'll flight-see the **Selawik Wildlife Range**, the **Great Kobuk Sand Dunes**, and **Kobuk Valley National Park**. You'll land at an Inupiat Eskimo village for lunch and a guided walk to view the villagers' subsistence lifestyle. The $225 cost includes the hotel in Kotzebue.

Another worthwhile extension tour, just outside of town, is Tour Alaska's ◆ **Kotzebue Cultural Fish Camp Experience,** where you learn firsthand about Inupiat tools, clothing, food preparation, and other aspects of traditional Native life in the Arctic. The cost, including an extra night at the hotel, is $140. Other opportunities in most packages include a **tundra walk** to see wild flowers and berries plus a stop at the **National Park Service visitor information center**.

The Northwest Alaska Native Association (NANA) regional Native corporation's ◆ **Museum of the Arctic** is certainly a must-see on anyone's Kotzebue itinerary. Here, in a two-hour program set within a huge, world-class **wildlife diorama** containing scores of mounted Alaskan animals, your Eskimo hosts put on a panoramic slide show and introduce you to Eskimo dancing, sewing, leathercraft, ivory carving, and the culture of the hardy people who live in these climes. Afterward the action moves to the attached **jade factory**, where you can see products made from the precious gem available in these parts. Finally, outdoors, you get to witness the famed **Eskimo blanket toss**.

Jumpers are propelled 20 or 30 feet into the air by pullers, including visitors, around a large, walrus hide blanket. The museum hours are 9:15 A.M. to 3:00 P.M. The admission charge, if you're not on an inclusive package tour, is $20. For more information, call (907) 442–3304.

More adventurous than the standard airline tour (or perhaps in addition to it) is LaVonne Hendricks' ◆ **Arctic Circle Adventures** tours, whose options range from one-day excursions labeled Tundra Hiking and Bird Watching, Local Ethnic Tour, and Inupiat Cultural Adventure to overnight tours at a beach-front commercial salmon fish camp about 5 miles from Kotzebue via a four-wheel-drive road. Hostess Hendricks is a former village public health nurse who traveled throughout the region for fourteen years. Her beach camp nestles beneath 250-foot bluffs. Guests stay in quaint rustic private cabins with "turn-of-the-century toilet facilities" (outhouses). Family-style meals, with local folks as dinner guests, feature meat, fish, and once-in-a-lifetime appetizers and greens harvested from the tundra. Breakfasts consist of sourdough pancakes, reindeer sausage, fresh trout and salmon. The cabin rate of $95 per person includes transportation from and to the airport, and meals. Call (907) 442–3509 in summer, (907) 276–0976 in winter.

In addition to having its own worthwhile attractions, Kotzebue serves as a major jumping-off place for expeditions to the surrounding bush. From the community, you can fly **Baker Aviation** (907–442–3108) to the nearby village of **Kiana** (the round-trip is $88) for modern lodgings and riverboat trips via **Kobuk River Jets**, hosted by Inupiat Eskimos Lorry and Nellie Schuerch. On their trips you can tour **Kobuk Valley National Park**, see incredible sand dunes in the Arctic, view wildlife, sample traditional foods, and experience the unique Inupiat culture. Overnight B&B rate is $85 per person. A tour on the Kobuk River, including one night's lodging in Kiana, costs $250 per person. Guided fishing is also available and the Schuerchs also rent kayaks and inflatables for do-it-yourselfers. Call (907) 475–2149 for more information.

Another backcountry option is Ed and Ruth Iten's **Kotzebue Sound Charters** aboard the 28-foot cabin vessel *Katie Marie* for sight-seeing remote Arctic beaches, fishing, and birding along Kotzebue Sound's major nesting sites for waterfowl, shorebirds, and songbirds. Rates start at $90 for a half day. In summer contact Arctic Travel at (800) 478–3501; in winter call the Itens in Ambler at (907) 445–2149.

Lower Forty-eight residents seem to know at least three things about **Nome**. First, It was the site of a lively gold stampede from 1898 through the early years of this century. Second, each year in March, the 1,000-mile Iditarod Sled Dog Classic finishes there under a massive timber-burled winner's arch, having started some ten days to two weeks earlier in Anchorage. And, third, Nome lies in the far, far north, well above the Arctic Circle.

Well, two out of three's not bad.

Although virtually everyone thinks of Nome as an Arctic community, it's actually a bit south of the Arctic Circle. The town does, however, experience Arctic-like weather, especially in the wintertime. Seas freeze solid off its shores well into late spring. Each year in March, in fact, the Nome Lions Club sponsors a **Bering Sea Ice Golf Classic**, during which shivering duffers play a six-hole, par 41 course consisting of fairways on frozen sea ice with flagged holes made from coffee cans sunk into the ice.

Nome, with a population of 4,500, is a fair-sized city by Alaska standards, but except for an occasional "far out" cruise ship, you can get there only by air. The air service, however, is excellent. Alaska Airlines jets fly to the city several times daily. And here's one of Alaska's best kept secrets: Once you've arrived here on the shores of the Bering Sea, there are hundreds of miles of good roads to explore. Places to visit and things to see include former gold mining sites, Native villages, impressive scenic vistas, even a hot springs. Nome is also one of the few places in North America where you can take a side trip to Russia.

A little history: One unconfirmed account records that Nome got its start in 1897, when John Hummel, an aging prospector suffering from scurvy, arrived in the area to search for gold, which many had predicted would be found there. But unlike others, Hummel did his panning on the beach, more hopeful of curing his ailments in the sun and salt air than of anything else. Incredibly, while sifting the beach sands he found gold. More incredible still, as he tested up and down the shoreline, he continued to see precious metal in every pan. In no time the rush was on! Another, more substantiated, version of Nome's beginning states that "three lucky Swedes"—Jafet Lindberg, Erik Lindblom and John

Brynteson—started the rush by finding gold in Anvil Creek in 1898, and that the beach finds came a year or so later.

However the rush began, it hasn't stopped yet. Mining remains a big part of Nome's economy. These days the rush consists of tourists eager to see where all the excitement took place. When you arrive in town, your first stop should be the Nome Convention and Visitor Bureau's **Visitor Information Center** (907–443–5535) located downtown on Front Street, across from City Hall. Lots of free brochures, walking maps, restaurant menus, antiques, and historic photos are available or on display Monday through Friday. Also on Front Street, in the basement of the library building, you'll find the **Carrie McLain Museum** (907–443–2566), with its wide variety of Alaskan artifacts and historical memorabilia. At the **XYZ Center** (907–443–5238) located in the north end of the City Hall building, fall, winter, and spring visitors can join Nome's elders for noon lunch and interesting conversation. (Please make a donation, even if you're a senior yourself.) The menu might include reindeer, blueberries, or other foods from the area. Any time of the year your most vivid memories of Nome may well be the ◆**gold dredges.** One old and abandoned dredge is within walking distance of town. Three dredges still operate in the area during summer twenty-four hours a day. The huge lumbering behemoths create their own ponds as they creep and float across the tundra, scooping up ore and extracting gold. And, of course, what could be more fitting for a visit to Nome than to buy a gold pan at one of the local stores and pan for some "color" of your own on the beaches where thousands once labored for nuggets and fortunes?

If you want to visit one of Alaska's best known saloons, but don't want your friends to know, simply tell them you stopped in at **Nome's Board of Trade**, also on Front Street.

About those highways: For a place you can't drive to, Nome has lots of miles to tour by auto. Three major roads offer access to wildlife viewing, rivers to fish, mining ruins to examine, plus awesome seascapes and landscapes to photograph. **Budget Rent A Car** (907–443–3858) rents compacts, vans, and campers, starting at $65 per day for autos. **Stampede Rent A Car** (907–443–5598) starts at $60.

153

The **Nome–Council Road**, which extends 72 miles east from Nome's main thoroughfare, Front Street, follows the coast for about 30 miles, then moves inland past rivers and sloping hills to the village of Council. About halfway out you'll come to the former community of Solomon, with its picturesque graveyard of old abandoned railroad engines and cars. Locals call this the Last Train to Nowhere. The 73-mile **Nome–Teller Road** leads to the village of Teller (population 200). You reach this highway from the west end of Front Street by turning north on Bering Street, which leads into the northwest-heading Teller Road.

A shorter driving option (about 3 miles one way) takes you to the top of **Anvil Mountain**, near an inoperative communications site. The rewarding view takes in the city of Nome, the Bering Sea, Sledge Island, and a colorful expanse of Arctic tundra.

Perhaps most rewarding, you can drive to ◆**Pilgrim Hot Springs** on the Kougarok Road, which is accessible about two miles north of town by turning north off Bering Street. The experience offers a lot of natural history, mining history, and vast fields of tiny colorful flowers growing wild on the tundra. The 36-mile drive will take about 45 minutes one way. Pack a snack to enjoy on the shores of Salmon Lake at the Bureau of Land Management campground. Farther down the road comes historic Pilgrim Hot Springs—once the site of a Catholic mission orphanage—and experimental gardens where tons of beets, carrots, turnips, cabbage, kale, rutabagas, rhubarb, onions, and potatoes were harvested from the hot springs-heated ground. Visitors are welcome to soak up the local atmosphere by spending quality time in a **Pilgrim Hot Springs hot tub.** (Bring your own towel.) There's time, as well, for bird-watching, trail hiking, and angling for trout or grayling in the Pilgrim River. During a drive north on the Kougarok Road, you'll pass through the Nome River Valley, where it's not uncommon to spot musk ox, moose, and reindeer.

Nome Custom Adventures' daylong tour covers a lot of territory, from a visit in the home of an Eskimo family where you can see an ivory carving demonstration to gold panning and watching a dogsled team in action. Too, you will visit the site of the original claim made by the "three lucky Swedes," explore a bit of tundra, take a quick glimpse at several small mining operations and get a close-up view of one of the few operating gold dredges left in Alaska. The cost is $82. For information about this and other tours, including escorted road trips, call (800) 443–5134.

Nome Tour & Marketing (907–443–2651) has a $25 tour that takes visitors along Nome's "golden beaches" to Iditarod musher Howard Farley's camp. There, in the summer, they can watch him mushing his team. Also on the schedule is Little Creek Mine, where Kitty Scott, a gold miner's daughter, will walk you back in time through slides and stories from Nome's past. You can also pan for gold on the trip and pet a reindeer.

If you want a dogsled ride yourself, contact Richard Burmeister's **Flat Dog Kennels** at (907) 443–2958. Summer on wheels or winter on the snow, you can mush for a half hour, 6 to 8 miles, for $25.

Nome is one of those places where you can flight-see to spot wildlife, take aerial photos of gold dredges and diggings, or even—during ❖**Olson Air Service's Siberian Sight-seer**—see two continents, experience two days in one (because you're flying over the international date line into "tomorrow"), and view two islands belonging to two different nations—Little Diomede, U.S.A., and Big Diomede, Russia—separated by 2 miles of sea. The tour, you guessed it, takes about two hours. The charter rate per person is $250 an hour, divided by the number of passengers (maximum six) aboard the plane. For more information, call (907) 443–2229.

Other air tours include **Cape Smythe Air** flights to **Gambell** and **Savoonga** villages on **St. Lawrence Island**, off the coast of Siberia. Call (907) 443–2414 for more information. Various carriers also offer trips to the villages of **St. Michael**, known for its grass baskets; **Shaktoolik,** where you'll find Eskimo dolls, parkas, and mukluks; and **White Mountain**, which has excellent earrings of porcupine quills, beads, and ivory. If you'd like to fly outbound and return by bus, **Grantley Harbor Tours** (800–478–3682) has a $99 tour (transportation only) between Nome and Teller, where explorer Roald Amundsen landed with his dirigible *Norge* following his famous transpolar flight.

Arranging flights from Nome to **Provideniya, Russia,** isn't quite as simple as booking a sight-seeing tour, but flights to the former Soviet Union are possible, and hundreds of Nome visitors book them every year. ❖**Bering Air** (907–443–5464) helped lift the "Iron Curtain" when the carrier transported American visitors across the international border in May 1988. The company has flown more than 600 such charter flights since and

155

now operates regularly scheduled flights each week. Upon request the airline will send literature explaining how to arrange permission from the Russians to enter the country. Passengers traveling individually and with flexible schedules may be able to travel on a seat-fare basis for as little as $250 each way.

Lori Egge's **Sky Trekking Alaska** (800–770–4966) is based in Wasilla, but she flies clients across the whole state. From Nome, for instance, she'll fly-trek you on an eight-day trip to Provideniya and to St. Lawrence Island in the Bering Sea. Her trips are not just sight-seeing. They can include dogsled rides, backpacking, fishing, and bush country photography hikes. There's nothing bushy, however, about the meals. They're planned by Chef Duncan Boyd of Nora's Restaurant, in Washington, D.C. And no matter how far back you are in the backcountry, Lori invariably brings a gas-powered espresso machine.

Several hotels offer lodging and dining accommodations in Nome, including the **Nome Nugget Inn** (907-443-2323), where most of the airline tourists stay. If you like more informal surroundings, consider Shirley Bronston's **Ocean View Manor,** a spacious home with a spectacular view of the Bering Sea. Room options include private or shared baths. Breakfasts are continental style, available anytime. Doubles cost $60; call (907) 443-2133. And who says there's no such thing as a real igloo in Alaska? **Betty's Igloo Bed and Breakfast** is situated in Betty and Michael Hannigan's home, with attractive, comfortable rooms, and a beautiful ocean view. The rate of $70 for a double includes a full breakfast. Call (907) 443-2419.

The Bush

Since 1973, the small Brooks Range bush outpost called **Bettles** has been the base of operations for ◆**Sourdough Outfitters**, one of the unquestioned pioneers in North Country guiding and outfitting. We sampled one of the company's expeditions some years ago—a trek into the towering, jagged, granite **Arrigetch Peaks** country—and have treasured the memory since as one of the great hikes of a lifetime. The outfitters' menu of more than two dozen choices range from easy—**Alatna River Canoeing**, for instance—to demanding—like the **Gates of the Arctic**

Winter Dogsledding trip. They also offer rental cabins in the Brooks Mountains wilderness, float trips on the storied **Kobuk River**, camping on the **Arctic Divide** to witness herds of caribou in migration, and exploring the environmentally controversial **Arctic National Wildlife Refuge** (where developers want to drill the coastal plains for oil and environmentalists want protection for the area's rich storehouse of wildlife). Sourdough Outfitters trips range from $1,250 per person for eight days of hiking to $3,200 for twenty days of canoeing. Call (907) 692-5252.

There are more options in the Brooks Range. **Alaska Discovery,** of Juneau, offers two hiking/rafting trips down the seldom-traveled ◆**Kongakut and Sheenjek Rivers**. Both trips are ten days and originate with a bush flight from Fairbanks to Arctic Village and beyond. The Sheenjek option is perhaps the more adventurous of the two. Said a recent participant, "During our trip . . . the tundra was ablaze with color, the river full of grayling, and we were never sure what would greet us around the next bend: possibly a caribou, a moose, sheep on a distant hillside." The costs, including bush plane charters, run $2,900 for the Kongakut and $2,700 for the Sheenjek. Call (800) 586–1911.

A Juneau friend spent a week or so in a camp called ◆**Peace of Selby** in the midst of **Gates of the Arctic National Park** and returned home full of its praises. There, on Selby/Narvak Lake in the Brooks Range you can book fully furnished, comfortable lodge accommodations, with meals included, for $275 per person, per night. Rustic sourdough cabins (bring your own food and sleeping bag) rent for $275 per group, per night and Arctic tent accommodations go for $110. From the camp the owners will arrange guided float trips, lake or river canoe excursions, overnight hikes, or fishing expeditions. Access, of course, is by air from Fairbanks or Bettles. Air rates vary with the size of the group. Call (907) 672–3206.

For birders in search of rare species, **Wilderness Birding Adventures** arranges tours from Prince William Sound in South-central Alaska and the Aleutians of the Southwest region to the far north Arctic. Among the latter is the opportunity for spectacular sightings on float trips down the **Colville, Kukpuk, and Koyukuk Rivers** as well as floats or base camp adventures on a small island of mountains protruding from the Arctic coastal plain in the **Arctic National Wildlife Refuge**. The company also packages tours of Gambell on St. Lawrence Island and of Nome, where rare species fly over from Siberia. Tours are priced as low as a two-day **Owls of the North** excursion from Anchorage at $395 or as high as $2,750 for a ten-day trip of **Kongakut River Rafting** through perhaps the most remote wilderness in the United States. Call (907) 694–7442.

Jim Campbell and Carol Kasza, husband and wife, have hiked and climbed mountains around the world, but to establish their own guiding business—**Arctic Treks**—they selected the Brooks Range. They offer a wide selection of wilderness hiking, backpacking, and rafting options from eight days to twenty-one. Prices range from $2,325 to $3,680, including air from Fairbanks. They take only six to nine clients per trip. Call (907) 455–6502.

Established in 1847 by the Hudson's Bay Company, ◆**Fort Yukon** is today one of Alaska's oldest settlements and the largest Athabascan Indian village in the state. Actually, the Gwich'in Athabascans have lived in this area for literally thousands of years. The town, which the people call *Gwichyaa Zhee* (meaning "house on the flats") lies 8 miles north of the Arctic Circle, and about 140 miles northeast of Fairbanks. You can get there by air via three scheduled carriers and four charter outfits or by boat. No roads lead to Fort Yukon.

If you enjoy buying souvenirs at the source, check out the Alaska Commercial Company store for beaded moose skin accessories. Most visitor services are available. One of the principal visitor attractions is a **replica of the original Fort Yukon**. Nearby is the old Hudson's Bay cemetery. Interestingly, Hudson's Bay built the fort not for protection from the Indians, but as a safeguard against the Russians who "owned" Alaska until 1867. Be sure also to see the **Old Mission School**, which is on the National Register of Historic Places. Ask to visit **St. Stephen's Territorial Episcopal Church,** where you can view exquisite and colorful Athabascan beaded embroidery on the altar cloth there. The Athabascans are renowned for their beadwork designs, which decorate boots, moccasins, jackets, and gloves.

Richard and Kathy Carroll's **Alaska Yukon Tours** (907–662–2727) range from two-hour guided tours around the village ($20) to riverboat rides across the mighty Yukon River ($30 minimum plus $10 per person) to a wilderness camp in the heart of the Yukon Flats National Wildlife Range ($30 per person per night). The firm offers a number of additional excursions, including ninety-mile riverboat trips between Circle City and Fort Yukon with a return by plane. On a longer trip between these two points, visitors experience three to five hours on the river, a stop at a Native fish camp, lunch, and the Fort Yukon village tour before flying back to Circle. This trip costs $175 per person, with a minimum of $700. Both of the Carrolls were born and raised in Fort Yukon, and Richard's father owns the only resort lodge in the Arctic National Wildlife Refuge. Richard can book you into the **Porcupine River Lodge** for fishing, hiking, exploring, and viewing wildlife for six day, at $3,000 for one or two persons and $1,100 for each additional guest. Fairbanks air carriers that serve Fort Yukon include Frontier Flying Service (907–474–9169), Larry's Flying Service (907–474–9169), and Warbelow's Air Ventures (907–474–0518).

ARCTIC VILLAGE

The northernmost Indian village in the world, ◆**Arctic Village,** in the foothills of the Brooks Range, is home to about 140 Gwich'in Athabascan Indians, who are doggedly determined to preserve their hunting/fishing/subsistence way of life. They're nonetheless willing to share their culture with a restricted number of visitors each year. Visits can be as brief as a fly-in, one-day excursion from Fairbanks to tour the village, sample traditional Native foods, and enjoy cultural presentations (including fiddling, borrowed from early Caucasian explorers), or trips can span several days with guided excursions into the wilderness to view caribou, moose, Dall sheep, and bears. Tours, which include a necessary visitor's entry permit, can be arranged by calling **Arctic Village Tours** at (907) 479–4648. A one-day summer tour, including round-trip flight, village tour, and lunch, is $280. Overnight visits (any season) run $260 for the first day, plus $150 for each additional day. The price includes air, food, lodging, guide service, and ground transportation. The same company offers new winter overnight excursions to the Native village of Venetie. This tour runs $190 for the first day, plus $150 per additional day.

THE DALTON HIGHWAY

This road—the only overland route into the Arctic from Alaska's highway network—is not for the timid or the unprepared. But the ◆Dalton Highway is one of the great, last adventure roads in the United States. If you have the right vehicle and plan ahead, it can be one of the most satisfying drives of a lifetime. *A little history:* Alaska began construction of the 414-mile road in April 1974 and had it operational that fall in order to expedite construction of the 800-mile pipeline from Prudhoe Bay to Valdez.

The Dalton is gravel, two lanes, hilly in places, bumpy in many more, lonely (you may not see another car for hours), and has few service facilities along the way. If you break down, you may not get help until an Alaska state trooper comes by on patrol. That's the bad news. The good news is that it is safely negotiable if you use common sense, and it opens up some of the most awesome northern mountain and tundra country in the world.

If you want to experience the highway but you don't want the hassle of planning, preparing, or driving the Dalton on your own, there's an easy option: Book reservations with one of several large or little tour companies that schedule motor-coach or van trips all summer long. Several of these offer drive-fly three-day itineraries during which you cruise the highway in one direction and fly between Fairbanks and Prudhoe Bay in the other. Among the companies that offer this and other options are **Princess Tours** (206–728–4202), **Gray Line of Alaska** (800–544–2206), **Northern Alaska Tour Company** (907–474–8600), and **Trans-Arctic Circle Treks, Ltd.** (907–479–5451). Prices vary with the different companies, points of origin, and whether you're traveling in a high or "shoulder" season. For a tour originating from Anchorage, for instance, Princess includes a flight leg to and from Fairbanks and charges $724 to $799; for a tour originating in Fairbanks costs vary from $624 to $699.

Until recent years, the northern half of the road was closed to any but commercial vehicles; private cars and RVs couldn't go beyond Disaster Creek at Mile 211. In December 1994, the road opened to unlimited access all the way to Deadhorse. It should be noted that some litigation has been filed to turn this decision around, but chances of rescinding access are considered slim. Just to be sure, however, you might wish to contact the Alaska

Department of Transportation at (907) 451–2210 before you start out. The folks there will give you the latest skinny on the legal situation as well as current road conditions along the way.

If you decide to drive the road yourself, make sure your car is in top mechanical condition. Especially if you're camping out along the way (in fact, even if you're not), bring lots of bug dope. (We like Cutters.) And by all means, pack plenty of film. It's a long, long drive to the nearest photo shop. If you don't plan to camp, make sure you've called ahead and reserved motel space in Coldfoot and Deadhorse. Be aware that gasoline is available along the way only at the Yukon River (mile 56), at Coldfoot (mile 175), and at Deadhorse at road's end (mile 414).

Whether you're in the family vehicle or an air-conditioned motor coach, the adventure begins when you leave the Elliott Highway past mile 73 and head north on the Dalton. Four miles later you're descending a steep incline into Lost Creek Valley, with the pipeline visible (as it frequently will be) to your right. From time to time, the pipe will crisscross under the road. Sometimes the line will be buried for many miles, and you won't see it at all.

About 48 miles out you begin your descent to the Yukon River, and at mile 55.6, there it is, the storied Yukon and an impressive 2,290-foot wood-decked bridge that rises (or falls, depending on which way you're driving) at a 6 percent grade.

Across the river on its northern bank, you can top off your fuel tank at **Yukon Ventures Alaska** (907–655–9001) as well as eat a restaurant meal and overnight in a motel. You can also take one of **Yukon River Tours'** daily 12-mile boat trips aboard the forty-nine-passenger cabin vessel *Yookene Spirit* to an Athabascan Indian fish camp. The boat trip costs $30; with an overnight tenting experience the cost is $45. Bring your own sleeping bag and food. For information, call (907) 452–7162.

At mile 115.3 you can expose a photo you'll be proud to hang on your living room wall. Here you will officially cross the **Arctic Circle** at 66 degrees, 33 minutes north latitude, and there's a big sign there to prove it.

At mile 175 you'll come to **Coldfoot**, which started life as an old-time mining camp and exists today as the major overnight spot for truckers and visitors on the Dalton Highway. The name, according to local legend, came about when early gold stampeders got this far north, then got "cold feet" and retreated south. Last time I overnighted in Coldfoot, a miner came in from his camp and told friends at the bar about a grizzly bear that had followed him all the way. The next day our own party saw a big grizzly sow and two roly-poly cubs nearby.

The *services* provided by **Coldfoot Services and Arctic Acres Inn** include gas, phone, tire and mechanical repair, RV hookups, motel, lounge, and lots of good contact with authentic bush-country Alaskans. Call (907) 678–5201. The National Park Service maintains a **visitor center** at Coldfoot, offering road and travel updates as well as programs each night about the Arctic.

Approaching mile 189 along the highway, you junction with a short access road to **Wiseman.** Like many others of its kind, this community once thrived as a trading center for prospectors and miners. These days, about two dozen determined souls still live there year-round, joined by others in the summer. **Wiseman Trading Company** survives and contains a museum of mining artifacts and photos. There's a campground nearby.

At Mile 235.3, just south of a highway turn-off, you'll see the northernmost spruce tree in Alaska. No others grow beyond this point. This is also the start of a long and very steep grade—10 percent. Be sure to give any downhill-traveling trucks you meet their full half of the road.

Another steep ascent begins just beyond mile 242 and ends at Atigun Pass, which at 4,800 feet is the highest in Alaska. Watch for Dall mountain sheep—on our last trip we saw dozens on Slope Mountain west of the highway, at the turnoff at mile 301.

About 75 miles later you'll see a pingo 5 miles west of the road. These curious circular mounds, more common the closer you get to the Arctic Ocean's shores, rise dramatically from surrounding table-top smooth terrain. They're caused by frozen water beneath the surface.

At mile 414 you've arrived at ◆ **Deadhorse,** the gathering point where crude oil from Prudhoe Bay, Kuparuk River, and other lesser oil fields is brought in by a network of smaller pipelines and directed into the 48-inch Trans-Alaska Pipeline for transport to Valdez, 800 miles to the south.

Truth to tell, you'll probably judge Deadhorse a pretty bleak and dreary place. Some of the Arco and BP oil company buildings (with self-contained dorms, cafeterias, libraries, and recreation centers) are modern and bright, even cheerful, and some of the subcontractor structures and quarters are on a par with counter-parts in industrial parks in the Lower Forty-eight. But a consid-erable number of Deadhorse's buildings and lots are unkempt, junky, littered, and strewn with unused or abandoned pipe, equipment, and building material. No one really seems to care, since almost no one lives here year-round. Virtually the entire population consists of crews and individuals who arrive or depart on periodic shift assignments. There are no church build-ings, schools, movie theaters, or any of the other trappings of a bona fide community. Few if any of the workers bring wives or family. They claim residence in Anchorage, Fairbanks, and even far-flung points like Dallas and Fort Worth.

So what's the attraction? Well, it may be drab, dreary, and des-olate, but in a strange sort of way, it's dramatic and absorbing. There's a lot of coming-going-moving-shaking activity, and if you take one of the organized tours available, you'll learn a lot about the place and the process from which the United States gets a whopping 1.8 million barrels of crude oil a day. You can have your picture taken at ◆ **Pipeline Mile Zero.** You'll likely see wild caribou grazing virtually in the shadow of oil rigs and pipelines just outside of town, and any number of waterfowl bird species resting or nesting on the tundra. And if you don't happen to have Point Barrow on your itinerary, where else will you be able to skip a stone on the **Arctic Ocean?** (Or, if you're a winter or very early summer visitor, actually take a few steps out onto the Arctic ice pack.)

You can't, by the way, just mosey around Deadhorse in your car on your own as you would back home. Much of this com-munity, including many roads, is private property, and you need permission to visit many sites, including the shores of the Arctic Ocean. This is the reason many visitors choose all-inclusive van or motor-coach drive-fly tours from Fairbanks or Anchorage. If you plan to drive here in your own vehicle, you should definitely make housing reservations ahead of time. The **Prudhoe Bay Hotel** (907–659–2449) is open year-round and accommodates visitors as well as petroleum workers. The man-agement offers tours of the area as well. Arctic Caribou Inn (907–659–2368) provides rooms, tours, breakfasts, dinners, and a gas station. These were modest but clean and comfortably fur-nished accommodations when I stayed in Deadhorse a few years

The Trans-Alaska Pipeline along the Dalton Highway

ago. **Alaska Petroleum Company** (907–659–2704) will fix
your car or your tires if you need repair services and **NANA Oilfield** (907–659–2840) has gasoline and diesel fuel for sale. Incidentally, no one uses street addresses here. To find these companies,
watch for signs or simply ask someone. It's a small community.
You won't have trouble locating whatever you're looking for.

The Dalton Highway, of course, is a north-south, single road.
There are no loops or alternate routes back. If you're driving,
when your visit ends, you simply retrace your path to the Elliott
Highway, to Fairbanks, or wherever.

SOUTHWESTERN ALASKA

Bethel
12

8
Pribilof Islands
9

10

5

11

1, 2
3, 4
Kodiak

Unalaska/
Dutch Harbor

Alaska Marine Hwy

7

1. Baranov Museum
2. Holy Resurrection Russian
   Orthodox Church
3. Kodiak Alutiiq Dancers
4. Fort Abercrombie
   State Park
5. *Tustumena*
6. Grand Aleutian Hotel
7. Holy Ascension Russian
   Orthodox Cathedral

8. St. Paul and St George Islands
9. St. George
10. Lake Clark National Park
    and Preserve
11. Aniakchak National
    Monument and Preserve
12. Yugtarvik Regional
    Museum

Southwestern Alaska

Strange opportunity you have in Southwestern Alaska. If you really want to, you can travel farther off the beaten path in this region than in any other in the nation. Farther west and—here's the strange part—farther *east.*

The Aleutian Islands, as you probably know, stretch from the end of the Alaska Peninsula almost to Japan. The westernmost point in the United States lies on one of those islands, Amatignak at 179 degrees, 10 minutes west.

Now about the easternmost point. Just across the 180th meridian that separates the earth's Western Hemisphere from the Eastern Hemisphere (and exactly halfway around the world from the prime meridian at Greenwich, England) is Semisopochnoi Island's Pochnoi Point, at 179 degrees, 46 minutes east. Thus the nation's most northern (at Point Barrow), western, and eastern real estate is located in Alaska. (The most southern, if you're curious, is on the southern side of the Big Island of Hawaii.)

Some other Alaska-sized statistics about this region include these: You can visit Alaska's largest island, Kodiak, in this region and in the process see the nation's biggest land carnivore, the Kodiak brown bear. You can photograph the biggest moose in Alaska on the Alaska Peninsula. Some of North America's most volatile volcanoes have blown their tops in this area—one of the most awesome, Katmais, has been designated a national park. Through the region flow some of the nation's wildest rivers. And way, way, *way* out in the Bering Sea you'll find two tiny islands on which you'll see more birds of more species than you ever thought possible. Every visitor comes home from the Pribilof Islands a confirmed bird-watcher.

Among Native residents in the region, you'll meet Yu'pik Eskimos on the western mainland, Aleuts on the Aleutian and Pribilof Islands, and Alutiiq Natives on Kodiak Island.

Kodiak Island, in fact, is a good place to start an exploration of the region. The island ranks not only as the largest in Alaska, it contains Alaska's earliest continuing European settlement, the **city of Kodiak**.

No roads or bridges from the Alaska mainland connect Kodiak Island, but, no matter, the Alaska Marine Highway System (800–642–0066) offers regular, dependable passenger and vehicle ferry service from Homer and Seward on the Kenai Peninsula several times each week. Alaska Airlines (through ERA Aviation) provides daily flights from Anchorage. There are visitor accommodations and services aplenty in the community. For information contact the **Kodiak Island Convention and Visitors Bureau**, at (907–486–4782) at 100 Marine Way.

Tourism as a major industry has not yet discovered Kodiak. It's clearly still off the beaten path. The result is, you can come away from a visit with a genuine feel for the way Alaskans live and work and play in this part of the "Last Frontier." It's fun simply to wander along the boat docks and cannery sites, watching the frantic, frenzied busyness of salmon, crab, halibut, shrimp, and other fisheries landings. More than 3,000 commercial vessels— some quite large—utilize Kodiak harbors and facilities each year, making it one of the busiest in the world.

A great deal of Alaska's early European history resides in Kodiak. The first Russian settlement, established in 1784, was at Three Saints Bay, but the Russian trader and manager Alexander Baranov relocated his headquarters to present Kodiak in 1792. One of Baranov's still-standing structures, originally a warehouse for precious sea otter pelts, now the ❖**Baranov Museum**, was constructed about 1808. It's at 101 Marine Way and contains antiques and artifacts of the Russian and pre-Russian era, including grand samovars, handcrafted silver jewelry, and fine-woven Alutiiq basketry. Price is $2.00. Phone (907) 486–5920 for information.

Kodiak's ❖**Holy Resurrection Russian Orthodox Church**, the oldest parish in Alaska, stands in the city's downtown district at Kashaveroff Street and Mission Avenue. Tour hours are 1:00 P.M. to 3:00 P.M., daily except Sunday in the summer. At other times, call (907) 486–3854. You'll see colorful religious trappings of the Orthodox faith, including icons that date back to Russia's czarist period. Additional icons, artifacts, and reminders of the area's Christian spiritual beginnings can be found at the **Saint Innocent Veniaminov Research Institute Museum** at Saint Herman Theological Seminary, on Mission Road north of the church. Father Herman was one of the early Orthodox monks who arrived to evangelize, educate, and provide medical attention to Alaska Natives. On August 9, 1970, he became the first North American religious to be canonized by the Russian Orthodox Church. For museum hours, check with the visitor center downtown.

169

Holy Resurrection Russian Orthodox Church, Kodiak

Of course, before the Americans and before the Russians, there were the Native residents of Kodiak, the Alutiiq people. In Kodiak you can learn a lot of indigenous history simply by attending the dances performed by a talented group called the ◆**Kodiak Alutiiq Dancers.** And these Alutiiq (pronounced Al-LOO-tig) performers are truly one of a kind in their stories and music and in their unique "snow falling" attire, with tassels of brilliant white Arctic fox descending over black parkas. Three dozen or so dancers perform daily, Monday through Saturday, at their *barabara*, or traditional Alutiiq dwelling, at 713 Rezanof Street near downtown. Performers range from six years to eighty and their dances run the gamut from an ancestral "kayaking" dance to more contemporary, enacted stories of rich humor, such as the tale of a little boy who eats pudding as fast as his frantic parents can make it. Admission is $15.00. For information, call (907) 486–4449.

New on the Kodiak scene is the **Alutiiq Museum and Archaeological Repository**, which opened in 1995 at 215 Mission Road. Housed there are artifacts from numerous archaeological sites around the Kodiak Island Archipelago, and plans are under way to repatriate additional artifacts and artwork that is now scattered in museums around the world. The new facility features a display gallery, state-of-the-art storage for sensitive artifacts, and a research laboratory. There's also a museum store which showcases the work of local artists. Hours are 10:00 A.M. to 4:00 P.M., Monday through Friday and noon until 3:00 P.M. on Saturday and Sunday. Admission is $2.00.

For some close-to-town hiking or exploring, walk across the bridge to **Near Island.** If, while you're trekking through the woods, you spot some large, furry brown shapes, don't be alarmed. They're resident ponies and cattle, not brown bears.

To view recent history, visitors can take a 4-mile drive out the Rezanof-Monashka Road to ◆**Fort Abercrombie State Park** to see the remains of World War II gun emplacements, restored bunkers, and other such artifacts. It's a toss-up which you'll find the more interesting, the massive concrete bunkers and fortifications that once protected Kodiak from a Japanese invasion, or the breathtaking, panoramic view from rugged cliffsides and gentle shores. The area is thickly forested with conifers, berry plants, and wildflowers. For $10 a night RVs and tenters can camp at the park, which also contains swimming and fishing sites, woodsy trails, and picnic facilities.

Several roads are worth exploring, including the **Chiniak Highway** that runs southwest from town then southeast. Particularly scenic points and beaches can be found from about miles 35 to the end of the 42-mile road. It's great for picnics, photography, and viewing more World War II gun battery emplacements. If you do your beach exploring at low tide, you'll be amazed at the sealife left behind in small pools after the tide has receded— tiny crabs, anemones, starfish, sea dollars, snails, itty-bitty fish, seaweeds, and all manner of other creepy-crawlies.

The **Anton Larsen Bay Road**, which begins about 5 miles from downtown at a junction with the Chiniak Highway, leads to Anton Larson Bay. Along the way you just may spot a brown bear. They don't call the golf course at mile 3 (from the junction) Bear Valley Golf Course for nothing. If you're into viewing natural history, drive the **Pasagshak Bay Road** (still another south-bound side road off the Chiniak Highway) all the way to the end, including the last .5 mile, which is not maintained. You'll find a beautiful beach with cliffs at either end. Countless thousands of ancient fossils are embedded in them. Be advised this is a low-tide excursion; check the tide tables.

If Kodiak has been, until recently, a lesser-known visitor destination, it has nonetheless been one of North America's best known hunting areas for decades. The reason is *ursus arctos middendorffi*, the Kodiak brown bear, which can weigh in at 1,500 pounds or more. Around 2,700 or more of the big bruins live on Kodiak Island, according to game professionals. Most reside in the 2,491-square-mile **Kodiak National Wildlife Refuge** on Kodiak and nearby Uganik, Ban, and Afognak Islands. Visitors can dwell among these critters if they like by renting one of several backcountry recreation cabins constructed by the U.S. Fish and Wildlife Service. Access, incidentally, is only by float-equipped airplanes or boats. For information, contact the Kodiak National Wildlife Refuge Manager, 1390 Buskin Road, Kodiak, AK 99615 (907–487–2600), or stop by the **U.S. Fish and Wildlife Service Visitor Center**, about 4.5 miles from downtown on Chiniak Highway.

If you don't want to arrange your own sight-seeing, fishing, or hiking expeditions, there are quite a number of outfitters ready to package a tour for you. Kodiak Island historian Lola Harvey operates **Island Terrific Tours** and offers one- and two-day Crown Jewel excursions from Anchorage for under $250 or $300, respectively. Sights include visitor centers, museums, harbor tours, the Orthodox church, secluded bays and country roads, plus "a sky full of eagles, puffins, gulls, ducks, and seabirds." Prices from Anchorage include round-trip airfare, hotel or B&B, transfers, and fees, but no meals. From out of town, book through Alaska Sightseeing/Cruise West (800–426–7702) or Gray Line of Alaska (800–544–2206). If you're already in Kodiak, call Island Terrific at (907) 486–7777. The Kodiak portion of the tour runs $70.

Linda Blessin, of **Kodiak Tours**, offers packages in the same general price range, with or without airfare from Anchorage. She also offers bear-viewing tours by air and charter vessel excursions. Call (907) 486–5989.

Saltery Lake Lodge offers fishing, photography, and (in season) hunting adventures on Saltery Lake, near Ugak Bay on the eastern side of Kodiak Island. The lodge operates a floatplane and fishing vessel to aid guests in their quests for sockeye, pink, chum, and silver salmon as well as Dolly Varden, rainbow, and steelhead. Three couples—the Beehlers, Franklins, and Hatfields—serve as hosts at the alcohol-free lodge. Prices for three-day stays begin at $885. Call (800) 770–5037.

Buskin River Inn's Kodiak Island Ultimate Adventures includes a number of "ultimate" tours, among them a two-hour introduction to kayaking by **Wavetamer Kayaking**, priced as low as $40. An $85 half-day trip includes paddling along remote shores and through tidal pools and cruising past Kittiwake rookeries and among sea lions, otters, eagles, and puffins. Another completely different trip takes you horseback riding at the 21,000-acre **Kodiak Cattle Company**, where you'll see not only ranch cattle but huge buffalo wandering over the range. The cost is $62.50, not including a car rental to get to the ranch. And to see Kodiak brown bears—guaranteed—there's **Sea Hawk Air's Guaranteed Bear Viewing and Flight-seeing**. Also on the flight agenda: sights of whales in the saltwater plus elk in the valleys and mountain goats on ridge tops. The charge is $125 for flight-seeing only, $350 for bear viewing.

Other Ultimate Adventures include underwater touring with **Scuba Do–Alpha Dive Charters**. The operator has Discover Dives for uncertified beginners at $110 and boat dives for experienced hands from $125. Above the surface **Pristine Charters** provides fishing and whale watching aboard the vessel *Three Bears*. The cost is $200 a day. Still another opportunity is **Eskimo Red's Muskomee Bay Lodge**, on the shores of nearby Afognak Island. The attractions here include a three-day stay at a brand new lodge plus, say the lodge operators, "incredible hiking, unequaled photography, and fantastic fishing." The cost is $350 per day.

Buskin River Inn also arranges mountain bike rentals, books guided bird-watching trips, rents cars for $47 a day, and offers its own lodging at $100 for a single, $110 for a double. Call (800) 544–2202.

173

Captain Chris Fiala departs Kodiak Harbor daily with up to sixteen passengers aboard his 43-foot charter vessel *U Rascal,* offering ocean salmon and "monster halibut" fishing, Alaska bird and marine mammal watching, and the chance to stalk Sitka blacktail deer and Roosevelt elk. The price is $175 per person and includes bait, tackle, lunch, and soft drink. For details from **Kodiak Island Charters**, call (907) 486–5380.

R&R Lodge is a small, personal, backcountry lodge on remote Ugak Bay. Host Robin Reed books only one party at a time and limits the size to four (maybe six by special arrangement). The attractions here are fishing, of course, plus unstructured sightseeing to observe seals, sea lions, sea otters, orca (killer) whales, grey and other whale species as well as Kodiak brown bears, deer, foxes, and even mountain goats. A sample charge, including the bush flight from Kodiak, would run $270 per night, per guest, each for a party of two persons staying three nights. For more information, call (907) 486–3704.

The Dog Salmon River drainage supports one of Kodiak Island's densest bear populations, and **Olga Bay Lodge** packages an eight-hour flight-seeing and on-the-ground bear viewing program that includes a morning forty-minute floatplane flight by **Island Air** over mountains, glaciers, and fjords en route to the river. Animals spotted during the flight may include bears, mountain goats, and deer. Once you've landed, an armed guide will take you to a bug-screen-enclosed site for spectacular bear viewing, during which the great carnivores may approach as close as twenty yards. A hot lunch is included before departure for a 4:30 P.M. arrival back in Kodiak. The cost is $480. Olga Bay Lodge's phone number in Kodiak is (907) 486–5373. Call Island Air at (800) 478–6196 for information about shorter flight-seeing excursions. Their one-and-a-half-hour trip to the middle of the island costs $175.

Katmai National Park

During the morning of June 1, 1912, a volcanic mountain in what is now **Katmai National Park** began a series of violent quakes and eruptions, the likes of which had seldom been recorded in earth's history. A full foot of volcanic ash fell on Kodiak, 100 miles distant, and darkened the sky to inky blackness. When the eruptions subsided, a valley at the site lay buried under 700 feet of ash. In 1916 when the first expedition entered the area, thousands of still-steaming fumeroles inspired the name "Valley of 10,000 Smokes." That valley, curiously, remains stark and desolate to this day, though the surrounding area now thrives with lush growth and beautiful lakes and rivers that teem with salmon and other fish. You can visit the park easily, though no roads lead to it. Propeller-equipped aircraft offer daily access from King Salmon (accessible by jet from Anchorage) and less frequent flights are also available from Kodiak.

Katmailand, concessionaire for Katmai National Park, offers accommodations at Brooks Lodge, Kulik Lodge, and Grosvenor Lodge. Rates, including air fare from Anchorage, begin at $1,526 for two days, one night. The company also schedules daily 23-mile motor coach tours into the eerie, moonlike Valley of 10,000 Smokes. The author arranged to camp in the stark valley (motoring in with a sight-seeing tour one day and out a day later), and it was one of the best—albeit most eerie—camp-outs of his life. Fishing in nearby lake and river waters is outstanding. National Park Service rangers offer talks and lead hikes to archaeological sites daily. For information, call (800) 544-0551.

Incidentally, if you want to bring a tent and camp in the Park Service **Brooks Campground** near the Brooks Lodge, be advised there's a lottery system now in effect and a four-day limit for campground reservations. For more details, call the superintendent's office at (907) 246-3305. The phone is often busy, so you can also request information by mail from Katmai National Park, P.O. Box 7, King Salmon, AK 99613.

Tom Watson of Wavetamer Kayaking and skipper Chaco Pearman of Pristine Charters have combined their services to offer a quality sea kayaking/cruising experience off the shores of Katmai National Park. Called **Kayak Katmai Adventures**, the tour—four days aboard the 53-foot charter vessel *Three Bears*—uses the boat as a floating base camp, and it includes a Grumman Goose flight over Kodiak Island, guided sea kayaking, bear viewing, saltwater fishing, clam digging, and coastal sight-seeing. The price is in the $1,500 range. Call (907) 486-2604.

Katmai Wilderness Lodge, headquartered in Kodiak and located on Kukak Bay on the eastern coast of Katmai National Park, limits its guest list to six visitors a day. The company promises abundant wildlife viewing both ashore and from the water, including brown bears digging for razor clams plus whales and sea otters. There are also glacier treks, nature hikes, and kayak trips. Birders have identified 231 species so far; maybe you'll spot the 232nd. The area is especially rich in archaeological resources. A one-day bear-viewing package from Kodiak costs $700; three nights and four days, in a comfortable log cabin, with cook and guide, costs $1,800. Prices include a floatplane trip from Kodiak. For details, call (800) 488–8767.

UNALASKA/DUTCH HARBOR

If you look just at location, **Unalaska** and its adjacent neighbor, **Dutch Harbor**, would seem the most unlikely of tourist destinations situated, as they are, out on the Aleutian chain. The two towns (actually, they're really just one; only a small bridge separates them) lie 800 air miles from Anchorage, about midway along the 1,000-mile Aleutian Islands chain that extends westerly from the Alaska Peninsula almost to Japan.

Don't, if you're a true fan of out of the way travel, overlook this destination. Unalaska/Dutch Harbor offers a surprising number of pleasurable places to see, lots of things to do, and an amazing comfort level. Although no roads or surface highways lead there, the towns enjoy excellent daily air service from Anchorage (via Alaska Airlines, Reeve Aleutian Airways, and PenAir plus weekly flights on Markair Express) as well as a monthly schedule of calls by the Alaska Marine Highway System's passenger and auto ferry ◆ *Tustumena*. Traveling aboard the stateroom-equipped Trusty Tusty, as she's called, is in fact a terrific way to see this part of Alaska. The vessel leaves Homer one Tuesday a month, April through September, en route to Kodiak, Chignik, Sand Point, King Cove, Cold Bay, False Pass, and Unalaska. She leaves Unalaska on a Saturday and arrives back in Homer the following Tuesday. One-way fare costs $242 from Homer, $250 from Seward, meals not included; cabins begin at $208 and $218. Call (800) 642–0066.

Now for some geography: Unalaska is located on Unalaska Island and Dutch Harbor is situated on Amaknak Island. The bridge that connects them is called the Bridge to the Other Side.

Rich in Aleut, early Russian, and World War II history, Unalaska/Dutch Harbor has become a major bustling seafood landing and processing center in recent years. It is, in fact, the number one port in the United States in terms of pounds and value of fish and crab landed. The year-round population totals more than 4,300 residents, and there are thousands of additional commercial fishermen coming and going at all times. Recently the community has enjoyed a small but growing visitor influx, particularly World War II veterans who served in this theater in the 1940s. Many return to see once again the site of Japanese bombing attacks and the defensive fortifications the U.S. troops built and manned along shorelines and on mountainsides.

Birders come from around the world to see the rare whiskered auklet and other species, and anglers journey here to land world-class halibut and three kinds of salmon.

Accommodations here are much more plush than you might imagine. The wonderfully named ◆ **Grand Aleutian Hotel,** in fact, offers uncompromising luxury in its 112 rooms, public areas, and gourmet restaurant, the **Chart Room,** where the chefs make innovative use of locally abundant seafood. The hotel offers rooms starting at $135 as well as tour packages for sight-seers, birders, and sportfishers. Call (800) 891–1194 for information and reservations.

New and located downtown is Carl's Bayview Inn. Carl's offers a variety of accommodations from standard rooms to suites. Prices range from $90 to $175. Call (800) 581–1230.

Not quite so new, but commendable nonetheless, is the **UniSea Inn**, both a hotel and a short-order sports bar and grill. The pizza, in particular, comes highly recommended. Rooms start at $125 for a double. Phone (907) 581–1325.

Among small inns available in Unalaska/Dutch Harbor is **Sheila's Guest House,** which promises spacious rooms, and a serene location at the base of General's Hill in Unalaska Valley. Rates are $75 a visit. Call (907) 581–2000.

Sights to see around the community include a vast array of WW II bunkers, gun emplacements, and structures still remaining on the island. Look closely at the cliffs below Bunker Hill and along Unalaska Lake for some of the many blocked tunnels that once provided protection from enemy bombs for U.S. soldiers and equipment. The **Marine Works,** on Airport Beach Road, houses an informal museum of wartime memorabilia, including weapons, a mine detector, soldiers' field gear, photos, and news-papers. It's open Monday to Friday 8:00 A.M. to 5:00 P.M. There's no admission charge. Call (907) 581–1749.

177

Surely the most compelling cultural and historical site is ◆ **Holy Ascension Russian Orthodox Cathedral**, constructed 1894–96. It contains an astonishing 697 documented icons, artifacts, and significant works of art, one of the largest and richest such collections in Alaska. Within the structure, too, are remnants of even earlier churches and chapels used in 1808, 1826, and 1853. Most ground tours offer a visit to this historic landmark. Call the Convention and Visitor Bureau at (907) 581-2612 for details.

Other possibilities in Unalaska/Dutch Harbor include nature excursions that focus on wildlife and geological features, marine adventures including World War II shipwrecks, gold mining claims, sportfishing aboard charter vessels, and visits to a state-of-the-art processing plant. Again contact the Convention and Visitors Bureau.

The community's new 30,000-square-foot **recreation center** is open for daily or weekly use, as well as mountain bike rentals for $10 a day. Call the office at (907) 581–1297 or stop by the recreation center at Broadway and Airport Beach Road.

Greg Hawthorne offers an option even farther afield. His **Volcano Bay Adventures** tour starts with a fifteen-minute float-plane ride around the end of Unalaska Island to a lake at the foot of Mt. Makushin. The camp there consists of three large wall tents, complete with kitchen-dining facilities, where a chef prepares hot meals daily. The main attraction, however, is stellar salmon fishing. Call (907) 581-3414.

Aleutian Air will take visitors to neighboring **Umnak Island** where you can see the well-preserved remains of a secret World War II air base, Fort Glenn. Aleutian Air also offers flight-seeing, volcano flights over Makushin, an active volcano, and World War II fighter base tours. Call (907) 581–1686.

Much of the land on Unalaska, Amaknak, and Sedanka Islands is privately owned by the **Ounalashka Corporation**, an Alaska Native corporation. It asks visitors who want to hike, ski, bike, or camp on this land to first obtain a permit from the corporate office. Permits may be requested by phone at (907) 581–1276 or from their office between 8:00 A.M. and 5:00 P.M., Monday through Friday. The office is located on Salmon Way.

C. Regan Newhouse, general manager of **Channel 8 TV**, extends an invitation for visitors to stop by Unalaska Community

Broadcasting, where they can be honorary newscasters. Call (907) 581–1888.

THE PRIBILOF ISLANDS

If you think the Aleutians are "far out," wait until you hear about ◆St. Paul and St. George Islands in the lonesome middle of the Bering Sea. Located about 800 air miles west-southwest of Anchorage and more than 200 miles north of the Aleutian chain, the Pribilof Islands are home to fewer than 1,000 people, but—in the summer at least—the islands provide a hauling out place for an estimated one and a quarter million howling, barking, fighting, breeding, birthing fur seals. In addition, the islands' craggy sea cliffs provide a summer nesting sanctuary for more than two million seabirds (211 species), some of which you'll see nowhere else in this hemisphere. Add to this, domestic reindeer and fascinating Native Aleut cultures and history, and you have a superb, offbeat travel destination.

It's surprisingly easy to visit the Pribilofs. Many hundreds do each year. Reeve Aleutian Airways (800–544–2248) offers three- to eight-day tours that include round-trip airfare from Anchorage to **St. Paul**, accommodations at the warm and rustic **King Eider Hotel**, and daily excursions to beaches and cliffs. From behind protective blinds at various beaches, you'll view thousands of fur seals, including bellowing "beachmasters," their "harems," and pups. At numerous cliffs you can easily photograph superabundant bird species. You'll also visit the ornate **Russian Orthodox Church**, and you'll meet members of the largest population of Aleuts anywhere. The three-day tour costs $838.52. The eight-day option goes for $1,593.77. Meals are extra and average $30 to $36 daily for breakfast, lunch, and dinner.

Reeve Aleutian also has a $1,380 **Pribilof Aleutian Adventure** tour that provides air transportation by Reeve to St. Paul, a one-way flight via Pen Air to Dutch Harbor, air from Dutch Harbor to Anchorage by Reeve, two hotel nights at the King Eider, two hotel nights at the Grand Aleutian in Unalaska/Dutch Harbor, plus transfers and guided tours at St. Paul and Dutch Harbor.

Dedicated offbeat travelers—especially birders—will want to extend their trips to ◆St. George, about 40 air miles south of St. Paul. Travelers (or their travel agents) will have to make more of their own arrangements, but the opportunity here is to view not only fur seals (250,000 come to the island each year) but the largest seabird colony in the Northern Hemisphere. On its precipitous cliffs, St. George hosts the largest colony of thick-billed murres in the North Pacific as well as 98 percent of the world's population of red-legged kittiwakes. It's also the the largest breeding colony for parakeet auklets . . . and the list goes on.

PenAir (800–448–4226) operates between St. George and St. Paul (round-trip fare, $120) and also provides regular service between Anchorage, St. George, St. Paul, and back for $599. Tours that include accommodations, tours, and meals unfortunately aren't available. The single hotel on St. George is the ten-room **Tanaq Hotel**, which can accommodate a total of eighteen guests, and although the hotel offers no meal service, guests have free use of the kitchen and dining room facilities. A grocery store is located about a block away. The rate is $89 per person per night. Call St. George Tanaq Corporation at (907) 562–3100. The company will also help you line up local guides. Especially if you're a photographer, you may want to join an annual **Joseph Van Os Photo Safari** to St. George. Air transportation from Anchorage, hotel accommodations, meals, tours, and the expertise of a professional wildlife photographer are included in the seven-day tour. Call (206) 463–5383 for details.

LAKE CLARK NATIONAL PARK

It's probably one of the National Park System's least known and visited parks—but that's one of the things that make ◆**Lake Clark National Park and Preserve** across Cook Inlet from the Kenai Peninsula special. Access is only by air (or water, on the shores of Cook Inlet), you certainly won't find Yellowstone- or Yosemite-type roads and trails within the park boundaries. This is some of the wildest and most breathtakingly beautiful country on earth, with saltwater shores, turquoise blue lakes, steaming volcanoes, and cascading waterfalls that drop from towering mountainsides. Three rivers in the park have been designated National Wild Rivers. You travel in this country by foot, by boat, or by air. Accommodations are tents; either you bring your own or book with an outdoor guiding service that provides everything from fly-in charters to shelter, food, and expertise.

Food cache at Lake Clark National Park and Preserve

Among the companies who offer this expertise is **Alaskan Sojourns, Wilderness Guides** operated by Rod and Sara Arno. At times, say the Arnos, campers in the Lake Clark region can witness the migration of hundreds of caribou. A short hike can bring Dall sheep within camera range. Moose forage everywhere. Their Saturday-to-Saturday package tours cost $2,500, including bush flights within the park. For the traveler seeking an even more challenging camping experience, Alaskan Sojourns offers a seven-day trip to ◆ **Aniakchak National Monument and Preserve** on the Alaska Peninsula west of Anchorage. The centerpiece of the monument is a massive active volcano caldera containing turquoise lake waters, cinder cones, lava plugs, and steaming hot springs. The caldera is, in fact, one of the largest in the world. This is a trip for strong, fit, and knowledgeable campers only, but for those who qualify it is truly one of earth's great outdoor destinations. The cost is $2,500, including bush flights from and to King Salmon. The Arnos also package fishing excursions, sea kayaking expeditions, and other hiking/camping options on the Kenai Peninsula, in Bristol Bay, Prince William Sound, and Katmai National Park. For brochures or information, call (907) 376-2913.

Eruk's Wilderness Float Tours takes small groups, including families, on floats from lakes in the park down the Chilikidrotna River. Along the way, says Eruk Williamson, "bears and wolves are particularly active and visible." Game trails and dry channels offer frequent opportunities to explore, notes Williamson, a wildlife biologist. Trips vary from seven to ten days; an eight-day float costs $2,300, including airfare from Anchorage. The company also offers trips to Aniakchak Crater and the Kuskokwim Mountains, both in Southwest Alaska, plus Gates of the Arctic National Park, the Brooks Range from Bettles, and Interior Alaska. Phone (907) 345-7678.

Based in the Soldotna–Kenai area, **Haeg's Wilderness Lodge**, on the north side of Chinitna Bay (a small inlet on the south edge of the Lake Clark National Park) can offer a fly-in as brief as an evening barbecue with brown bear viewing and photography ($175 per person, for groups of four or five) or as long as seven days overnight in Robert Haeg's lodge and cabins. A longer trip includes fishing, flight-seeing, clam digging, and hiking in verdant, glacier-carved valleys. The weeklong visit runs $1,700, including airfare from Kenai/Soldotna. Call (907) 262-9249.

BETHEL

The city of **Bethel** and the surrounding Yukon–Kuskokwim delta country really doesn't come readily to mind when one compiles a list of Alaska's better known visitor destinations. Located 400 air miles from Anchorage on the banks of the mighty Kuskokwim River, this city of nearly 5,000 mostly Yu'pik Eskimo residents is primarily a commercial fishing, trading, and government center. None of the Goliaths of the travel industry have offices here. Fact is, there aren't many Davids either.

But of course that's what attracts a good number of us. That and the community's location about 90 miles inland from the Bering Sea and the mouth of the Kuskokwim River. Bethel sits in the midst of the United States' largest game refuge, the twenty-million-acre **Yukon Delta National Wildlife Range.**

The range, incidentally, is another of those places where you really ought not to venture on your own—not, at least, without knowledgeable local advice. Fortunately, such information is readily available. **Kuskokwim Wilderness Adventures** (owned by longtime Alaskans John McDonald, Beverly Hoffman, Mike Hoffman, and Jill Hoffman) rents a variety of outdoor equipment, including rafts, life jackets, tents, cooking tents, and Coleman stoves. If you'd rather not venture out on your own, they can arrange custom tours. In town, they put together Bethel city tours that run two hours to a half day and start at $25. Call (907) 543-3900.

Whether you take a package tour or not, don't fail to include the city's ◆**Yugtarvik Regional Museum** in your itinerary. (*Yugtarvik,* in Yu'pik, means "place for peoples' things.") Located in an elevated log structure and operated by the Bethel Council on the Arts, the museum is chock-full of Eskimo art, artifacts, tools, and household items from the past and present. There's a full-size kayak, complete with a realistic paddler in it, paddle, grass mat, ice picks, and other accessories. You will also find a mounted musk ox head and cape on the wall, mounted birds of the region, dolls, masterfully woven grass baskets, ivory work, and beaded items. Admission is free, but donations are gratefully accepted. Many crafts items are for sale. Phone (907) 543-2098.

There are several hotel and B&B accommodations in Bethel, among them **Pacifica Guest House**, operated by Bob and Diane Carpenter. We knew these friendly folk in their early

183

Alaska days in Ketchikan during the fifties. Bob's dental practice took them to Bethel where they now offer a convenient B&B between the airport and downtown. Accommodations include a hot tub, van service, and even such electronic niceties as computer and fax capability. All-you-can-eat breakfasts feature home-baked breads and pastries. Summer room rates start at $80 for a single, $100 for a double. There's also a dorm that sleeps twelve, at $40 per. Phone (907) 543–4305.

If you're in the Markair Express airport terminal, climb the stairs to the second floor and head for the **Bush Flight Coffee Shop** (907–543–3200). The place is a veritable museum in its own right, with displays of very old fur parkas, mukluks (Eskimo leather boots), mittens, a canoe, weapons, baskets, and early kitchen items such as old-time pans, pots, and cooking utensils. The food is first rate, too.

ADDITIONAL SOURCES OF INFORMATION

State of Alaska on the internet: htpp://www.state.ak.us

Alaska Department of Fish and Game, P.O. Box 25526, Juneau, AK 99802-5526. Phone: (907) 465–4112; fax (907) 465–3088.

Alaska Division of Tourism, P.O. Box 110801, Juneau, AK 99811-0801. Phone: (907) 465–2010; fax: (907) 465–2287. Ask for their free Official State Guide and Vacation Planner.

Alaska Marine Highway System (state ferries), P.O. Box 25535, Juneau, AK 99802-5535. Phone: (800) 642–0066 (U.S.), (800) 665–6414 (Canada); fax: (907) 277-4829.

Alaska Natural History Association (mail order service), 605 West Fourth Avenue, Suite 85, Anchorage, AK 99501. Sells guidebooks and natural history publications.

Alaska Railroad, Passenger Service Department, P.O. Box 107500, Anchorage, AK 99510-7500. Phone: (800) 544–0552; fax: (907) 265–2323.

Alaska State Parks, 3601 C Street, Suite 1200, Anchorage, AK 99503-5921. Phone: (907) 269–8400; fax: (907) 269–8901.

Alaska Wilderness Recreation and Tourism Association, P.O. Box 1353, Valdez, AK 99686. Phone: (907) 835–4300; fax: (907) 835–5679.

Tourism Yukon, P.O. Box 2703, Whitehorse, Yukon Territory, Canada Y1A 2C6. Phone: (403) 667–5340; fax: (403) 667–3546.

STATEWIDE OUTFITTERS AND TOUR ORGANIZATIONS

Adventure Alaska: Tours and adventures for very small groups by riverboat, raft, kayak, and canoe; as well as air, rail, and road. Call (800) 365–7057.

AlaskaPass: Based somewhat on the concept of Europe's Eurail Pass, the company offers unlimited travel for a given number of days on a variety of ferries, buses, and trains from Seattle to and through British Columbia, the Yukon, and Alaska. Prices vary depending on the number of consecutive days purchased. Call (800) 248–7598.

Alaska Highway Cruises: Combination of an Inside Passage or Vancouver-Anchorage cruise on a major (Holland America Line) cruise ship one way, travel by late-model recreation vehicle the other, from ten to twenty-one nights. RV portions can be Alaska only, Alaska and Yukon, or Alaska to Seattle. Call (800) 323–5757.

Alaska-Yukon RV Caravans: Escorted groups of up to twenty-one RVs through Alaska, the Yukon, and British Columbia, with Alaska Marine Highway System ferry access as an option. Independent RV tours and rentals are also available. Call (800) 426–9865.

Alaska Up Close: A range of options from a ten-day Southeast journey in the footsteps of John Muir to a seven-day "A Gathering of Eagles" tour to see literally thousands of eagles in the Chilkat Valley near Haines to fourteen days of touring, flight-seeing, and cruising in three of Alaska's national parks—Denali, Kenai Fjords, and Glacier Bay. Call (907) 789–9544.

CampAlaska Tours: Small group, daytime travel by van, or overnight camping excursions to a variety of destinations. Tours range from six to twenty-two days. Mountain bike, fly-in, and raft options are also available. Call (907) 376–9438.

Equinox Wilderness Expeditions: More than two dozen educational, small group adventures ranging from springtime skiing on Ruth Glacier to summer backpacking and paddle trips in the Arctic and Katmai National Park. Photo floats in the Kobuk Valley and sea kayaking on the "Lost Coast of Icy Bay" are also available. Call (907) 274–9087.

Hugh Glass Backpacking Company: Treks and raft trips to a variety of destinations, plus wilderness fishing adventures. Call (907) 344–1340.

National Outdoor Leadership School: Teaches outdoor and survival skills through courses in wild and rugged terrain from the Arctic to Argentina and even Africa. Many of the courses are in Alaska and vary from hiking in the Arctic or ascending Denali (Mt. McKinley) to master's kayaking in Prince William Sound. Courses range from ten days to three months. Call (907) 745–4047.

Nova Riverunners of Alaska: River running trips from gentle floats to Class V whitewater. Trips range from a half-day to ten days and include Matanuska Valley, the Kenai Peninsula, Wrangell-St. Elias mountains, Denali in the Interior and the Kobuk River in the Arctic. Call (907) 745–5753.

Mountain Travel-Sobek: International rafting, canoeing, trekking. Tours include "Wilds of the Yukon" tours in Kluane National Park; Tatshenshini River and Alsek River rafting; an expedition to the top of Denali (Mt. McKinley), and Glacier Bay sea kayaking. Call (800) 227–2384.

VanGo Custom Tours: Day tours and longer packages in small groups in a variety of locations. Some tours feature home visits, others feature Native villages and river experiences. Call (907) 455–6499.

Wilderness: Alaska/Mexico: Summer Alaska backpacking, rafting, and kayaking expeditions in the Arctic National Wildlife Refuge and other Arctic areas plus Prince William Sound. Call (907) 479–8203.

INDEXES

Entries for Museum and State and National parks will be found in the special indexes on page 196.

A

Admiralty Island Canoeing, 28
Adventuress, 30
Adventures Afloat, 31
Adventures and Delights Eco Tours, 96
Aimee's Guest House, 49
Air Adventures, 100
Alaska Airlines' Vacations, 150
Alaska Bed and Breakfast Association, 32
Alaska Brewing Company, 26
Alaska Chilkat Bald Eagle Preserve, 37, 58
Alaska Cruises, 4
Alaska Discovery, 27, 38, 49, 157
Alaska Fly 'n' Fish Charters, 28
Alaska Highway, 35, 57, 59, 120, 128, 137
Alaska Indian Arts, 36
Alaska Marine Highway ferry *LeConte*, 32, 84
Alaska Maritime Tours, 103
Alaska Native Arts and Crafts Association, 79
Alaska Native Medical Center, 79
Alaska Ocean View Bed and Breakfast, 23
Alaska Peak and Seas, 15
Alaska Petroleum Company, 165
Alaska Public Lands Information Centers
 Anchorage, 78
 Fairbanks, 121
 Tok, 128
Alaska Railroad, 93
Alaska Railroad Depot, 78
Alaska Railroad "piggyback train," 91
Alaska Rainforest Tours, 32
Alaska Raptor Rehabilitation Center, 23
Alaska Renown Charters, 96
Alaska Rivers Company, 97
Alaska Sojourns, Wilderness Guides, 182
Alaska Star Charters, 15
Alaska Travel Adventures, 5, 21, 29
Alaska Scenic Waterways, 17
Alaska Serenity Kayak Company, 29
Alaska Sightseeing/Cruise West, 3, 82
Alaska State Fair, 111
Alaska Tolovana Adventures, 134
Alaska Two Wheel Tours, 81
Alaska Underwater Adventures, 15
Alaska Wild Berry Products, 102
Alaska Wildland Adventures, 97

Alaska Yachting and Fishing, 14
Alaska Yukon Tours, 158
Alaska-Denali Guiding, Inc., 133
Alaskaland, 123
Alaskan Hotel and Bar, 26
Alaska's Mainstreet Visitor Center, 129
Alatna River Canoeing, 156
Aleutian Air, 178
Allen Marine, 22
Alsek and Tatshenshini Rivers, 38
Alyeska Bed and Breakfast, 90
Alyeska Booking Company, 90
Alyeska Home Hostel, 90
Alyeska Pipeline Service Company, 86
Alyeska Pipeline Service Company information center, 140
Alyeska Resort, 89
Anadyr Adventures, 87
Anan Creek Bear Observatory, 6, 14, 15
Anaktuvuk Pass, 125
Anchor Point State Recreation Site, 102
Anchor River Beach Road, 102
Anchorage, 77–83
Anchorage Fur Rendezvous, 82
Anchorage International Hostel, 81
(Anchorage) log cabin visitor information center, 78
Angoon, 32, 34
Aniakchak National Monument and Preserve, 182
Annabelle's Famous Keg and Chowder House, 6
Anton Larsen Bay Road, 171
Anvil Mountain, 154
Arctic Brotherhood Hall, 44
Arctic Caribou Inn, 163
Arctic Chalet, 70
Arctic Circle, 69, 161
Arctic Circle Adventures, 151
Arctic Circle Hot Springs, 141
Arctic Divide, 157
Arctic National Wildlife Refuge, 157, 158
Arctic Ocean, 163
Arctic Roadrunner, 80
Arctic Safari Tours, 149
Arctic Treks, 158
Arctic Village, 157, 159
Arctic Village Tours, 159
Armadillo Cafe, 26
Arrigetch Peaks, 156
Athabasca Cultural Journeys, 125
Atlin, 56
Atlin Road, 56

Auke Bay Kayaking, 29
Aurora, 9
Aurora Express, 127

B
Bake Shop, 90
Baker Aviation, 151
Bald Eagle Preserve Raft Trips, 37
Baranof Island, 19
Barren Islands, 103
Barrow, 148
Barrow Airport Inn, 149
Bartlett, 84
Bayshore Lodge and Oasis
    Restaurant, 74
Beachcomber Inn, 19
Bear Bight Camps, 8
Bear Creek, 67
Bear Creek Camp and International
    Hostel, 41
Beaver Creek, 74
Beaver Creek Canada Customs and
    Immigration, 74
Begich-Boggs Visitor Center, 91
Belinda V. Charters, 14
Beluga Lookout, 100
Beluga Point, 89
Bering Air, 155
Bering Sea Ice Golf Classic, 152
Bethel, 183
Bettles, 156
Betty's Igloo Bed and Breakfast, 156
Beyer Lake Campground, 108
Bidarka Boats, 21
Big Delta State Historical Park, 138
Big Game Alaska, 91
Big Lake, 106
Big Lake Houseboat Rental, 106
Birch Trails Bed and Breakfast, 81
Birch Trails Sled Dog Tours, 81
Bird Creek State Campground, 89
Blind Sough recreation area, 18
Blue Moon Cafe, 34
Blueberry Lake State Recreation Site,
    114
Bodenburg Butte, 110
Bove Island, 56
Brooks Campground, 175
Budget Rent A Car, 153
Bunkhouse, 115
Bunk 'n' Breakfast, 112
Burgess Bauder's Lighthouse, 23
Burnt Paw, 129
Burwash Landing, 74
Bush Flight Coffee Shop, 184
Buskin River Inn, 173

C
Caines Head State Recreation Area, 94

Camp Denali, 131
Canada Customs, 56
Canada Customs and Immigration, 58
Canada—U.S. border, 74
Canteen Show, 62
Cantwell, 108, 144, 145
Cantwell Lodge, 145
Cape Fox Tours, 3
Cape Smythe Air, 155
Captain Benjamin Moore's cabin, 43
Captain Cook State Recreation Area,
    99, 100
Carcross, 56, 57
(Carcross) visitor reception centre, 56
Carcross Barracks Gift Shop, 56
Carcross Desert, 57
Carl's Bayview Inn, 177
Carmacks, 64
Carriage House, 135
Cassiar Highway, 9
Castle Hill, 21
Cathedral Peaks Bed and Breakfast, 40
Catholic Church, 70
Chair 5 Restaurant, 90
Channel 8 TV, 178
Chapel on the Hill, 117
Chart Room, 177
Chatanika, 140
Chena Hot Springs Road, 139
Chena Lakes Recreation Area, 139
Chena River Recreation Area, 139
Cheryl's Old Fashioned Bed and
    Breakfast, 130
Chichagof Island, 22, 34
Chicken, 73
Chicken Creek Cafe, 73
Chicken Discount Gas and Propane,
    73
Chicken Mercantile Emporium, 73
Chicken Saloon, 73
Chief Shakes Hot Springs, 15
Chief Shakes Island, 11
Childs Glacier, 85
Chilkat Center for the Arts, 36
Chilkat Eagle Bed and Breakfast, 40
Chilkat Guides, Ltd., 37, 38
Chilkat Indian Dancers, 36
Chilkat Pass, 58
Chilkat Restaurant and Bakery, 39
Chilkat Valley Inn, 41
Chilkoot Charlie's, 80
Chilkoot Lake Tours, 39
Chilkoot Sled Dog Adventures, 42
Chilkoot Trail, 44
Chiniak Highway, 171
Chitina, 114
Chuk Campground, 70
(Chugach) Forest Service
    Information Center, 5

Chugach State Park Visitor Center, 109
Circle, 141
Circle City, 159
Circle Hot Springs Road, 141
Clam Gulch State Recreation Area, 101
Classic Tours, 7
Cleft of the Rock Bed and Breakfast, 130
Climber Bunkhouse, 107
Coldfoot, 161
Coldfoot Services and Arctic
    Acres Inn, 162
Colville River, 157
Cooper's Landing, 97
Copper Center, 117
Copper Center Lodge, 117
Copper Oar, 117
Cordova, 85
Council, 154
Country Charm Bed and Breakfast, 65
Craig, 8
Cranes' Crest Bed and Breakfast, 104
Creamer's Field Migratory
    Waterfowl Refuge, 122
Crooked Creek & Whiskey Island
    Railroad, 123
Crystal Lake Fish Hatchery, 18
Creek Street, 6
Crow Creek Mine, 89, 90

D
Dall mountain sheep, 89
Dalton City, 37
Dalton Highway, 121, 160
Dawson City, 65, 69, 70
Dawson City Bed and Breakfast, 68
Dawson City walking tour, 66
Dawson Creek, British Columbia, 59
Dawson Visitor Reception Center, 66
Deadhorse, 162
Deer Mountain Trail, 4
Deishu Expeditions, 41
Delta Bison Range, 138
Delta International Hostel, 137
Delta Junction, 54, 113, 130, 137
Delta Junction Information Center, 137
Dempster Highway, 69
Denali Highway, 121, 137, 144
Denali Hostel, 133
Denali (Mt. McKinley), 120
Denali Parks and Resorts, 131
Denali Princess, 131
Denali Raft Adventures, 133
Denali Wilderness Lodge, 132
Dezadeash Lake, 58
Diamond Tooth Gertie's, 66
Discovery Campground, 100
Discovery Claim, 68
Discovery Voyage, 86
Dog Sled Saloon, 125

Dolly's House, 6
Double Musky, 90
Douglas Cafe, 27
Duncan Creek Golddusters, 65
Dutch Harbor, 176
Dyea, 44

E
Eagle, 72
Eagle Island, 5
Eagle Plains Hotel and Restaurant, 69
Eagle Summit, 141
Eagle River, 109
Eaglecrest Ski Area, 29
Eagle's Nest Car Rental, 39
Eagle's Nest Motel, 39
Eagle's Roost Bed and Breakfast, 6
Eagle's Roost Park, 17
Earth Tours, 81
East Turner Lake, 27
Edgerton Highway, 114
Eielson Visitor Center, 131
Eklutna Village Historical Park, 109
El Capitan Cave, 6
El Capitan Lodge, 6
El Dorado Gold Camp, 124
El Dorado Gold Mine, 143
El Sombrero Cafe, 26
Elderberry Park, 78
Elliott Highway, 121, 142
Elsa, 65
Emerald Lake, 57
End of the Road Bed and Breakfast, 136
Engine Number 1, 78
ERA Helicopters, 30
Eruk's Wilderness Float Tours, 182
Eskimo blanket toss, 150
Eskimo Red's Muskomee Bay Lodge, 173
Ester Gold Camp, 135
Evergreen Lodge, 112
Exit Glacier, 95
Explore Air Statewide Tours, 107

F
Fairbanks, 113, 120, 121, 135
Fairbanks Convention and Visitor
    Bureau Information Center, 121
Fairbanks Flight Train, 126
Fairbanks Golf and Country Club, 124
Fairview Inn, 107
Fairweather Adventures, 50
Falls Creek Fish Ladder, 18
Far North Tours, 83
Father Duncan's Cottage, 5
Favorite Bay Inn, 34
Fiddlehead Restaurant and Bakery, 27
Finnish Alaskan Bed and Breakfast, 134
Fireweed Inn Bed and Breakfast, 90
Fireweed Lodge, 8

189

First Out, Last In Fishing Charters, 39
Fishhook Road, 111
Five Mile Lake Campground, 65
Flat Dog Kennels, 155
Forget Me Not Bed and Breakfast, 127
Fort Kenay, 100
Fort McPherson, 69
Fort McPherson Tent and Canvas, 69
Fort Seward Bed and Breakfast, 40
Fort Seward Condos, 40
Fort Seward Lodge, Restaurant, and
    Saloon, 40
Fort William Henry Seward, 35, 36
Fort Yukon, 158
Fort Yukon, replica of the original, 158
Frontier Flying Service, 125
Frontier Heritage Park, 57

G
Gajaa Heen Dancers, 22
Gakona Junction, 135, 136
Gakona Lodge & Trading Post, 135
Galatea Charters, 33
Gambell, 155
Gastineau Guiding, 26
Gates of the Arctic Winter
    Dogsledding, 156, 157
Geophysical Institute, 123
George Parks Highway, 104, 120, 130
Georgeson Botanical Garden, 123
Gilmore Hotel, 6
Girdwood, 89
Glacier Bay Adventures, 50
Glacier Bay Airways, 35, 50
Glacier Bay Country Inn, 48
Glacier Bay Lodge, 47
Glacier Bay Sea Kayaks, 49
Glacier Bay Tours and Cruises, 3, 30, 47
Glacier Bay Tug Charters, 50
Glacier Park Resort, 112
Glenn Highway, 108
Glenn Highway–Tok Cutoff, 121, 135
Glennallen, 113, 118, 135
G. O. Shuttle Service, 127
Gold Creek Salmon Bake, 29
Gold Dredge #8, 124
Gold Dredge #4, 67
gold dredges, 153
Gold Panning and Gold History Tour,
    29
Gold Rush Cemetery, 44
Gold Rush Town, 123
Golden Circle Tour, 39
Golden North Hotel, 45
Good Riverbed and Breakfast, 49
Grand Aleutian Hotel, 177
Grand Pacific Charters, 48
Grandview Inn, 9
Grantley Harbor Tours, 155
Gray Line of Alaska, 160

Great Alaska Cedar Works Bed and
    Breakfast, 7
Great Kobuk Sand Dunes, 150
Grizzly Lake Ranch, 135
Growler Island, 86
GuggieVille, 65
Gulkana Fish Guides, 136
Gustavus, 46–47
Gustavus Inn, 48
Gusto Tours and Charters, 50
Gwennie's Old Alaska Restaurant, 80

H
Haeg's Wilderness Lodge, 182
Haines, 35
Haines Highway, 35, 57
Haines Junction, 58, 73
Haines Shuttle and Tours, 38
(Haines) visitor center, 35
Halibut Cove, 103
Halsingland Hotel, 37
Harbor Dinner Club, 95
Harbor House Lodging, 14
Harbor House Rentals, 15
Harding Lake, 138
Hatcher Pass Lodge, 111
Hawkins House Bed and Breakfast, 63
Herschel Island, 70
Hidden Lake, 98
Holy Ascension Russian Orthodox
    Cathedral, 178
Holy Assumption of the Virgin Mary
    Russian Orthodox Church, 100
Holy Resurrection Russian
    Orthodox Church, 169
Homer, 93, 102
Homer Spit, 102
Hoonah, 32, 33
Hope, 92
Hope Highway, 92
Hot Bite, 27
Hubbard Glacier, 50
Hubbard's Bed and Breakfast, 33
Huck Hobbit's Homestead
    Campground and Retreat, 136
humpback whales, 16
Hungry Beaver, 13
Hudson Air Service, 108
Hyder, 9

I
Iditarod, 82
Ingamo Hall, 70
Independence Mine, 105
Independence Mine State
    Historical Park, 111
Independent Rental, Inc., 124
Iditarod Sled Dog Classic, 152
Iditarod Trail Committee Head--
    quarters and Visitor Center, 105

190

Inn at the Waterfront, 27
Institute Creek Trail, 11
Inuvik, 69, 70
Island Air, 174
Island Terrific Tours, 172

J
Jack London's cabin, 66
Jack Wade Junction, 72
jade factory, 150
Jake's Corner, 57,60
J&B Bike Rentals, 23
Jon James Adventures, Ltd., 97
Joseph Van Os Photo Safari, 180
Juneau, 24
(Juneau) Forest Service Information
    Center, 5
Juneau International Hostel, 32
Juneau Raptor Center, 29
Juneau Sea Kayaking, 28

K
Kachemak Bay Ferry *Danny J.*, 103
Kachemak Bay Natural History Tour, 103
Kalifornsky Beach Road, 99, 101
Kantishna Roadhouse, 132
Katmai Wilderness Lodge, 175
Katmailand, 175
Kayak Katmai Adventures, 175
Kenai, 99, 100
Kenai Bicentennial Visitors and
    Cultural Center, 100
Kenai Fjords Tours, 95, 96
Kenai National Wildlife Refuge, 98
Kenai National Wildlife Refuge
    Visitor Center, 99
Kenai Peninsula, 87
Kenai Peninsula Guided Hikes, 94
Kenai Princess Lodge, 97
Kenai Princess RV Park, 97
Kenai Spur Highway, 99, 100
Kennicott, 114, 116
Kennicott Glacier Lodge, 116
Kenny Lake Mercantile and RV Park, 114
Keno City, 65
Ketchikan, 2
Ketchikan Air, 6
Ketchikan Hostel, 7
(Ketchikan) Visitor Information
    Center, 4
Keystone Raft and Kayak Adventure,
    87
Kiana, 151
Kincaid Park, 79
King Eider Hotel, 179
King Salmon, 175
Klawock, 8
Klondike Express, 84
Klondike Gold Rush National
    Historical Park, 42, 43, 44

Klondike Highway, 46, 55, 64
Klondike Summit to Sea Cruise, 46
Klondike Trail of '98 Road Relay, 46
Kluane Bed and Breakfast, 74
(Kluane National Park) visitor
    reception centre, 73
Kluane Park Adventure Center, 73
Knight Riders Horse and Buggy Rides,
    135
Knik Glacier, 105, 110
Knik Glacier Adventures, 106
Knik Kennels, 105
Knik Road, 105
Knudson Cove, 6
Kobuk River, 157
Kobuk River Jets, 151
Kodiak, 168
Kodiak Alutiiq Dancers, 170
Kodiak Cattle Company, 173
Kodiak Island Charters, 174
Kodiak Island Convention and
    Visitors Bureau, 169
Kodiak National Wildlife Refuge, 172
Kodiak Tours, 172
Kongakut River, 157
Kongakut River Rafting, 158
Kotzebue, 150
Kotzebue Cultural Fish
    Camp Experience, 150
Kotzebue Sound Charters, 151
Kougarok Road, 154
Koyukuk National Wildlife Refuge, 126
Koyukuk River, 157
Kruzof Island, 21
K2 Aviation, 107
Kukpuk River, 157
Kuskokwim Wilderness Adventures, 183

L
L.A.B. Flying Service, 42
Lake Louise, 112
L&L Fishing & Hunting Plus, 141
Leblondeau Glacier, 38
LeConte, 34
LeConte Bay, 16
LeConte Glacier, 15, 16
LeConte Outfitters, 18
Legacy Tours, 99
Large Animal Research Station, 123
Larry's Flying Service, 125
Liberty Falls State Recreation Site, 115
Little Norway Festival, 16
Livengood, 143
Log Cabin RV Park and Resort, 8
Long Rifle Lodge, 102
Lorna's at the Skagway Inn, 45
Lower Dewey Trail, 44
Lucky Husky Racing Kennel, 106
Lucky Wishbone, 80

M
Ma Johnson Hotel, 115
Mahay's Riverboat Service, 107
Major Marine Tours, 85, 96
Malemute Saloon, 125
Manley Hot Springs, 143–144
Manley Hot Springs Resort, 144
Manley Road House, 143
Mariah Charters and Tours, 96
Marine Works, 177
Mary's McKinley View Lodge, 108
Mary Carey's Fiddlehead Farm, 106
Marx Brothers, 80
Mascot Saloon, 43
Matanuska Glacier, 112
Matanuska Glacier State
    Recreation Site, 112
Mat-Su Visitors Center, 105
Mayo, 65
Mayo Bed and Breakfast, 65
McCarthy, 114, 115
McCarthy Air, 117
McCarthy Lodge restaurant
    and saloon, 115
McCarthy Road, 114, 115
McDonald's, 24
McFarland's Floatel, 8
Mendenhall Glacier, 25, 26
Mendenhall Glacier Float Trips, 29
Metlakatla, 5
Midnight Dome, 65
Milepost 0 Monument, 59
Miles Glacier, 85
Million Dollar Bridge, 85
Million Dollar Falls Campground, 58
Minto, 143
Minto Landing Campground, 64
Misty Fjords National Monument, 4, 6
Mitkof Highway, 18
Mitkof Island, 15, 17
Mosquito Lake, 38
M.V. Galatea, 33
M.V. Tarahne, 57
Mt. Dewey, 11
Mt. Edgecumbe National
    Recreation Trail, 21
Mt. Juneau Trail, 26
Mt. Marathon, 94
Mt. Roberts Trail, 26
Moose Pass, 93
Mountain Bike Adventure, 17
Mountain Trip, Inc., 134
Mukluk Annie's Salmon Bake, 60
Mukluk Land, 129

N
Naabia Niign Athabascan
    Indian Crafts, 128
Nabesna Road, 135
NANA Oilfield, 165

National Park Service, 115
National Park Service Ranger
    Station, 135
National Park Service Glacier Bay
    Visitor Center, 47
National Park Service visitor
    information center, Kotzebue, 150
National Park Service Visitor Center,
    Seward, 95
Near Island, 171
Nenana, 134
1901 Post Office, 66
1901 Territorial Administration
    Building, 67
Ninilchik, 101
Ninilchik State Recreation Area, 101
Ninilchik Village, 101
Noland House, 57
Nome, 152
Nome Convention and Visitor
    Bureau's Visitor Information
    Center, 153
Nome Custom Adventures', 154
Nome Nugget Inn, 156
Nome Tour & Marketing, 155
Nome-Council Road, 154
Nome-Teller Road, 154
Nome's Board of Trade, 153
Nordic House Bed and Breakfast, 19
North Pole, 139
North Slope Borough, 148
North Star Golf Club, 124
North Woods Lodge, 127
Northern Alaska Tour Company, 149,
    160
Northern Bikes, 17
Northern Light Runners Dog Sled
    Rides and Kennel Tours, 140
Northern Nomad Adventures, 95
Northern Splendor Reindeer Farm, 63
Northwest Territories Information
    Centre, 66
Nullagvik Hotel, 150

O
Ocean View Manor, 156
Old Chena Indian Village, 122
Old F.E. Gold Camp, 140
Old Glenn Highway, 110
Old Log Church, 63
Old Mission School, 158
Old Richardson Highway, 117
Old Sourdough Lodge, 14
Olga Bay Lodge, 174
Olson Air Service's Siberian
    Sight-seer, 155
Oomingmak Musk Ox Producers' Coop,
    78
Oscar Anderson House, 78
Osprey Expeditions, 133

Otter Cove Bed & Breakfast, 35
Ounalashka Corporation, 178
Our Collections, 13
Out of Bounds, Inc., 30
Owls of the North, 158

P
Pacific Wing, 17
Pacifica Guest House, 183
Pack Creek, 28
Packhouse Restaurant, 138
Palace Grand Theatre, 66
Palace Theatre and Saloon, 123, 125
Palmer, 111
Palmer musk ox farm, 111
Park Service visitor center, 131
Pasagshak Bay Road, 172
Patching Lake Cabin, 5
Paxson, 137, 144
Paxson Llama Works, 137
Paxson Lodge, 137
Peace of Selby, 157
Pearson's Pond Luxury Inn, 32
Peggy's Alaskan Cabbage Patch Bed
    and Breakfast, 138
Pelican, 34
Pepe's North of the Border, 149
Petersburg, 15
Patching Lake Cabin, 5
Paxson, 144
Perseverance Trail, 26
(Petersburg) Visitor Information
    Center, 16
Petroglyphs, 11
Petroglyph Beach, 11
Pikes Landing, 127
Pilgrim Hot Springs, 154
Pilgrim Hot Springs hot tub, 154
Pipeline Mile Zero, 163
Plate and Palette Gallery Cafe, 127
Porcupine River Lodge, 159
Port Alexander, 24
Portage Glacier, 91
Portage Glacier Road, 91
Port of Whittier, 91
Potter Marsh, 89
Pribilof Aleutian Adventure, 179
Pribilof Islands, 179
Prince of Wales Island, 6, 7
Prince Rupert, 5
Prince William Sound, 83
Princess Tours, 160
Pristine Charters, 173
Provideniya, Russia, 155
Prudhoe Bay, 148
Prudhoe Bay Hotel, 163
Ptarmigan, 92
public harbors, 16
Puffin's Bed and Breakfast, 49
Pullen House, 44

R
R&R Lodge, 174
Rafter T Ranch Trail Rides, 111
Rainbow Falls Trail, 11
Rainbow Tours, 103
Rainforest Retreat Bed and
    Breakfast, 24
Raven's Roost, 18
Ray's Waterfront, 95
recreation center, 178
Red Dog, 26
Reeve Aleutian Airways, 179
Reluctant Fisherman Inn, 85
Resurrection Bay, 95
Resurrection Pass Trail, 92
Revillagigedo Island, 2
Richardson Highway, 113, 130, 136
Rika's Roadhouse, 138
Rita's Campground and RV Park, 130
River Adventures, 38
Robert Service's Cabin, 66, 67
Rock Glacier Trail, 58
Rocky Point Resort, 19
Rooney's Roost Bed and Breakfast, 13
Rosie's, 34
Russel Fjord, 50
Russian Bishop's House, 21
Russian blockhouse, 21
Russian Orthodox Church, 179

S
St. Elias Alpine Guides, 117
St. Elias Lake Trail, 58
St. George Island, 179
St. Lawrence Island, 155
St. Lazaria National Wildlife Refuge, 22
St. Mark's Episcopal Church, 134
St. Michael, 155
St. Michael's Russian Orthodox
    Cathedral, 21
St. Nicholas Chapel, 100
St. Paul Island, 179
St. Stephen's Territorial Episcopal
    Church, 158
Saga Alaskan Bicycle Adventures, 82
salmon bake, 37
Salmon Glacier, 9
Salmon River Smokehouse, 49
Saltery Lake Lodge, 173
Salty Dawg Saloon, 103
Sandy's Beyond Good River, 49
Santa Claus House, 139
Saturday Market, 79
Savoonga, 155
Sawyer Glaciers, 30
Saxman Native Village, 3
Scuba Do-Alpha Dive Charters, 173
Sea Hawk Air's Guaranteed Bear
    Viewing and Flight-seeing, 173
Sea Otter and Wildlife Quest, 22

Seaside Farm Hostel, 104
SeeAlaska, 17
Selawik Wildlife Range, 150
Seldovia, 103
Sepal Hollow Bed and Breakfast, 32
Seven Glaciers Restaurant, 90
Seward, 93
Seward Trolley, 94
Seward Highway, 88
Shaktoolik, 155
Sheenjek River, 157
Sheep Mountain Lodge, 112
Sheep Mountain Visitor Centre, 74
Sheila's Guest House, 177
Sheldon Jackson College, 19
Sheldon, Steve, 36
Shxat'Kwaan Native dancers, 11
Sights Southeast, 16
Sign Post Forest, 59
Silver Trail, 65
Silverbow Inn, 27
Sitka, 19
Sitka Hostel, 24
Sitka National Historical Park, 21, 22
Sitka'S native village, 22
Sitka Sea Kayaking Adventure, 21
Sitka's Secrets, 22
Sitka Sportfishing, 23
Sitka Tribe of Alaska, 21
Six Bar E Ranch Bed and Breakfast, 81
Skagway, 42
Skagway Hostel, 45
Skagway Inn Bed and Breakfast, 45
Skagway's City Hall, 45
Skagway Convention and Visitors
    Bureau, 34, 46
Skilak Lake, 98
Skilak Lake Loop Road, 98
Skyline Trail and A.B. Mountain, 44
Sky Trekking Alaska, 156
Smuggler's Cove, 5
Snow River Hostel, 96
Snyder Mercantile Company, 34
Sockeye Cycle, 39, 46
Soldotna, 93, 98, 99
Solomon, 154
Sons of Norway Hall, 16
Sound Adventure Charters, 85
Sourdough Cabins, 131
Sourdough Outfitters, 156
Sourdough pancake breakfast with
    Alaska reindeer sausage, 129
Southeast Alaska State Fair, 37
Southeast Exposure, 4
Southeast Retreat, 8
Southwestern Alaska, 168–184
Spirit of Adventure, 47
Spirit Walker Expeditions, 50
Stampede Rent A Car, 153
Stan Stephens Cruises, 86

Starrigavan Bay, 20
Starrigavan Estuary trail, 20
S.S. Klondike, 60
S.S. Nenana, 123
Steamer *Keno*, 67
S.O.B., 27
Steese Highway, 120, 140
Sterling Highway, 96
stern-wheeler Discovery III cruise, 121
Stewart, 9
Stewart Crossing, 64
Stikeen Wilderness Adventures, 14
Strawberry Island, 41
Sugarloaf Wilderness Trail Rides, 134
Summit, 27
Summit Lake Lodge, 92
Sunrise Aviation, 15
Swan Lake Canoe Trail, 98
Swanson River Canoe Trail, 98
Syd Wright's *Chan IV*, 18

T
Tack's General Store and
    Greenhouse Cafe, 140–41
Tagish, 56
Takhini Hot Springs, 63
Takhini-Wud Bed and Breakfast, 63
Taku Wilderness Lodge, 30
Talkeetna, 106
Talkeetna Roadhouse, 107
Tanana Valley Fairgrounds, 122
Tanana Valley Farmer's Market, 122
Tanaq Hotel, 180
Tangle Lakes Lodge, 145
Taquan Air, 5
Taylor Highway, 72, 128
Teller, 154, 155
Temsco Helicopters, 30
Tenakee Hot Springs Lodge, 34
Tenakee Springs, 32–33
"Tent Lady" Donna Blasor-
    Bernhardt, 129
Tern Junction, 93
Tern Lake, 96
Tetlin Junction, 72, 73, 128
33-Mile Roadhouse, 39
The Farm Bed and Breakfast, 93
The Resort at Chena Hot Springs, 140
Thompson Pass, 114
Thorne Bay, 8
Tides Inn, 18
Tok, 128, 135
Tok Cutoff, 113
Tok Cutoff-Glenn Highway, 128
Tok International Hostel, 129
Tokeen, 8
Tolovana Lodge, 134
Tolsona Wilderness Campground, 113
Tongass Heritage Center, 3
Tongass Kayak, 17

Tongass National Forest, 4
Tongass Traveler, 18
Tony Knowles Coastal Trail, 78
Top of the World Highway, 70, 128
Top of the World Hotel, 149
Tormented Valley, 56
Totem Village Tribal House, 36
Tour Arctic, 150
(Tourism Yukon) visitor
    reception center, 74
Tours on the Kenai, 99
Tracy Arm Fjord, 30
Trail Inn and Pack Train Saloon, 43
Trail Lake Lodge, 93
Trans-Alaska Pipeline, 86, 140
Trans-Alaska Pipeline
    pumping station, 138
Trans-Arctic Circle Treks, Ltd., 125, 160
True North Kayak Adventures, 103
Trumpeter Swan Observatory, 18
Tsirku River and Leblondeau Glacier,
    38
Tuktoyaktuk, 70
Tundra Taxi and Limo Service, 149
Tundra Tours, 149
tundra walk, 150
Turnagain Tidal Bore, 89
Tustumena, 103, 176
Two Rivers Lodge, 128

U
Umnak Island, 178
U.S.—Canada border, 56, 58
U.S.Customs, 56, 58
U.S. Customs and Immigration
    Station, 128
U.S. Forest Service cabins, 4, 8, 15, 20,
    27
U.S. Fish and Wildlife Service, 128
U.S. Fish and Wildlife Service
    information station, 98
U.S. Fish and Wildlife Service
    Visitor Center, Kodiak, 172
Unalaska, 176
UniSea Inn, 177

V
Valdez, 86, 113
(Valdez) visitor information center, 86
Valley of 10,000 Smokes, 175
Van Gilder Hotel, 96
Venus mine, 56
Viking Room, 19
Viking sailing vessel, 16
Viking Travel, 17
Villa Nova Restaurant, 80
Village/Wilderness Excursion, 150
visitor center, Coldfoot, 162
visitor center, Glennallen, 135
visitor center, Nenana, 134

Volcano Bay Adventures, 178
Voyager Hotel, 80

W
Walking tours, Sitka, 21
Wasilla, 105
Waterfall Resort, 7
Water Taxi and Scenic Cruise, 42
Watson Lake, 59
(Watson Lake) visitor reception
    centre, 59
Wavetamer Kayaking, 173
Weeping Trout Retreat and Golf Course,
    41
Western Arctic Nature Tours, 70
West Glacier Trail, 26
West Turner Lake, 27
Westmark Hotel, 129
Whalers Cove Sportfishing Lodge,
    34
Whales Resort, 8
Whalesong Lodge, 48
White Mountain, 155
White Pass & Yukon Route, 43
White Pass & Yukon Route
    Caboose, 45
WP&YR Depot, 43
White Ram Manor Bed and
    Breakfast, 68
White Sulphur Springs cabin, 22
Whitehorse, 60
Whitehorse Chamber of Commerce
    Information Centre, 60
Whitehorse Heritage Buildings
    Walking Tours, 62
Whittier, 84
Wickersham Courthouse, 72
Wickersham House, 25
Wilderness Birding Adventures, 157
Wilderness Explorer, 47
Wilderness Swift Charters, 28
Wildlife diorama, 150
Wildwood General Store and
    Fox Farm Tour, 143
Williams Reindeer Farm, 110
Wings of Alaska, 35
Winter Cabin Bed & Breakfast, 129
Wiseman, 162
Wiseman Trading Company, 162
Wonder Lake, 131
World Championship Sled Dog Race,
    82
World Extreme Skiing
    Championships, 114
Worthington Glacier State
    Recreation Site, 114
Wrangell, 9
Wrangell Garnet Ledge, 13
Wrangell Hostel, 13
Wrangell Mountain Air, 117

Wrangell Ranger District, 15
(Wrangell) Chamber of Commerce
    Visitor Information, 10
Wrangell-St. Elias National Park and
    Preserve headquarters
    and visitor center, 117

X
XYZ Center, 153

Y
Your Wilderness Connections, 30
Yukon Adventure Bed and Breakfast,
    72
Yukon Arts Centre, 62
Yukon Conservation Society, 62
Yukon Delta National Wildlife Range,
    183

Yukon Don's Bed and Breakfast Inn,
    106
Yukon Gardens, 62
Yukon Permanent Art Collection, 62
Yukon Queen River Cruise, 68
Yukon River Cruise and
    Pleasure Island narrated tour, 68
Yukon River Tours, 161
Yukon Territory, 54, 74
Yukon Ventures Alaska, 161
Yukon Visitor Reception Centre, 60
Yukon Wildlife Preserve, 62
Yukon-Charley National Preserve, 72

Z
Zimovia Highway, 12

SPECIAL INDEXES

Museums

Alaska Railroad Museum, 134
Alaska State Museum, 25
Alutiiq Museum and
    Archaeological Repository, 171
Anchorage Museum of History and Art,
    79
Atlin Historical Museum, 56
Baranov Museum, 169
Carrie McLain Museum, 153
City of Wrangell Museum, 10
Clausen Memorial Museum, 17
Corrington Museum of Alaska
    History, 44
Dorothy G. Page Museum, 105
Elmendorf Wildlife Museum, 79
Fort Richardson Alaska Fish and
    Wildlife Center, 79
George Ashby Memorial
    Museum, 117
George Johnston Museum, 59
Hyder Museum and Information
    Center, 9
Juneau-Douglas City Museum, 25
Kluane Museum of Natural
    History, 74
Knik Museum and Sled Dog
    Mushers' Hall of Fame, 105
MacBride Museum, 60
McCarthy Museum, 115
Mining Museum, 65
Museum of Alaska
    Transportation and
    Industry, 106
Museum of the Arctic, 150
Museum of Yukon Natural
    History, 57
Pratt Museum, 102

St. Innocent Veniaminov Research
    Institute Museum, 169
Reeve Aviation Picture Museum, 78
Sheldon Jackson Museum, 20, 22
Sheldon Museum and Cultural
    Center, 36
Soldotna Historical Society Museum,
    99
Stewart Historical Society Museum, 9
Talkeetna Historical Society Museum,
    107
Tongass Historical Museum, 3
Trail of '98 Museum, 44
University of Alaska Museum, 122
Valdez Museum, 86
Yugtarvik Regional Museum, 183
Yukon Transportation Museum, 60

National and State Parks

Denali National Park and
    Preserve, 108, 130, 144
Gates of the Arctic National Park, 157
Glacier Bay National Park and
    Preserve, 46
Katmai National Park, 174
Kenai Fjords National Park, 95
Kluane National Park, Canada, 58,
    73
Kobuk Valley National Park, 150, 151
Lake Clark National Park and
    Preserve, 180
Wrangell-St. Elias National Park, 117,
    135
Chilkat State Park, 37, 41
Chugach State Park, 79, 109
Denali State Park, 108, 130
Fort Abercrombie State Park, 171